Adobe®
Dreamweaver® CS5
Digital
Classroom

Adobe®
Dreamweaver® CS5
Digital
Classroom

Jeremy Osborn and AGI Creative Team

with Greg Heald

WILEY

Wiley Publishing, Inc.

Adobe Dreamweaver® CS5 Digital Classroom

Published by
Wiley Publishing, Inc.
10475 Crosspoint Boulevard
Indianapolis, IN 46256

Copyright © 2009 by Wiley Publishing, Inc., Indianapolis, Indiana
Published by Wiley Publishing, Inc., Indianapolis, Indiana
Published simultaneously in Canada
ISBN: 978-0-470-60774-9
Manufactured in the United States of America
10987654321

For general information on our other products and services or to obtain technical support, please
contact our Customer Care Department within the U.S. at (800) 762-2974, outside the U.S. at (317)
572-3993 or fax (317) 572-4002.

Please report any errors by sending a message to errata@agitraining.com

Library of Congress Control Number: 2010921236

About the Authors

Jeremy Osborn is the Content Director at American Graphics Institute (*agitraining.com*). He has more than 15 years of experience in web and graphic design, filmmaking, writing, and publication development for both print and digital media. He has contributed to several of the Digital Classroom book series. Jeremy holds a MS in Management from the Marlboro College Graduate Center and a BFA in Film/TV from the Tisch School of the Arts at NYU.

Greg Heald has 20 years of design and production experience in both Web and print environments. He has served as a contributing author or editor on a number of books on Dreamweaver, Flash, InDesign, and Acrobat. Greg has contributed to the development of Adobe's certification exams, and as Training Manager for American Graphics Institute, he oversees the delivery of professional development training programs for individuals and organizations. Greg holds a degree in Advertising Design from the acclaimed College of Visual and Performing Arts at Syracuse University.

The AGI Creative Team is composed of Adobe Certified Experts and Adobe Certified Instructors from American Graphics Institute (AGI). The AGI Creative Team has authored more than 10 Digital Classroom books, and previously created many of Adobe's official training guides. They work with many of the world's most prominent companies, helping them to use creative software to communicate more effectively and creatively. They work with marketing, creative, and communications teams around the world delivering private customized training programs, and teach regularly scheduled classes at AGI's locations. They are available for professional development sessions at schools and universities. More information at *agitraining.com*.

Acknowledgments

Thanks to Web and interactive Czar Fred Gerantabee for providing guidance along with much of the foundation for this book. A special thanks and shout-out to our many friends at Adobe Systems, Inc. who made this book possible and assisted with questions and feedback during the writing process. To the many clients of AGI who have helped us better understand how they use Dreamweaver and provided us with many of the tips and suggestions found in this book. And thanks to the instructional team at AGI for their input and assistance in the review process and for making this book such a team effort.

Thanks to iStockPhoto for the use of their exclusive iStockPhoto.com photographers' images.

Credits

Additional Writing
Greg Heald

President, American Graphics Institute and Digital Classroom Series Publisher
Christopher Smith

Executive Editor
Jody Lefevere

Technical Editors
Barbara Holbrook, Kelley Lawrence, Haziel Olivera

Editor
Marylouise Wiack

Editorial Director
Robyn Siesky

Business Manager
Amy Knies

Senior Marketing Manager
Sandy Smith

Vice President and Executive Group Publisher
Richard Swadley

Vice President and Executive Publisher
Barry Pruett

Senior Project Coordinator
Lynsey Stanford

Graphics and Production Specialist
Lauren Mickol

Media Development Project Supervisor
Chris Leavey

Proofreading
Jay Donahue, Barnowl Publishing

Indexing
Broccoli Information Management

Stock Photography
iStockPhoto.com

Contents

Lesson 2: Setting Up a New Site

Lesson 3: Adding Text and Images

Lesson 4: Styling Your Pages with CSS

Lesson 5: Creating Page Layouts with CSS

Lesson 6: Advanced Page Layout

Lesson 7: Working with Tables

Lesson 8: Fine-Tuning Your Workflow

Lesson 9: Adding Flash, Video, and Sound Content

Lesson 10: Maximizing Site Design

Lesson 11: Working with Code-editing Features

Lesson 12: Building Web Forms

Lesson 13: Working with the Spry Framework

Lesson 14: Managing Your Web Site: Reports, Optimization, and Maintenance

Lesson 15: Using Legacy Tools: Frames and Tables

Starting up 367

Legacy sites. 368

How frames work 368

Advantages and disadvantages of frames. 368

Common frame usage 370

Creating framesets 371

Selecting frames 373

Selecting framesets 375

The Frames panel 375

Setting frameset properties. 376

Setting frame properties. 380

Splitting a frame 382

Dragging a frame border 383

Specifying frame content 385

Targeting frames 385

Linking to outside web pages 387

Using _top to replace a frameset 388

Adding <noframes> content 389

Using tables for layout. 389

Tables versus CSS 390

Inserting a table 390

Selecting tables 393

Modifying tables 396

Setting table borders 397

Merging cells 397

Nesting a table inside a row. 398

Specifying column widths 399

Adding content to tables 400

Adding another table. 405

Formatting tables 407

Self study. 412

Review 413

Lesson 16: Dreamweaver CS5 New Features

Starting up

About Dreamweaver Digital Classroom

Adobe® Dreamweaver® CS5 lets you design, develop, and maintain web pages and web sites. Designers and developers both use Dreamweaver CS5, which lets you create and edit content using either a visual layout or a coding environment. Dreamweaver CS5 also provides tight integration with other Adobe products such as Photoshop® CS5 and Flash® CS5 Professional.

The *Adobe Dreamweaver CS5 Digital Classroom* helps you to understand these capabilities, and how to get the most out of your software, so that you can get up-and-running right away. You can work through all the lessons in this book, or complete only specific lessons. Each lesson includes detailed, step-by-step instructions, along with lesson files, useful background information, and video tutorials.

Adobe Dreamweaver CS5 Digital Classroom is like having your own expert instructor guiding you through each lesson while you work at your own pace. This book includes 16 self-paced lessons that let you discover essential skills, explore new features, and understand capabilities that will save you time. You'll be productive right away with real-world exercises and simple explanations. Each lesson includes step-by-step instructions and lesson files available on the Digital Classroom web site at *digitalclassroombooks.com*. The *Adobe Dreamweaver CS5 Digital Classroom* lessons are developed by the same team of Adobe Certified Instructors and Dreamweaver experts who have created many of the official training titles for Adobe Systems.

Prerequisites

Before you start the *Adobe Dreamweaver CS5 Digital Classroom* lessons, you should have a working knowledge of your computer and its operating system. You should know how to use the directory system of your computer so that you can navigate through folders. You also need to understand how to locate, save, and open files, and you should also know how to use your mouse to access menus and commands.

Before starting the lesson files in the *Adobe Dreamweaver CS5 Digital Classroom*, make sure that you have installed Adobe Dreamweaver CS5. The software is sold separately, and not included with this book. You may use the free 30-day trial version of Adobe Dreamweaver CS5 available at the *Adobe.com* web site, subject to the terms of its license agreement.

System requirements

Before starting the lessons in the *Adobe Dreamweaver CS5 Digital Classroom*, make sure that your computer is equipped for running Adobe Dreamweaver CS5. The minimum system requirements for your computer to effectively use the software are listed on the following page.

System requirements for Adobe Dreamweaver CS5

These are the minimum system requirements for using the Dreamweaver CS5 software.

Windows OS

- Intel® Pentium® 4, AMD Athlon® 64 processor
- Microsoft® Windows® XP with Service Pack 2 (Service Pack 3 recommended); Windows Vista® Home Premium, Business, Ultimate, or Enterprise with Service Pack 1; or Windows 7
- 512MB of RAM (1GB recommended)
- 1GB of available hard-disk space for installation; additional free space required during installation (cannot install on removable flash-based storage devices)
- 1280x800 display with 16-bit video card
- DVD-ROM drive
- Broadband Internet connection required for online services

Macintosh OS

- Multicore Intel® processor
- Mac OS X v10.5.7 or v10.6
- 512MB of RAM (1GB recommended)
- 1.8GB of available hard-disk space for installation; additional free space required during installation (cannot install on a volume that uses a case-sensitive file system or on removable flash-based storage devices)
- 1280x800 display with 16-bit video card
- DVD-ROM drive
- Broadband Internet connection required for online services

Starting Adobe Dreamweaver CS5

As with most software, Adobe Dreamweaver CS5 is launched by locating the application in your Programs folder (Windows) or Applications folder (Mac OS). If you are not familiar with starting the program, follow these steps to start the Adobe Dreamweaver CS5 application:

Windows

1 Choose Start > All Programs > Adobe Dreamweaver CS5.

2 Close the Welcome Screen when it appears. You are now ready to use Adobe Dreamweaver CS5.

Mac OS

1 Open the Applications folder, and then open the Adobe Dreamweaver CS5 folder.

2 Double-click on the Adobe Dreamweaver CS5 application icon.

3 Close the Welcome Screen when it appears. You are now ready to use Adobe Dreamweaver CS5.

Menus and commands are identified throughout the book by using the greater-than symbol (>). For example, the command to print a document appears as File > Print.

Resetting the Dreamweaver workspace

To make certain that your panels and working environment are consistent, you should reset your workspace at the start of each lesson. To reset your workspace, choose Window > Workspace Layout > Designer.

Loading lesson files

The *Dreamweaver CS5 Digital Classroom* DVD includes files that accompany the exercises for each of the lessons. You may copy the entire lessons folder from the supplied DVD to your hard drive, or copy only the lesson folders for the individual lessons you wish to complete.

For each lesson in the book, the files are referenced by the file name of each file. The exact location of each file on your computer is not used, as you may have placed the files in a unique location on your hard drive. We suggest placing the lesson files in the My Documents folder (Windows) or at the top level of your hard drive (Mac OS).

Copying the lesson files to your hard drive:

1   Insert the *Dreamweaver CS5 Digital Classroom* DVD supplied with this book.

2   On your computer desktop, navigate to the DVD and locate the folder named dwlessons.

3   You can install all the files, or just specific lesson files. Do one of the following:

- Install all lesson files by dragging the dwlessons folder to your hard drive.

- Install only some of the files by creating a new folder on your hard drive named dwlessons. Open the dwlessons folder on the supplied DVD, select the lesson(s) you wish to complete, and drag the folder(s) to the dwlessons folder you created on your hard drive.

Unlocking Mac OS files

Macintosh users may need to unlock the files after they are copied from the accompanying disc. This only applies to Mac OS computers and is because the Mac OS may view files that are copied from a DVD or CD as being locked for writing.

If you are a Mac OS user and have difficulty saving over the existing files in this book, you can use these instructions so that you can update the lesson files as you work on them and also add new files to the lessons folder

Note that you only need to follow these instructions if you are unable to save over the existing lesson files, or if you are unable to save files into the lesson folder.

1   After copying the files to your computer, click once to select the dwlessons folder, then choose File > Get Info from within the Finder (not Dreamweaver).

2   In the dwlessons info window, click the triangle to the left of Sharing and Permissions to reveal the details of this section.

3   In the Sharing and Permissions section, click the lock icon, if necessary, in the lower right corner so that you can make changes to the permissions.

4   Click to select a specific user or select everyone, then change the Privileges section to Read & Write.

5   Click the lock icon to prevent further changes, and then close the window.

Working with the video tutorials

Your *Dreamweaver CS5 Digital Classroom* DVD comes with video tutorials developed by the authors to help you understand the concepts explored in each lesson. Each tutorial is approximately five minutes long and demonstrates and explains the concepts and features covered in the lesson.

The videos are designed to supplement your understanding of the material in the chapter. We have selected exercises and examples that we feel will be most useful to you. You may want to view the entire video for each lesson before you begin that lesson. Additionally, at certain points in a lesson, you will encounter the DVD icon. The icon, with appropriate lesson number, indicates that an overview of the exercise being described can be found in the accompanying video.

DVD video icon.

Setting up for viewing the video tutorials

The DVD included with this book includes video tutorials for each lesson. Although you can view the lessons on your computer directly from the DVD, we highly recommend copying the folder labeled *Videos* from the *Dreamweaver CS5 Digital Classroom* DVD to your hard drive for best performance.

Copying the video tutorials to your hard drive:

1   Insert the *Dreamweaver CS5 Digital Classroom* DVD supplied with this book.

2   On your computer desktop, navigate to the DVD and locate the folder named Videos.

3   Drag the Videos folder to a location onto your hard drive.

Viewing the video tutorials with the Adobe Flash Player

The videos on the *Dreamweaver CS5 Digital Classroom* DVD are saved in the Flash projector format. A Flash projector file wraps the Digital Classroom video player and the Adobe Flash Player in an executable file (.exe for Windows or .app for Mac OS). However, please note that the extension (on both platforms) may not always be visible. Projector files allow the Flash content to be deployed on your system without the need for a browser or prior standalone player installation.

Playing the video tutorials:

1   On your computer, navigate to the Videos folder you copied to your hard drive from the DVD. Playing the videos directly from the DVD may result in poor quality playback.

2   Open the Videos folder and double-click the DWvideos_PC.exe (Windows) or DWvideos_Mac.app (Mac OS) to view the video tutorial.

3   Press the Play button to view the videos.

The Flash Player has a simple user interface that allows you to control the viewing experience, including stopping, pausing, playing, and restarting the video. You can also rewind or fast-forward, and adjust the playback volume.

A. Go to beginning. B. Play/Pause. C. Fast-forward/rewind. D. Stop. E. Volume Off/On. F. Volume control.

Playback volume is also affected by the settings in your operating system. Be certain to adjust the sound volume for your computer, in addition to the sound controls in the Player window.

Hosting Your Web sites

While you can work on everything in this book using only your computer, you will eventually want to create Web sites that you share with the world. To do this, you will need to put your Web site on a computer connected to the Internet that is always accessible. This is known as a Web server. If you don't want to get involved in hosting a Web site, you can pay a company to provide space on their Web servers for you. A good place to look for a hosting provider is here: *http://www.microsoft.com/web/jumpstart/hosting.aspx*. If you want to set up your own computer for hosting a Web server and you are using any Windows computer, you can turn it into a Web server at no cost by using the Web Platform Installer available at: *http://www.microsoft.com/web*. If you are a Mac OS user, you can get Mac OS X server from Apple to use a Mac OS computer as a Web server.

If you are just getting started, you don't need to worry about Web hosting just yet. But you'll find this information useful once you start creating sites and you learn how to manage sites using Dreamweaver.

Additional resources

The Digital Classroom series goes beyond the training books. You can also continue your learning online, with training videos, at seminars and conferences, and in-person training events.

Book series

Expand your knowledge of creative software applications with the Digital Classroom training series. Learn more at *digitalclassroombooks.com*.

Seminars and conferences

The authors of the Digital Classroom seminar series frequently conduct in-person seminars and speak at conferences, including the annual CRE8 Conference. Learn more at *agitraining.com* and *CRE8summit.com*.

Resources for educators

Visit *digitalclassroombooks.com* to access resources for educators, including instructors' guides for incorporating Digital Classroom into your curriculum.

What you'll learn in this lesson:

- Exploring Dreamweaver's primary features
- Introducing new features in CS5
- Understanding how web sites and web pages work
- Coding HTML/XHTML: the basics

Dreamweaver CS5 Jumpstart

Whether you are a novice web designer or an experienced developer, Dreamweaver is a comprehensive tool you can use for site design, layout, and management. In this lesson, you'll take a tour of Dreamweaver's key features and get a better understanding of how web pages work.

Starting up

Before starting, make sure that your tools and panels are consistent by resetting your workspace. See "Resetting the Dreamweaver workspace" on page 3.

You will work with several files from the dw01lessons folder in this lesson. Make sure that you have loaded the dwlessons folder onto your hard drive from the supplied DVD. See "Loading lesson files" on page 3.

Note: If you want to get started creating a page, jump ahead to "Tag structure and attributes" on page 18. Otherwise, the next few pages provide you with an overview of key capabilities and features of Dreamweaver CS5.

See Lesson 1 in action!

Use the accompanying video to gain a better understanding of how to use some of the features shown in this lesson. The video tutorial for this lesson can be found on the included DVD.

What is Dreamweaver?

Dreamweaver is an excellent coding and development tool for new and experienced users alike, and it has quickly become the preferred web site creation and management program, providing a creative environment for designers. Whether you design web sites, develop mobile phone content, or script complex server-side applications, Dreamweaver has something to offer.

Design and layout tools

Dreamweaver's many icon-driven menus and detailed panels make it easy to insert and format text, images, and media (such as video files and Flash movies). This means that you can create great-looking and functional web pages without knowing a single line of code—Dreamweaver takes care of building the code behind the scenes for you. Dreamweaver does not create graphics from scratch; instead, it is fully integrated with Adobe Photoshop CS5, so you can import and adjust graphics from within the application.

The Insert panel features objects in several categories that let you easily add images, web forms, and media to your page.

Site management and File Transfer Protocol

Dreamweaver has everything you need for complete site management, including built-in file transfer protocol (FTP) capabilities between a server and your local machine, reusable objects (such as page templates and library items), and several safety mechanisms (such as link checkers and site reports) so that you can ensure that your site works well and looks good. If you're designing your pages with Cascading Style Sheets (CSS), the Browser Compatibility Check and CSS Advisor features will help you to locate and troubleshoot any potential display issues that may occur across different web browsers.

Coding environment and text editor

Dreamweaver lets you work in a code-only view of your document that acts as a powerful text editor. Edit HTML code directly and switch views to see the results of your code as you work. Features such as color-coding, indentation, and visual aids make Dreamweaver a perfect text editing or coding environment for web designers of any level.

For more experienced developers, Dreamweaver also supports popular coding and scripting languages, such as JavaScript, and several server-side languages, including ColdFusion, PHP, and ASP.NET. Specialized insert menus and code panels help you to build pages and applications in the language of your choice.

```
BasicHTML.html ×                         C:\Users\agiaquent\Desktop\dwlessonfiles\dw01lessons\BasicHTML.html

 Code   Split   Design     Live Code  ⊞⌐   Live View   Inspect   ⦿,  ⦿  C    Title: Put a title here

 ⇦ ⇨ ⊗ ⌂ Address: file:///C|/Users/agiaquent/Desktop/dwlessonfiles/dw01lessons/BasicHTML.html ▾ ⊞▾

  1   <!DOCTYPE html PUBLIC "-//W3C//DTD XHTML 1.0 Transitional//EN"
      "http://www.w3.org/TR/xhtml1/DTD/xhtml11-transitional.dtd">
  2   <html xmlns="http://www.w3.org/1999/xhtml">
  3   <head>
  4   <meta http-equiv="Content-Type" content="text/html; charset=utf-8" />
  5   <title>Put a title here</title>
  6   </head>
  7
  8   <body>
  9   <p>My text and pictures go here...</p>
 10   <p><strong>My Bold Title</strong></p>
 11
 12
 13   <p>This text will appear inside of its own paragraph</p>
 14
 15
 16   </body>
 17   </html>
 18   |
```

Code view is a full-featured text editor that color-codes tags and scripts for editing that's easier to decipher.

Scripting languages, such as those used to build interactive web pages or e-commerce sites, fall into two categories: client-side and server-side. Client-side languages (such as JavaScript) run in your browser, while server-side languages (such as ColdFusion) require special software installed on the server to run.

Who uses Dreamweaver?

Dreamweaver's popularity is a result of its diversity. Its ability to take a site from conception through to launch—and maintenance afterward—makes it a preferred tool among industry professionals, businesses, and educational institutions. However, it remains easy and accessible enough for novice designers to get up-and-running quickly. It's not unusual to see Dreamweaver utilized for personal projects or by small businesses and media professionals, such as photographers and painters, to maintain a web presence.

An overview of features

This book is dedicated to exploring, learning, and putting to use all that Dreamweaver has to offer. This section looks at some of the application's key features.

Three different points of view: When you edit a document, Dreamweaver lets you see your work in one of three views: the Design, Split, or Code view. Dreamweaver's easy-to-use Design view lets you build visually and see everything come to life as you create your pages. More experienced web designers and coders can use the Code view to edit a document's HTML code and scripts directly, enhanced with easy-to-read color-coding and visual aids.

For those who like something in between, the Split view provides a split-pane Design and Code view all at once. You can easily change views at any time with a single click in the Document toolbar.

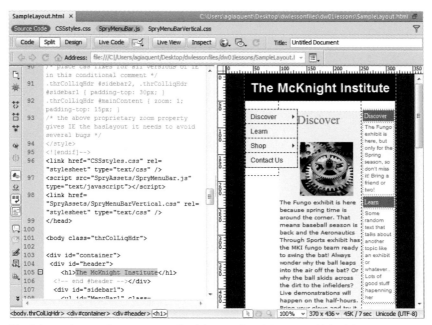

The Split view lets you edit your page visually while seeing the code being created behind the scenes.

Built-in FTP: You can easily upload and download files to and from your web server using the Files panel's drag-and-drop interface, or use the Get/Put button at any time to post pages you're currently working on. There's no need for separate software. Dreamweaver also provides Check In/Check Out functionality and synchronization features for easy management.

Page and code object Insert panels: You can find intuitive icons for most common web page elements in a categorized Insert panel, from which you can add elements to your page with a single click. You can use additional panels to fine-tune any page element to ensure that you see exactly what you want. Included in the default Insert panel are tools for formatting text, building forms, and creating layouts. Customize a Favorites tab with your most-used icons.

The Insert panel is divided into several categories geared toward specific tasks.

Customizable workspace layouts: You can save combinations and positions of panels and toolbars for easy recall at any time. Save multiple workspace layouts for different users, or create different workspaces for specific tasks, such as coding or designing page layouts.

You can customize the Favorites panel with icons from any of the other Insert panel categories.

Powerful visual aids: Take advantage of the precision you're accustomed to in other design programs through Dreamweaver's guides, rulers, measuring tools, and customizable positioning grid. Dreamweaver's Design-Time style sheets let you customize the look of your page exclusively for the editing process, making layout quicker and easier without permanently altering the page's appearance.

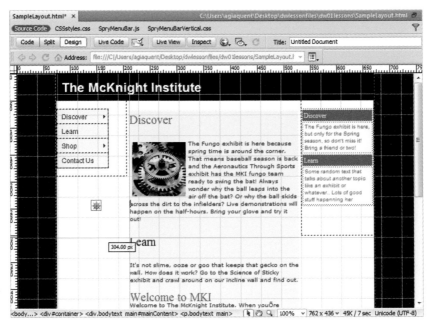

Rulers, a document grid, and guides help you to size and position page items with precision.

CSS Styles panel: Take advantage of the vast design and formatting options that CSS provides through Dreamweaver's full-featured CSS Styles panel, which lets you create, edit, and manage styles on-the-fly from a single panel.

Live View

Experience tells you that visual web editors often display differently from the browsers they're emulating. As script-driven interactivity gains popularity, the need to accurately design the different states of your page (including menus, panels, and interface elements) has become increasingly important. The static nature of Design view in Dreamweaver might no longer meet users' advanced needs.

Dreamweaver's Live View mode uses the WebKit rendering engine (which is also the basis for the Safari web browser and Adobe AIR) to give you a more accurate preview of your page, usually just as a browser would render it.

Live View enables you to interact with your pages.

When you select Live Code while in Live View mode, you can see, in real time, how visually changing your page affects the code behind the scenes. You can preview your code as classes are added and removed using JavaScript, as dynamic content is inserted using Spry, and much more.

It's one thing, however, to preview these states, and another to effectively work with them. The Freeze JavaScript button (or the F6 key) freezes your page in a particular state (for example, with a menu locked open and a hover effect in place). You can then edit those interactively displayed elements directly in Dreamweaver, without having to use the Preview in Browser feature (F12) and your favorite web browser.

Related files

Web-based projects are becoming more complex than ever before, and you often find that even a single page is composed of a variety of assets. These assets can include Cascading Style Sheets (CSS), external JavaScript files, or even server-side includes. Dreamweaver CS5 has a feature that will help you be much more effective at designing and managing sites and applications with multiple assets.

The Related Files bar runs across the top of your document window, just below the document tabs. The bar shows you all the various files that combine to create your finished page. Switch between these files using the Related Files bar without losing the visual preview of their parent page. Design view (or Live View) always shows the parent file, but you can now edit any of the related files without losing their important visual context.

The Related Files bar shows you the various files that are part of your finished page.

Code Navigator

Using the Code Navigator, you can easily jump to any of the related files (including the specific rules within) that combine to create the final display of a selected element. It is not necessary to look through multiple style sheets to find a specific rule. It's now just a context menu-click away in Dreamweaver. With the Code Navigator, when you hover over a CSS rule you are able to see the properties and values and click on them to navigate to that specific code. As with related files, you an do this without losing the visual context that's so important to creating interactive experiences.

The Code Navigator allows you to easily jump to any of your related files.

Photoshop smart objects

Dreamweaver CS5 offers support for Photoshop smart objects, meaning you can drag a PSD file into a web page within Dreamweaver, optimize the image for the web, and even resize it. If you later update the original PSD file, a red arrow appears on the image in Dreamweaver, indicating that the source file has changed. You can then click the Update from Original button in the Property Inspector, and a new version of the image is created.

Smart objects provide easier optimizing and updating of graphics.

How web sites work

Before embarking on the task of building web pages (and in turn, a web site), it's a good idea to know the basics of how web sites work, how your users view them, and what you need to know to make sure your web site looks and works its best.

A simple flow chart

What happens when you type in a web site address? Most people don't even think about it; they just type in a URL, and a web site appears in a flash. They likely don't realize how many things are going on behind the scenes to make sure that pages gets delivered to their computers so that they can do their shopping, check their e-mail, or research a project.

When you type in a URL or IP address, you are connecting to a remote computer (referred to as a server) and downloading the documents, images, and resources necessary to reconstruct the pages you will view at that site. Web pages aren't delivered as a finished product; your web browser (Internet Explorer, Firefox, Safari, and so on) is responsible for reconstructing and formatting the pages based on the HTML code included in the pages. HTML (Hypertext Markup Language) is a simple, tag-based language that instructs your browser how and where to insert and format pictures, text, and media files. Web pages are written in HTML, and Dreamweaver builds HTML for you behind the scenes as you construct your page in the Design view.

An Internet Service Provider (ISP) enables you to connect to the Internet. Some well-known ISPs include America Online and Earthlink. You view web pages over an Internet connection using a browser, such as Internet Explorer, Firefox, or Safari. A browser can decipher and display web pages and their content, including images, text, and video.

Domain names and IP addresses

When you type in a web site address, you usually enter the web site's domain name (such as *eBay.com*). The web site owner purchased this domain name and uses it to mask an IP address, which is a numerical address used to locate and dial up the pages and files associated with a specific web site.

So how does the web know what domains match what IP address (and in turn, which web sites)? It uses a Domain Name Service (DNS) server, which makes connections between domain names and IP addresses.

Servers and web hosts

A DNS server is responsible for matching a domain name with its companion IP address. Think of the DNS server as the operator at the phone company who connects calls through a massive switchboard. DNS servers are typically maintained by either the web host or the registrar from which the domain was purchased. Once the match is made, the request from your user is routed to the appropriate server and folder where your web site resides. When the request reaches the correct account, the server directs it to the first page of the web site, which is typically named index.html, default.html, or whatever the server is set up to recognize as a default starting page.

A server is a machine very much like your desktop computer, but it's capable of handling traffic from thousands of users (often at the same time!), and it maintains a constant connection to the Internet so that your web site is available 24 hours a day. Servers are typically maintained by web hosts, companies that charge a fee to host and serve your web site to the public. A single server can sometimes host hundreds of web sites. Web hosting services are available from a variety of providers, including well-known Internet service companies, such as Yahoo!, and large, dedicated hosting companies, such as GoDaddy. It is also common for a large company to maintain its own servers and web sites on its premises.

The role of web browsers

A web browser is an application that downloads and displays HTML pages. Every time you request a page by clicking a link or typing in a web site address, you are requesting an HTML page and any files it includes. The browser's job is to reconstruct and display that page based on the instructions in the HTML code, which guides the layout and formatting of the text, images, and other assets used in the page. The HTML code works like a set of assembly instructions for the browser to use.

An introduction to HTML

HTML is what makes the Web work; web pages are built using HTML code, which in turn is read and used by your web browser to lay out and format text, images, and video on your page. As you design and lay out web pages in Design view, Dreamweaver writes the code behind the scenes that is necessary to display and format your page in a web browser.

Contrary to what you may think, HTML is not a programming language, but rather a simple text-based markup language. HTML is not proprietary to Dreamweaver—you can create and edit HTML in any text editor, even simple applications such as Windows Notepad and Mac OS X's TextEdit. Dreamweaver's job is to give you a visual way to create web pages without having to code by hand. If you like to work with code, however, Dreamweaver's Code view, discussed earlier, is a fully featured text editor with color-coding and formatting tools that make it far easier to write and read HTML and other languages.

Tag structure and attributes

HTML uses tags, or bracketed keywords, that you can use to place or format content. Many tags require a closing tag, which is the keyword preceded by a forward slash (/).

1 Choose File > Open. When the Open dialog box appears, navigate to the dw01lessons folder. Select BasicHTML.html and press Open.

2 Select the Split button in the Document toolbar to see the layout as well as the code that makes up the page.

Take a look at line 10 (indicated at the left edge of the Code panel). The text *My Bold Title* is inside a Strong tag, which is simply the word *strong* contained within angled brackets. Any words or characters inside these tags are formatted in bold, and appear as shown in the Design view.

A look at the code reveals the tags used to format text in your page.

Tags can also accept CSS rules that specify additional information for how the tag should display the content. CSS rules can take a number of different values, such as a size, a color, or a direction in which to align something. Take a look at the line that reads *This text will appear inside of its own paragraph*. This line is enclosed in a *p* (paragraph) tag, which separates it from the other text by a line above and below. You can add a class rule to this to align the text in whichever direction you want.

3 Highlight the entire line that reads *This text will appear inside of its own paragraph* at the bottom of the Design view.

4 With the CSS button selected in the Property Inspector, locate the paragraph align buttons. Press the Align Center button (≣).

5   In the New CSS Rule dialog box, type **.center** into the Selector Name text field, and press OK.

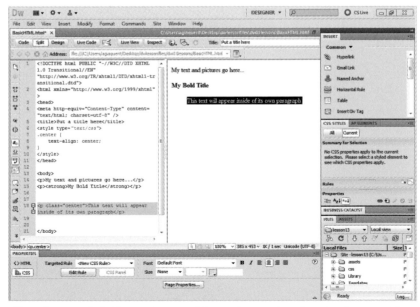

Name a newly created style in the New CSS Rule dialog box.

6   The text is now centered. Take a look at the Code view, and notice that the .center rule has been added to the opening *<p>* tag.

Align or format text in the Property Inspector, and then see the appropriate rules and attributes created in your code.

For more information on formatting text with CSS rules, please see Lesson 3, "Adding Text and Images."

7   Choose File > Save to save your work, then choose File > Close.

The structure of an HTML document

Although you use many HTML tags to format text, certain tags are devoted to establishing structures, such as lists, tables, or, most importantly, the HTML documents themselves. The HTML tag is the most fundamental tag. It is used to specify the beginning and end of HTML in a document:

```
<html></html>
```

Inside the main HTML tags are two tags that define the key areas of your web page: the head and the body. The head of your page contains items that are not visible to your user, but are important nonetheless, such as search engine keywords, page descriptions, and links to outside scripts or style sheets. You create the head of the document inside the HTML tags using the *<head>* tag:

```
<html>
<head></head>
</html>
```

The body of your page is where all the visible elements of your page are contained. Here is where you place and format text, images, and other media. You define the body of the page using the *<body>* tag:

```
<html>
<head></head>
<body>

My text and pictures go here...

</body>
</html>
```

Whenever you create a new HTML document in Dreamweaver, this framework is created automatically before you add anything to the page. Any visual elements you add to the page are added, using the appropriate HTML code inside the *<body>* tags.

Placing images in HTML

You use some tags in HTML to place items, such as pictures or media files, inside a web page. The *<img>* tag is the most common example; its job is to place and format an image on the page. To place an image and see the resulting code, follow these steps:

1   Choose File > Open. When the Open dialog box appears, navigate to the dw01lessons folder. Select the Images.html file and press Open to edit the file.

2   If necessary, click the Split button in the Document toolbar so that you're viewing both the layout and the code for your page. In the Design view portion of the Split view, click below the line of text to place your cursor underneath it. This is where you'll place a new image.

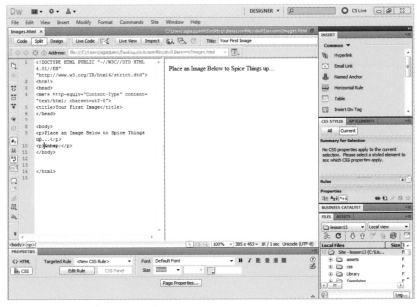

Enter the Split view before you insert the image onto your page.

3   From the Common category in the Insert panel on the right side of the screen, click on the Images element (▣) and choose Image. When the Select Image Source dialog box appears, select the file named gears.jpg, located in the images folder within the dw01lessons folder.

Choose Image from the Common tab on the Insert bar.

4   Press OK (Windows) or Choose (Mac OS); when the Image Tag Accessibility Attributes dialog box appears, type the words **Gears Image** in the Alternate text field, and press OK to place the image.

Attach alternate text to your image.

The Image Tag Accessibility Attributes dialog box appears when you add images, to provide additional information for users with special needs (such as the visually impaired). You should always provide each image with alternative text, but you can disable this panel by choosing Edit > Preferences (Windows) or Dreamweaver > Preferences (Mac OS). In the Accessibility category, uncheck the Images *option.*

5   The code shows that the HTML *<img>* tag has been used to place the image. Click once on the image in the document window to select it. The Property Inspector at the bottom of the page displays and sets the properties for the image.

6   In the Border text field of the Property Inspector, type **3** to set a three-pixel border around the image, then press Enter (Windows) or Return (Mac OS). Click on the background of the page to deselect and note the appearance of the border. The *<img>* tag now contains the border attribute, which is set to a value of 3, just the way you typed it in the Property Inspector.

As you change or add options to a selected image, Dreamweaver changes code behind the scenes.

7   Choose File > Save to save your work, then choose File > Close.

Note that in HTML, images and media are not embedded, but placed. This means that the tags point to files in their exact locations relative to the page. The tags count on those files always being where they're supposed to be in order to display them. This is why HTML pages are typically very lightweight in terms of file size.

Colors in HTML

In Dreamweaver's various panels and in your code, each color is referred to by a six-character code preceded by a pound sign. This code is called hexadecimal code, and is the system that HTML pages use to identify and use colors. You can reproduce almost any color using a unique hexadecimal code. For example, you represent dark red in HTML as #CC0000.

The first, middle, and last two digits of the hexadecimal code correspond to values in the RGB spectrum. For instance, white, which is represented in RGB as R:255 G:255 B:255, is represented in HTML as #FFFFFF (255 | 255 | 255). Choosing colors is easy, thanks to a handy Swatches panel, which you can find in many places throughout the work area.

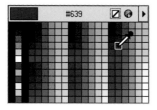

The Swatches panel makes it easy to work with colors.

The color pickers in Adobe Photoshop and Illustrator also display and accept hexadecimal codes, making it easy to copy and paste colors between these applications and Dreamweaver.

Case sensitivity and whitespace rules

HTML is a flexible language that has very few rules regarding its own appearance. Based on how strictly you want to write it, HTML can be either very specific about whether tags are written in upper- or lowercase (called case sensitivity), or not specific at all. To see how HTML treats whitespace, follow these steps.

1   Choose File > Open. When the Open dialog box appears, navigate to the dw01lessons folder. Select the Whitespace.html file, then press Open.

2 If your file is not in Split view, press the Split button in the Document toolbar, so that you can view both the layout and the code. Notice three seemingly identical tags beneath line 9 in your code:

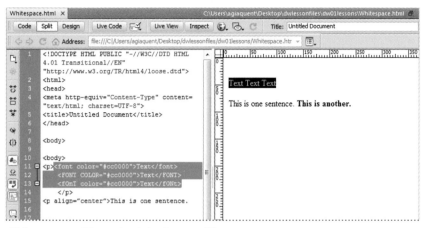

All these tags are valid, even though they have very different case structures.

All three tags use a completely different case structure, but all are valid and are treated in the same way. Take a look at the text that reads *This is one sentence. This is another.* The code shows a lot of space between the two lines, but the Design view shows no space at all. This is because both whitespace and line returns between two pieces of text or tags are not recognized.

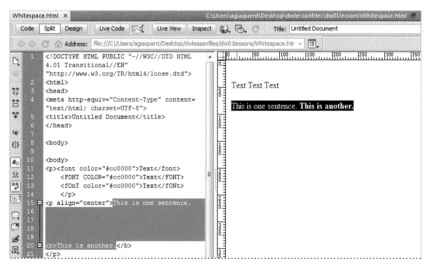

Despite the large amount of space between the two sentences, they appear side-by-side in the Design view.

3   To create a line return, or a new paragraph, you need to enter the necessary HTML tags. In the Design view at the bottom, position your cursor after the first sentence, then press Shift+Enter (Windows) or Shift+Return (Mac OS) twice. This creates two line returns—you can see that each line return is created in your code by a *
* (break) tag. When rendered in the browser, the *
* tag adds blank lines between the sentences, however the sentences are technically within the same paragraph.

To create a line return, hold down the Shift key while pressing the Enter or Return key.

4   To create a new paragraph, position your cursor before the phrase, *This is another*, and press Enter (Windows) or Return (Mac OS). The text is separated by a line above and below, and is wrapped inside a set of *<p>* (paragraph) tags.

Dreamweaver creates a new paragraph each time you press the Enter or Return key.

Other than a standard single space (such as the ones used between words), several consecutive spaces created by the spacebar are ignored, and are displayed as only one space in Design view and in a browser.

5   Choose File > Save to save your work then choose File > Close.

Tag hierarchy

HTML tags follow a certain order of weight, or hierarchy, to make sure that everything displays as it should. The tag at the top of the hierarchy is the *<html>* tag, and every other tag you create is contained within it. Tags such as the *<body>* tag always hold smaller tags, such as the *<p>* (paragraph), *<img>* (image), and *<strong>* (bold) tags. In addition, structural tags (such as those that create paragraphs, lists, and tables) hold more weight than formatting tags such as *<strong>* (bold) and *<em>* (italic). Take this line of code, for example:

```
<strong><p>Big bold paragraph</p></strong>
```

Although code such as this may work in certain browsers, it isn't recommended, because the *<strong>* tag technically holds less weight than the *<p>* tag. The following code represents a safer and more proper way to include the bold type:

```
<p><strong>Big bold paragraph</strong></p>
```

Dreamweaver generally does a great job of keeping tags properly nested, or contained within each other. When you choose to manipulate the code by hand, you should always keep good coding techniques in mind.

XHTML 1.0 Transitional

The latest recommended version of HTML is XHTML 1.0, a stricter version of HTML that makes the language more compatible with newer platforms, such as mobile phones and handheld devices, which require code to be perfectly formed. XHTML combines elements of HTML and XML, a language used to describe data. XML, or Extensible Markup Language, has become a popular method of exchanging information among seemingly unrelated applications, platforms, and systems. By default, Dreamweaver creates new web pages using the XHTML 1.0 Transitional standard.

What's the difference?

Although tags and attributes remain the same, the structure of the language changes with XHTML, becoming stricter. Whereas HTML was very forgiving of sloppy coding practices such as overlapping or unclosed tags, XHTML requires all tags to be closed and properly nested. HTML doesn't care which case you use when constructing tags, but in XHTML, all tags must be lowercase.

For example, a *
* (break) tag, which normally doesn't require a closing tag, now must be closed. You can write tags to *self-close* by using a forward slash—making sure there is a space between the (*br*) and the forward slash—and then closing the bracket like so:

```
<br />
```

The result is a well-formed language that takes advantage of newer browsers and device platforms, while remaining compatible with older browsers. Working with XHTML in Dreamweaver requires nothing more than selecting XHTML 1.0 Transitional as the Document Type (DocType) when creating a new page.

Explorations in code

Although this book occasionally refers to the code for examples, hand-coding is not a primary goal of the included lessons. The best way to learn how code represents the layouts you are building visually is to switch to the Code view and explore what's happening behind the scenes.

It's important to remember that every button, panel, and menu in Dreamweaver represents some type of HTML tag, attribute, or value; very rarely will you learn something that is unrelated or proprietary to Dreamweaver alone. Think of the Dreamweaver workspace as a pretty face on the HTML language.

A look at the Welcome Screen

A common fixture in most CS5 applications is the Welcome Screen, which is a launching pad for new and recent documents. In Dreamweaver, the Welcome Screen appears when the application launches or when no documents are open. From the Welcome Screen, you can create new pages, create a new site, open a recent document, or use one of Dreamweaver's many starter pages or layouts.

The Welcome Screen appears when you launch the application, or when no documents are open.

Here's what you'll find on the Welcome Screen:

Open a Recent Item: A list of the last few documents you worked on appears in the leftmost column, or you can browse to open a different file using the Open button (📁) at the bottom.

Create New: In addition to HTML pages, you can choose from a variety of new document formats, such as CSS, JavaScript, and XML. Dreamweaver is not just a web page-building tool, but also a superior text editor, making it ideal for creating many non-HTML files. You can also define a new Dreamweaver site using the link at the bottom, or choose the More folder for even more new file options.

Top Features (videos): On the far right side of the Welcome Screen, there is a column that contains Top Features videos. These videos explore some of the new top features of Dreamweaver CS5, such as CSS Inspect Mode, Dynamically-Related Files, and BrowserLab Integration. The videos are located on Adobe's web site, *adobe.com*, and when you click on one, Dreamweaver launches the site in your web browser to give you access to the video.

Creating, opening, and saving documents

The lessons throughout this book require that you create, save, and open existing files. You can accomplish most file-related tasks from the File menu at the top, or from the Welcome Screen that appears when you launch Dreamweaver.

Creating new documents

Dreamweaver creates text files, commonly in the form of HTML files (or web pages). It can also create files in a variety of text-based languages, including CSS, XML, JavaScript, and even Flash ActionScript.

You can create blank files that you build from the ground up, or get started with a variety of layout templates and themes. You can create new documents from the File menu or from the Welcome Screen.

The New Document dialog box gives you a choice of new files in a variety of formats and templates.

1   To create a new document, choose File > New. The New Document dialog box appears.

2   Select Blank Page and under the Page Type column, choose HTML. Under Layout, choose <none> to start a new blank document. Leave the DocType drop-down menu at its default. Press Create.

3   Choose File > Save or File > Save As to start the process of saving your document.

4   When prompted, choose a location for your file and assign it a name. Note that you must save HTML files with an .html extension, or they will not be interpreted properly in a browser. This rule applies for files of any type (such as .xml, .css, and .cfm).

Opening a recently opened document

To open a document you've worked on recently, Choose File > Open Recent or, from the Welcome Screen, select a document under the Open a Recent Item column.

Dw
ADOBE® DREAMWEAVER® CS5

Open a Recent Item
dw01lessons/Whitespace.html
dw01lessons/Images.html
dw01lessons/SampleLayout.html
dw01lessons/PhotoshopDoc.html
dw01lessons/BasicHTML.html
dw13lessons/ex4_sticky.html

File	Edit	View	Insert	Modify	Format	Comm

New...   Ctrl+N
Open...   Ctrl+O
Browse in Bridge...   Ctrl+Alt+O
Open Recent   ▶   1 Whitespace.html
Open in Frame...   Ctrl+Shift+O   2 BasicHTML.html
Close   Ctrl+W   3 Images.html
Close All   Ctrl+Shift+W   4 SampleLayout.html
                                             5 SampleLayout.html
Share My Screen...   6 BasicHTML.html

                                             Reopen Documents on Startup

Choose a file from the Welcome Screen or choose File > Open Recent to select a recently opened file.

Now that you've seen what Dreamweaver can do, it's time to put what you've learned into practice. Move to the next lesson so that you can begin building your first Dreamweaver site!

Self study

Explore the ready-to-use CSS layouts available in Dreamweaver by choosing File > New, then selecting HTML from the Page Type column. Browse the options listed in the Layout column and open a few layouts. Identify some that you'd like to use as a starting point for any future project.

Review

Questions

1 From what two locations in Dreamweaver can a new document be created?

2 In what three views does Dreamweaver allow you to view and edit documents?

3 True or False: When a web page is requested, it is delivered to a user's browser as a completed, flat file ready for viewing.

Answers

1 From the Welcome Screen or by choosing File > New.

2 Design, Split, and Code views.

3 False. Files are delivered individually; the browser uses HTML code to assemble the resources together to display a finished page.

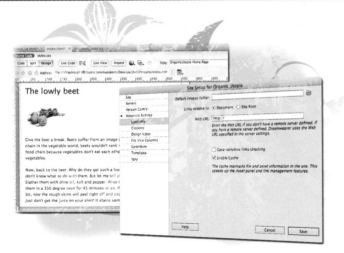

What you'll learn in this lesson:

- Defining site settings

- Establishing local root and remote folders

- Adding pages

- Selecting, viewing, and organizing files with the Files panel

- Uploading and downloading files to and from your remote server

Setting Up a New Site

Dreamweaver's strength lies in its powerful site creation and management tools. You can use the software to create everything from individual pages to complete web sites. The pages you create within your site can share similar topics, a cohesive design, or a common purpose. And, once your Dreamweaver site is complete, you can efficiently manage and distribute it from within the program.

Starting up

Before starting, make sure that your tools and panels are consistent by resetting your workspace. See "Resetting the Dreamweaver workspace" on page 3.

You will work with several files from the dw02lessons folder in this lesson. Make sure that you have loaded the dwlessons folder onto your hard drive from the supplied DVD. See "Loading lesson files" on page 3.

See Lesson 2 in action!

Use the accompanying video to gain a better understanding of how to use some of the features shown in this lesson. The video tutorial for this lesson can be found on the included DVD.

Creating a new site

In Dreamweaver, the term *site* refers to the local and remote storage locations where the files that make up a web site are stored. A site can also include a testing server location for processing dynamic pages. To take full advantage of Dreamweaver's features, you should always start by creating a site.

The easiest way to create a new site in Dreamweaver is to use the Site Setup dialog box. Choose Site > New Site, and the dialog box appears.

You can also use the Manage Sites dialog box to create a new site. This and other functions of the Manage Sites dialog box are discussed later in this book.

In this lesson, you begin by using the Site Setup dialog box to accomplish the following tasks:

• Define the site

• Name the site

• Define the local root folder

• Set up a remote folder

• Explore advanced settings

• Save the site

By default, the Site Setup dialog box opens with the Site Settings available. The options available here will help guide you through the essentials of defining your site. The Servers, Version Control and Advanced Settings options allow you to set up local, remote, and testing servers directly.

The first screen you see in the Site Setup dialog box allows you to name your site. Avoid using spaces (use underscores instead), periods, slashes, or any other punctuation in your site name, as doing so will likely cause the server to misdirect your files.

1   Launch Dreamweaver CS5, if it is not already open, then choose Site > New Site. First, you have to name the site. In the Site Name text field, type **Organic Utopia**.

Site Setup for Organic_Utopia	
Site	A Dreamweaver site is a collection of all of the files and assets you use in your website. A Dreamweaver site usually has two parts: a local folder on your computer where you store and work on files, and a remote folder on a server where you post the same files to the web.
Servers	
Version Control	
▶ Advanced Settings	Here you'll select the local folder and a name for your Dreamweaver site.

Site Name: Organic_Utopia

Local Site Folder: /Users/jeremyosborn/Documents/Unnamed Site 2   📁

Help   Cancel   Save

Type the Site Name into the text field.

Next, you need to set up a local root folder, which is where Dreamweaver stores the files with which you're currently working. The Local Site Folder field allows you to enter information regarding where you'll be working with your files during development.

To ensure that the links you set up on your computer will work when you upload the site to a web server, it is essential that you store all the site's resources in one main folder on your hard drive, then identify it within Dreamweaver. This is because the links will only work properly if all the site's elements remain in the same relative location on the web server as with your hard drive.

2   Click on the folder icon (📁) to the right of the Local Site Folder text field to navigate to your pre-existing files.

If you did not click on this folder and went on to the next step, Dreamweaver would simply create a new folder on your system where you could begin to create new pages in your site. In this case, you will be pointing to a preexisting folder that already has files within it.

It is important to distinguish between adding a new site (which is what you are doing now) and creating a new site from scratch. In both cases, the important part is that Dreamweaver knows where this folder is on your system. This folder is known as the root folder and will always contain the content that will eventually be your website.

3 Navigate to your desktop and locate the dw02lessons folder you copied to your desktop earlier.

4 Select the dw02lessons folder. On the Windows platform, click Open to open this folder, then press Select (Windows). On the Mac OS platform, press Choose (Mac OS) to choose this as your local root folder. The field now shows the path to your newly defined local root folder.

5 Click on the Servers tab. This section allows you to define the remote server where your website will end up being hosted. Take a moment to read the heading in the dialog box. Note that it says you do not need to fill in this information to begin creating a website. It is only necessary if you are connecting to the Web.

You are not connecting to the web in this lesson, but you should take a look at the screen anyway to understand the information needed.

6 Click on the + button and the Basic site settings window appears. Here there are fields for Server Name, Connect Using, FTP Address, Username and Password, along with other options. These settings allow you to choose both a destination and a method (FTP being the most common) for Dreamweaver to use to transfer files.

Set up access to your remote folder.

7   As noted earlier, you do not have to define your remote folder at this stage. Dreamweaver allows you to define your remote folder at a later time, such as when you're ready to upload. Click on the Advanced tab. Click on the Server Model menu in the Testing Server section. Here there are choices for different scripting languages such as PHP and Asp pages. If you are an advanced user, this is where you would set up the connections to your testing server.

   Again, you won't be making any changes here, so press Cancel.

8   Click on the Version Control option on the left to access Subversion settings. Subversion, a VCS or version control system, keeps track of changes made to files, enabling users to track changes and return to previous versions of any file. For this exercise, make sure the Access pull-down in this window is set to None, as you won't be using Subversion.

   You've now completed the site setup process, using basic settings. Don't close the Site Setup dialog box yet, though, as you'll now explore the options found under the Advanced Settings option.

Advanced site-creation options

Chances are if you are new to Dreamweaver or web design you won't need these advanced settings. If you are in this category, press Save and skip to the Creating Pages section. Other users may be curious what these settings are and should proceed.

1   Click on the arrow next to Advanced Settings in the Site Setup dialog box.

2   From the categories listed below Advanced Settings, choose Local Info.

The information you entered using the wizard is reflected here.

The information you set in the Local Info window identifies your Default Images folder, what your links are relative to, and a Web URL to be used if you don't have a remote server defined. One of the more important Local Info settings, though, is case-sensitive link checking.

The case-sensitive link checking feature ensures that your links will work on a Unix server, where links are case-sensitive. If you're using a Windows or Mac OS server, this doesn't matter as much, but it is a good idea to follow the strict naming and linking conventions of a Unix system in case you ever move your site to a different server.

The remaining categories to the left of the Advanced tab of the Site Setup dialog box help to define your site's production, collaboration, and deployment capabilities. They include the following:

Cloaking allows you to specify file types or specific files that you do not want uploaded to the server.

Design Notes is a collaboration tool that keeps notes regarding the development of the page or site.

File View Columns is an organizational tool. If you want to share the custom columns with others, you must enable Design Notes as well.

Contribute is a separate application that enables users with basic word processing and web browser skills and little or no HTML knowledge to create and maintain web pages.

Templates can be automatically updated with rewritten document paths using this option.

Spry is a JavaScript library for web designers. It allows designers to build pages that provide a richer experience for their users.

At this point, you are finished defining your settings, so press Save; Dreamweaver creates a site with the settings you have defined.

You are now ready to build pages for your web site.

Adding pages

Dreamweaver contains many features to assist you in building pages for your site. With these features, you can define properties for those pages, including titles, background colors or images, and default text and link colors.

The first step for creating a new page correctly was taken when you defined the site in the last exercise. By defining the root folder, Dreamweaver will always create new pages in your site automatically. These pages are now visible in the Files Panel in the lower right of your screen.

The Files panel.

1   Choose File > New. The New Document dialog box opens.

Use the New Document dialog box to add a page to your site.

2   You can create a new page using a predesigned layout, or start with a blank page and build a layout of your own. In this exercise, you'll start with a blank page. Click on the Blank Page category on the left side of the New Document dialog box.

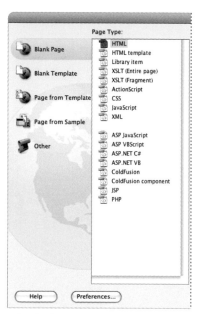

Select the Blank Page *category on the left side of the New Document dialog box.*

3   In the Page Type column, you can select the type of page you want to create (for example, HTML, ColdFusion, and so on). Select HTML.

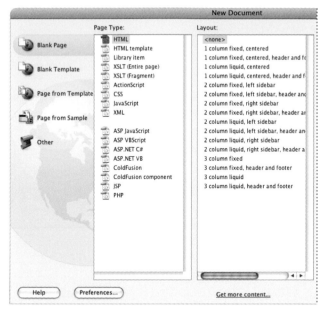

Choose the type of page you want to create (HTML).

In the Layout column, you can choose to base your page on a prebuilt design (created using Cascading Style Sheets [CSS], which are discussed in detail later in this book). These predesigned layouts fall into one of two categories:

Fixed columns do not resize based on the user's browser settings. They are measured in pixels.

Liquid columns resize if the user resizes the browser window, but not if the user changes the text settings.

4   Click on <none> in the Layout column to build the page without using a
prebuilt layout.

Select <none> from the Layout column.

5   Leave the DocType setting at XHTML 1.0 Transitional. The DocType drop-down menu
defines the document type and compliance with different versions of HTML. XHTML
1.0 Transitional is the default setting and is suitable in most cases.

Choose XHTML 1.0 Transitional as your DocType.

*The Layout CSS and Attach CSS settings are irrelevant here, as you didn't choose a CSS-based
layout for this page.*

6   Press Create to create a new, blank HTML page. You will learn more about Workspaces a bit later, but to make sure you are working as we are choose Window > Workspace Layout and choose Reset Designer. Your screen should now look like ours.

Your new, blank HTML page.

Saving a page to your site

You should get accustomed to saving pages to your local root folder early and often. It is very important that you store all your site's resources in one main folder on your hard drive so that the links you set on your computer will work when your site is uploaded to a server.

1   Choose File > Save.

2   In the Save As dialog box, you should be saving within your dw02lessons folder which was defined earlier in the Site Settings.

   Note that if this is not the case, navigate to your desktop and locate the dw02lessons folder.

3   In the Name text field, name your file **about_us.html**.

4   Click Save to save the page in your local root folder. In the Files panel note that the file about_us.html has now been added. Again, this is why site settings are so important in Dreamweaver.

Defining page properties

Now that you've created a page in Dreamweaver, you'll use the Page Properties dialog box to specify its layout and formatting properties. You use this dialog box to define page properties for each new page you create, and to modify the settings for pages you've already created.

1   Use the Page Properties dialog box to set page titles, background colors and images, text and link colors, and other basic properties of every web page. To access the Page Properties dialog box, choose Modify > Page Properties, or use the keyboard shortcut Ctrl+J (Windows) or Command+J (Mac OS). The Page Properties dialog box appears, with the Appearance (CSS) category selected by default.

The Page Properties dialog box.

Settings found in the Appearance (CSS) category will automatically create a Cascading Style Sheet that defines the appearance of your page. Using a CSS to define these page properties adds flexibility to your design, as styling can be changed more easily, and more universally, than if your defaults are defined using HTML code.

2   The Page font and Size fields define the default appearance of text on your page. For now, leave these settings at their defaults. You'll be styling type with CSS in later lessons in this book.

3   The Text color option allows you to set a default color in which to render type. To set a text color, click on the color swatch next to Text; the Swatches panel appears. You can choose your default text color by clicking on the appropriate swatch from the Swatches panel. Try this by clicking on any color swatch, and press Apply to apply your desired default text color.

You can also type the hexadecimal notation for your desired color into the text field. Type the hex code **666666** in the text field to specify a dark gray as the default text color.

You'll see the effects of this change later in this lesson, when you add text to your page using the Files panel.

Set a default text color using the Swatches panel.

4   Use the Background color option to choose a background color for your page. Click on the color swatch next to the Background text field; the Swatches panel appears. You can choose your background color by clicking on the appropriate swatch from the Swatches panel. Try this by clicking on any color swatch, then press Apply to see the results.

You can also choose the background color by typing the hexadecimal notation for your desired color into the Background text field. Type the hex code **739112** in the Background text field, then press Apply to specify a green as the background color.

Set a background color for your page.

5   The Background image field allows you to set a background image for your page. Dreamweaver mimics a browser's behavior by repeating, or tiling, the background image to fill the window. To choose a background image, click the Browse button next to the Background image text field. The Select Image Source dialog box appears.

6   Navigate to the images folder within dw02lessons and select bg_gradient.gif for your page background; then press Apply. You will see the background image which is a gradient appear on the page. It stops partway, however, so you will fix this with the Repeat property.

7   From the Repeat drop-down menu, choose repeat-x. Click Apply to see the change.

Choose a background image for your page (background.gif).

You can also type the path to your background image into the Background image text field.

8   By default, Dreamweaver places your text and images in close proximity to the top and left edges of the page. To build in some extra room between your page edges and the content on them, use the Margin settings in the Page Properties dialog box. In the Left margin text field, type **25** to place your content 25 pixels from the left edge of the page. In the Top margin text field, type **25** to place your content 25 pixels from the top edge of the page.

The Appearance (HTML) category in the Page Properties dialog box contains many of the same settings you just defined. Setting default page attributes with HTML code, however, does not automatically create a Cascading Style Sheet, and is therefore less flexible than using CSS. For more information on this difference, see Lesson 15, "Using Legacy Tools: Frames and Tables."

The Links (CSS) category allows you to define the appearance of linked text within your document. For more information on creating hyperlinks, see Lesson 3, "Adding Text and Images."

9 Click on the Links category on the left-hand side and leave the Link font and Size settings at their defaults (same as Page font). This ensures that your hyperlinks will display in the same typeface and size as the rest of the text on your page.

10 Set the colors for your different link types in the following fields:

Link Color: Type **#fc3** for the default link color applied to linked text on your web page.

Visited links: Type **#ccc** for the color applied to linked text after a user has clicked on it.

Rollover links: Type **#f03** for the color applied to linked text when a user rolls over it.

Active links: Type **#ff6** for the color applied when the user clicks on linked text.

11 Because you're using CSS formatting, you can choose whether or not (and/or when) you want your links to be underlined. This is not possible with HTML formatting. Choose the default setting of Always Underline in the Underline style drop-down menu.

Choose default colors for links, visited links, and active links.

The Headings (CSS) category allows you to define the font, style, size, and color of heading text within your document.

12 Leave the settings in the Headings category at their defaults for now. You'll be using CSS to style your heading text later in this book.

Define the default appearance of heading text on your page.

13 Click on the Title/Encoding category to the left of the Page Properties dialog box to expose more settings:

- Type **Organic Utopia: About Us** in the Title text field. This sets the title that appears in the title bar of most browser windows. It's also the default title used when a user bookmarks your page.

- Leave the Document Type (DTD) set to XHTML 1.0 Transitional. This makes the HTML document XHTML-compliant.

- Choose Unicode (UTF-8) (Windows) or Unicode 5.1 UTF-8 (Mac OS) from the Encoding drop-down menu. This specifies the encoding used for characters in your page.

- Make sure the Unicode Normalization Form is set to None and that Include Unicode Signature (BOM) is unchecked. Both settings are unnecessary for this lesson.

The Title/Encoding category allows you to title your page and/or specify the encoding used.

14 Click on the Tracing Image category in the left part of the Page Properties dialog box. A tracing image is a JPEG, GIF, or PNG image that you create in a separate graphics application, such as Adobe Photoshop or Fireworks. It is placed in the background of your page for you to use as a guide to recreate a desired page design.

15 Press the Browse button next to the Tracing image text field. You can also type the path to your image directly into this text field.

16 In the Select Image Source dialog box, navigate to your dw02lessons folder, select the file named tracing.gif; then press OK (Windows) or Choose (Mac OS).

17 Set the transparency of the tracing image to **50** percent by sliding the Transparency slider to the left.

```
                          Page Properties
  Category         Tracing Image

  Appearance (CSS)
  Appearance (HTML)    Tracing image: tracing.gif            ( Browse... )
  Links (CSS)
  Headings (CSS)       Transparency:  ══════════○══════  50%
  Title/Encoding
  Tracing Image              Transparent           Opaque




    ( Help )                      ( Apply ) ( Cancel ) ( OK )
```

Place a tracing image in the background of your page.

18 Press Apply to see the results. Tracing Images can be useful tools for building layout. Oftentimes, you can import a page mockup created originally in Photoshop or another application and use it as a visual guideline.

19 When activated, the tracing image replaces any background image you've added to your page, but only in Dreamweaver. Tracing images are never visible when you view your page in a browser. Now that you have a sense how the tracing feature works, you'll remove it. Select the path within the Tracing Image field and press Delete to remove it.

20 Press OK to close the Page Properties dialog box.

21 Choose File > Save. Now that you've finished setting up your page properties, you'll examine your page in Dreamweaver's three different work view modes.

Work views

In this book's lessons, you'll do most of your work in the Design view, as you're taking advantage of Dreamweaver's visual page layout features. You can, however, easily access the HTML code being written as you work in the Design view, and use it to edit your pages through Dreamweaver's other work views. You'll switch views, using the Document toolbar.

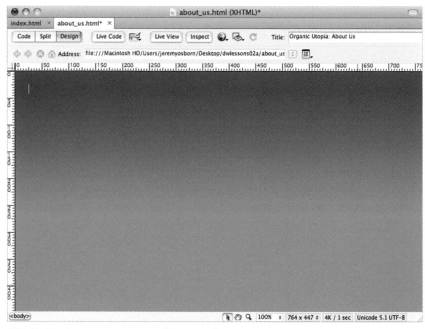

The Document toolbar.

1   In the Document toolbar, press the Design View button, if it is not currently selected. Design View is a fully editable, visual representation of your page, similar to what the viewer would see in a browser.

With Design view, you see your page as the viewer will see it.

2 Click on the Code View button to switch to the Code view. Your page is now displayed in a hand-coding environment used for writing and editing HTML and other types of code, including JavaScript, PHP, and ColdFusion.

```
1  <!DOCTYPE html PUBLIC "-//W3C//DTD XHTML 1.0 Transitional//EN"
   "http://www.w3.org/TR/xhtml1/DTD/xhtml1-transitional.dtd">
2  <html xmlns="http://www.w3.org/1999/xhtml">
3  <head>
4  <meta http-equiv="Content-Type" content="text/html; charset=UTF-8" />
5  <title>Organic Utopia: About Us</title>
6  <style type="text/css">
7  body,td,th {
8      color: #666;
9  }
10 body {
11     background-color: #739112;
12     background-image: url(images/bg_gradient.gif);
13     background-repeat: repeat-x;
14     margin-left: 25px;
15     margin-top: 25px;
16 }
17 a:link {
18     color: #FC3;
19 }
20 a:visited {
21     color: #CCC;
22 }
23 a:hover {
24     color: #F03;
25 }
26 a:active {
```

Code view shows the HTML code generated to display your page.

3   Click on the Split View button to split the document window between the Code and
     Design views. This view is a great learning tool, as it displays and highlights the HTML
     code generated when you make a change visually in Design mode, and vice versa.

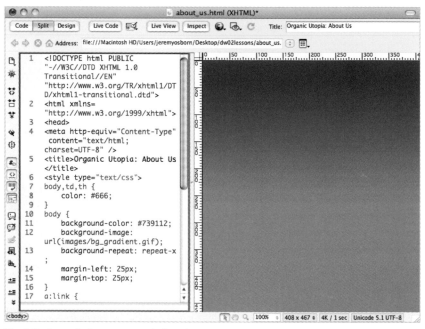

Use Split view to display your page in both modes at once.

4   Switch back to the Design view to continue this lesson.

A deeper look into the Files panel

You have already seen how Dreamweaver populates the Files panel when you define a new site.
The Files panel is more than just a window into your root folder however, it also allows you to
manage files locally and transfer them to and from a remote server. The Files panel maintains a
parallel structure between local and remote sites, copying and removing files when needed to
ensure synchronicity between the two.

The default workspace in Dreamweaver displays the Files panel in the panel grouping to the
right of the document window.

When you chose to use the dw02lessons folder as your local root folder earlier in this lesson,
Dreamweaver set up a connection to those local files through the Files panel.

Viewing local files

You can view local files and folders within the Files panel, whether they're associated with a Dreamweaver site or not.

1   Click on the drop-down menu in the upper-left part of the Files panel, and choose Desktop (Windows) or Computer > Desktop folder (Mac OS) to view the current contents of your Desktop folder.

2   Choose Local Disk (C:) (Windows) or Macintosh HD (Mac OS) from this menu to access the contents of your hard drive.

3   Choose CD Drive (D:) (Windows) from this menu to view the contents of an inserted CD. On a Mac, the CD icon and the name of the CD appears in the menu.

4   Choose Organic_Utopia to return to your local root folder view.

Selecting and editing files

You can select, open, and drag HTML pages, graphics, text, and other files listed in the Files panel to the document window for placement.

1   Double-click on the index.html file, located in the Files panel. The page opens for editing. Click beneath the heading the *lowly beet*.

2   Click on the arrow to the left of the images folder to expand it and then click and drag the beets.jpg image file from the Files panel to the index.html document window. If an Image Tag Accessibility Attributes dialog box appears when you release the mouse, press OK to close it. The image is added to the open page.

If you have an image editor such as Photoshop or Fireworks installed on your computer, you can double-click on the space.jpg image file to open for editing and optimizing.

3   Double-click on the lowly_beet.txt file in the Files panel to open it directly in Dreamweaver.

4   Choose Edit > Select All to select all the text in this file. You could also use the keyboard shortcuts, Ctrl+A (Windows) or Command+A (Mac OS)

5   Choose Edit > Copy to copy the text to the clipboard. You could also use the keyboard shortcuts, Ctrl+C (Windows) or Command+C (Mac OS)

6   Click on the index.html tab of the document window to return to the index page. Click on your page to the right of the image to place an insertion cursor.

7   Choose Edit > Paste. You could also use the keyboard shortcuts, Ctrl+V (Windows) or Command+V (Mac OS) The text is added to the open page, beneath the image in the default text color you chose earlier.

Paste the new text in the page.

8   Choose File > Save and then close this file.

Congratulations! You have finished this lesson. You will get a chance to work much more with text and images in the next lesson.

Self study

Using your new knowledge of site creation techniques in Dreamweaver, try some of the following tasks to build on your experience:

1   Choose Site > New Site to invoke the Site Setup dialog box, and use it to create a new local site called Practice_Site on your desktop. Make sure you understand the difference between creating an empty site from scratch (as you are doing here) and adding a preexisting site (as you did in the opening exercise of this lesson).

2   Use the File > New command to create a new, blank HTML page, and save it to your Practice_Site. Then choose Modify > Page Properties to access the Page Properties dialog box, and experiment with the background, link, margin, and title options available. Finally, switch to the Code and Design view in the document window to view the code generated by your experimentation.

Review

Questions

1   What characters should you avoid using when naming your site, and why?

2   How is the local root folder essential to the creation of your site?

3   What happens if you've chosen both a background color and a background image for a page within your site?

4   Where can you view, select, open, and copy files to and from your local root folder, and to and from remote and/or testing servers?

Answers

1   Avoid using spaces (use underscores instead), periods, slashes, or any other unnecessary punctuation in your site name, as doing so will likely cause the server to misdirect your files.

2   It's essential that you store all your site's resources in your local root folder to ensure that the links you set on your computer will work when your site is uploaded to a server. This is because all the elements of your site must remain in the same relative location on the web server as they are on your hard drive, for your links to work properly.

3   If you've added both a background color and a background image for your page, the color will appear while the image downloads, at which time the image will then cover the color. If there are transparent areas in the background image, the background color will show through.

4   Dreamweaver provides the Files panel to help you not only manage files locally, but also transfer them to and from a remote server. You can view, select, open, and copy files to and from your local root folder and to and from remote and/or testing servers in this panel.

What you'll learn in this lesson:

- Previewing pages
- Adding text
- Understanding styles
- Creating hyperlinks
- Creating lists
- Inserting and editing images

Adding Text and Images

Text and images are the building blocks of most web sites. In this lesson, you'll learn how to add text and images to web pages to create an immersive and interactive experience for your visitors.

Starting up

Before starting, make sure that your tools and panels are consistent by resetting your workspace. See "Resetting the Dreamweaver workspace" on page 3.

You will work with several files from the dw03lessons folder in this lesson. Make sure that you have loaded the dwlessons folder onto your hard drive from the supplied DVD. See "Loading lesson files" on page 3.

Before you begin, you need to create site settings that point to the dw03lessons folder from the included DVD that contains resources you need for these lessons. Go to Site > New Site, and name the site **dw03lessons**, or, for details on creating a site, refer to Lesson 2, "Setting Up a New Site."

See Lesson 3 in action!

Use the accompanying video to gain a better understanding of how to use some of the features shown in this lesson. The video tutorial for this lesson can be found on the included DVD.

Typography and images on the web

Dreamweaver CS5 offers some convenient features for placing images and formatting text. In this lesson, you'll be building a web site with some photos and text for the front page of a fictional store.

Adding text

You should already have created a new site, using the dw03lessons folder as your root. In this section, you'll be adding a headline and formatting the text on the events.html page.

1 If it's not already open, launch Dreamweaver CS5.

2 Make sure your dw03lessons site is open in the Files panel. If not, open it now.

3 Double-click on the events.html file in your Files panel to open it in the Design view. Without any formatting, the text seems random and lacks purpose. First, you'll add a headline to give the first paragraph some context.

4 Click to place your cursor in front of the word *There's* in the first paragraph. Type **OrganicUtopia Events** and press Enter (Windows) or Return (Mac OS) to create a line break.

5 Click and drag to highlight the phrase you just typed. You will now format your text using the Property Inspector. Located at the bottom of the screen, the Property Inspector allows you to format your text using a combination of HTML and CSS. HTML stands for Hypertext Markup Language, and CSS stands for Cascading Styles Sheets. You will learn much more about the use of HTML and CSS in the next lesson; however, you will need to have a basic understanding of these two languages in order to use the Property Inspector to format your text.

6   In the Property Inspector, click on the HTML button on the left side to see your HTML formatting options. Choose Heading 1 from the Format drop-down menu. The text gets larger and becomes bold. By default, the style of any HTML text formatted as Heading 1 is generic: the color is black and the font-family is Times New Roman.

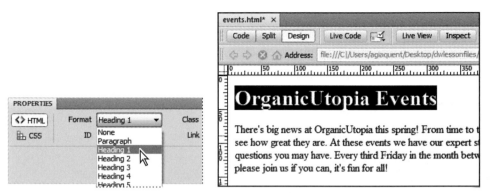

Use the Format drop-down menu in the Property Inspector to make the selected text a level-1 heading.

Although you are working in Dreamweaver's Design view, you have actually changed the HTML code for this page. Elements such as text are wrapped in opening and closing tags, and everything between these two tags is controlled by the properties of the tags. The text *OrganicUtopia Events* originally had an opening and closing tag defining it as a paragraph. The code looked like this:

```
<p>OrganicUtopia Events</p>
```

The first *<p>* is the opening tag for a paragraph element, and the second *</p>* is the closing tag for a paragraph. You then selected the text and formatted the text as a Heading 1 element, and so the HTML code changed to this:

```
<h1>OrganicUtopia Events</h1>
```

So now, the text OrganicUtopia Events is wrapped in an *<h1>* tag. Headings are important structural elements in HTML. The largest heading is H1, and the subsequent headings become smaller with H2, H3, and so on. For the next step, you will format this text in order to change the font style of this heading to Arial; however, you will not be using HTML to accomplish this, but rather CSS.

7   Click anywhere inside the heading OrganicUtopia Events; you do not need to have it selected. In the Property Inspector, click on the CSS button to access the formatting options. Choose Arial, Helvetica, sans-serif from the Font drop-down menu.

The CSS section of the Property Inspector allows you to change the font.

The New CSS Rule dialog box appears.

The New CSS Rule dialog box appears the first time you style text.

8   From the Selector Type drop-down menu, choose Tag. In the Selector Name text field, the selector h1 has been chosen for you. Dreamweaver does this because you placed your cursor inside the text formatted as H1. Press OK. Your heading is now styled in Arial.

Dreamweaver allows you to format text in a way that is similar to desktop publishing and word processing applications, but there are important differences to keep in mind. When you chose the styling, Arial, Helvetica, and sans-serif, they were listed together as one option in the Font drop-down menu. When a web page is rendered in a browser, it uses the fonts installed on the user's computer. Assigning multiple fonts allows you to control which font is used if the person viewing your page doesn't have a specific font installed. In this case, if the user doesn't have Arial, Helvetica displays instead. Sans-serif is included as the last option in case the user doesn't have Arial or Helvetica. A generic font family is listed at the end of all the options in the Font drop-down menu.

You will now change the text color using the Property Inspector.

9   Highlight *OrganicUtopia Events* and click on the Text Color button to the right of the Size drop-down menu. When the Swatches panel appears, hover over the color swatches. At the top of the Swatches panel, a different hexadecimal color value appears for each color. When you locate the value labeled #9C3 (an olive green), click once to apply the color.

10 Choose File > Save. Keep this file open for the next part of this lesson.

An introduction to styles

You have styled the first element on your page by first formatting text as a Heading 1 in HTML, and then you changed the font and color using CSS. It's important to realize that every change you make in the Design view creates or modifies code. In the next exercise, you'll begin to explore the HTML and CSS code behind the Design view. To help put this exercise in context, a little background on HTML and CSS is in order.

The HTML language has been around since the dawn of the web. It's easiest to think of HTML as the structure behind the pages that are rendered in your web browser. An HTML page at its most basic is a collection of text, images, and sometimes multimedia such as Flash or video files. The different sections of a web page, such as a paragraph, a heading, or a list, are all *elements*. Another way to define an element in HTML is as a set of tags such as the *<h1>* tag used in the last exercise.

CSS is also a language, but it has not been around as long as HTML. In many ways, CSS was created in order to fill in some of the shortcomings of HTML. CSS is a simple language that works in combination with HTML to apply style to the content in web pages, such as text, images, tables, and form elements. CSS creates rules, or style instructions, that the HTML elements on your page follow. The most important thing to remember is that HTML and CSS are two separate languages but they are very closely aligned and work together very well.

In the last exercise, you were introduced to this interplay between HTML and CSS. There was an HTML element for the Heading 1 formatting. In the code it looks like this:

```
<h1>OrganicUtopia Events</h1>
```

That was the HTML element. The CSS *rule* that defines the appearance of the *<h1>* element looks like this:

```
h1

{
font-family: Arial, Helvetica, sans-serif;
color: #9C3;
}
```

CSS has a different syntax than HTML. In HTML, tags are defined by angled brackets, and you have opening tags, *<h1>*, and closing tags, *</h1>*. In CSS code, brackets are not used. In the CSS code above, the h1 is referred to as the *selector* because it is selecting the HTML element and then changing the appearance. Because you've established that HTML and CSS are two separate languages and have different syntax, it's important that you see where this code lives in your web page. You will do this by changing Dreamweaver's workspace.

1   Click on the Split button in the Document toolbar to open up the Split view. The Split view allows you to see your code and the design of your page simultaneously.

2   Click quickly three times in the paragraph beneath OrganicUtopia Events in the Design view. In the Code view the text is highlighted between the opening and closing paragraph tags. As noted above, this is referred to as the paragraph element. On the line below is an h2 element.

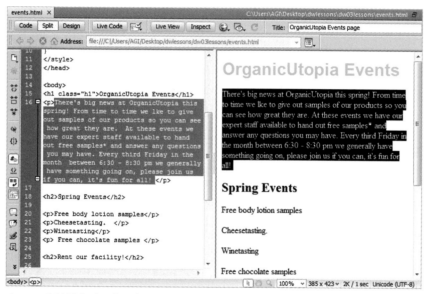

A paragraph highlighted in the Split view.

You will now change the font size of your paragraphs.

3   Choose 18 from the Size drop-down menu in the Property Inspector. The New CSS Rule dialog box appears again. This dialog box appears because it is the first time you have attempted to style a paragraph. After you define the properties, all text formatted as a paragraph will appear the same.

4   From the Selector Type drop-down menu, choose Tag. Since there are different categories of CSS rules, Dreamweaver wants to know which one you would like to use. You will stick with Tag for now (as you did in the last exercise). In the Selector Name text field, the selector p has been chosen for you because your cursor was inside a paragraph. Press OK to apply the changes; in this case, the font size is set to 18 pixels. Now let's look at the CSS code that is defining this font size.

5   Within the Code view of the split screen is all the HTML and CSS code that defines the appearance of this page. On the right side of the Code view, scroll up by clicking on the up arrow or by clicking the scroll bar and dragging upwards. Toward the top of the page, you are looking for a few lines of code that look like this:

```
<style type="text/css">
h1

{
font-family: Arial, Helvetica, sans-serif;
color: #9C3;
}

p   {
font-size:18px;
}

</style>
```

Between the two *<style>* tags are all the CSS rules you have created up to this point. Previously, you learned that CSS has a different syntax than HTML: because all the CSS rules are actually contained within an opening *<style>* tag and a closing *</style>* tag, they are allowed to have a different syntax. Additionally, the style tag itself is nested inside of an opening and closing *<head>* tag. In the world of HTML, nothing contained within head tags is rendered on a web browser's screen. You will explore this further in the next lesson, but this is referred to as an internal style sheet.

You will now see that changes made in Dreamweaver's Code view apply to the Design view as well.

6   In the Code view, locate the line *font-size:18px* in the rule for p, and select the value 18 by clicking and dragging over it. Type **14** to change the value. Although you made a change in the Code view, it has not yet been automatically updated in your Design view. You need to refresh your page in order to see the changes occur in the Design view.

7   In the Property Inspector, press the Refresh button to apply the changes; your paragraph text becomes smaller.

Changes made in the Code view are reflected in the Design view after pressing the Refresh button.

On the web, font sizes are specified differently than they are in print. The numerical choices in the Size drop-down menu refer to pixels instead of points. Also, the xx-small through larger options may seem oddly generic if you are accustomed to the precision of print layout. Because web pages are displayed on a variety of monitors and browsers, relative measurements can be a useful way for designers to plan ahead for inevitable discrepancies in the rendering of pages.

8   Click inside the first paragraph in the Design view. You will now change the color of the paragraph slightly to a dark gray rather than the default pure black. In the Property Inspector, click on the color swatch, and in the top-left corner, locate the dark gray swatch, which is hexadecimal color #666. Click on the swatch to apply the color. Notice that not only does the appearance in the Design view change, but in your Code view a new line of CSS has also been created (color: #666;).

Working in the Split view can be a great way to learn about hand-coding without diving in headfirst. Even if you're not quite comfortable editing code, keeping an eye on the code that Dreamweaver writes for you can give you a better understanding of how things like CSS affect your web pages.

9   Click the Design view button to return to Design view.

10 Choose File > Save. Keep this file open for the next part of this lesson.

Previewing pages in a web browser

Viewing your pages in the Design view is helpful, but visitors to your site will be using a web browser to access your site. In Lesson 1, "Dreamweaver CS5 Jumpstart," you learned how browsers use HTML code to render a page. Unfortunately, not every browser renders HTML code in exactly the same way, so it's important to test-drive your pages in a number of different browsers to check for inconsistencies and basic functionality.

Next, you'll use Dreamweaver's Preview in Browser feature to see how the OrganicUtopia site looks in a web browser.

1   With events.html open in Dreamweaver, choose File > Preview in Browser and select a browser from the available options. This list varies, depending on the browsers you have installed on your hard drive.

Preview in Browser allows you to see how a selected browser would render your page.

The options found under File > Preview in Browser can be customized by choosing File > Preview in Browser > Edit Browser List.

2   When events.html opens in the browser of your choice, look for differences between the Design view preview and the version rendered by your browser. At this stage, there shouldn't be anything too surprising, but there may be subtle differences in spacing and font weight. Close your web browser.

There is another method to preview your pages: using the Live View feature. Live View allows you to preview your page without having to leave the Dreamweaver workspace. You can think of Live View as a browser within Dreamweaver (in fact, it is the same WebKit rendering engine found in browsers such as Apple's Safari and Google's Chrome, among others).

3   Press the Live View button located in the Document toolbar. You will not see a dramatic shift, but your text will be slightly closer to the left edge of the window. Select the first heading in the window and try to delete it; you will be unable to, because Live View is a non-editable workspace. Live View does allow you to edit your page when you are in Split View. Here, you are allowed to edit in the Code View and changes will be reflected in real time. An additional advantage is that your document does not have to be saved in order to see the changes.

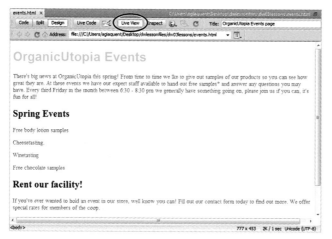

When Live View is enabled, Dreamweaver simulates a web browser.

4   Click on Live View again to deactivate this view. While Live View is a useful addition to Dreamweaver, it does not replace the need to preview your page in a browser. Web pages might be rendered differently depending on your visitor's browser, and so a good habit to get into is checking your page occasionally as you make changes to your design. As you become more skilled at styling your pages with CSS, you'll learn how to compensate for some of these discrepancies in web browser display.

Understanding hyperlinks

When people visit a web site, they usually expect to see more than one page. Imagine trying to shop for a new book by your favorite author on a site that consisted of nothing more than a single order form with every book offered by a retailer like *Amazon.com*. This might seem absurd, but without hyperlinks you wouldn't have much choice.

Hyperlinks make the web a truly interactive environment. They allow the user to freely navigate throughout a web site, or jump from one site to another. There are a number of ways to create links in Dreamweaver, but before you get started, you should be aware of some fundamentals.

Links rely on directory paths to locate files. A directory path is simply a description of a file's location that can be understood by a computer. A classic, real-world example is an address. If you wanted to send a letter to your friend Sally in Florida, you would have to specify the state, city, street, and house where Sally can be found. If Sally lived at 123 Palm Street in Orlando, the path would be:

Florida/Orlando/123 Palm Street/Sally

This simply means that inside Florida, inside Orlando, in the house numbered 123 on a street named Palm Street, you can find a person named Sally. Hyperlinks follow the same logic:

www.somewebsitesomewhere.com/photos/mydog.jpg

This URL address is a link to a JPEG image named mydog.jpg, which is inside a folder named photos on a web site named somewebsitesomewhere.com.

Creating hyperlinks

Later in this lesson, you'll be creating a gallery page to showcase some of the sample products mentioned in the main paragraph. Before you work on that page, you'll link it to the home page by creating a hyperlink.

1 In the Property Inspector, click on the HTML button to access the HTML properties.

2 In the first paragraph, highlight the word *products* in the second sentence.

3 In the Property Inspector, type **products.html** in the Link text field. Press Enter (Windows) or Return (Mac OS). The highlighted word *products* automatically becomes underlined. It is important to note that we have created this page for you and it is currently inside your site folder, you are simply linking to it.

*Type **products.html** into the Link text field in the Property Inspector.*

4 Choose File > Save and then File > Preview in Browser.

5 Click on the new *products* link. The products page appears in your browser window. This is because a previously existing page named products.html was located in this folder.

Now visitors can easily navigate to the products page, but what happens when they want to go back to the events page? It looks like you'll need another link.

6   Return to Dreamweaver and double-click on products.html in the Files panel. Click to the right of the word *Produce* and press Enter (Windows) or Return (Mac OS) to create a new line. Choose Insert > Hyperlink to open the Hyperlink dialog box.

The Hyperlink dialog box is one of the many ways to create a link in Dreamweaver. It offers all the options found in the Property Inspector, with a few additions.

7   Type **Events** in the Text field.

The Hyperlink dialog box is one of the many ways to create links in Dreamweaver.

8   Click on the Browse button to the right of the Link text field to open the Select File dialog box. The dw03lessons folder you defined as the root for this site should be selected for you by default. If not, locate it on your hard drive. Select events.html and press OK (Windows) or Choose (Mac OS). A link to events.html has been created for you, using the text entered into the Text field in the Hyperlink dialog box. Press OK.

9   Choose File > Save and keep this file open for the next part of this lesson.

Relative versus absolute hyperlinks

After reading about the fundamentals of hyperlinks and directory paths a few pages ago, you may have been surprised by the simplicity of linking events.html and products.html. Instead of entering a long directory path in the Link text fields, you merely typed the name of the file. This kind of link is called a *relative* link. Let's go back to the address example to see how this works.

Remember Sally from Orlando? Imagine you were already standing on Palm Street, where she lives. If you called her for directions to her house, she probably wouldn't begin by telling you how to get to Florida. At this point, all you need is a house number. Relative links work the same way. Because events.html and products.html both reside in the dw03lessons folder, you don't need to tell the browser where to find this folder.

Now you'll create an absolute link that will allow visitors to access the Adobe web site to learn more about Dreamweaver CS5.

1   Click on the events.html tab above the Document toolbar to bring the page forward. Scroll down to the bottom of the page if necessary. Create a new line at the bottom of the page after the text that reads "Occasionally we gather…", and type **This page was created with Adobe Dreamweaver**.

2   Highlight the words *Adobe Dreamweaver* and in the Common section of the Insert panel on the right side of the screen, click on the Hyperlink icon to open the Hyperlink dialog box.

The Hyperlink icon in the Insert panel is another convenient way to create links.

3   The Hyperlink dialog box opens. Notice that Adobe Dreamweaver has been entered into the Text field for you. In the Link text field, type the text **http://www.adobe. com/products/dreamweaver/index.html**. Make sure to include the colon and the appropriate number of forward slashes.

The absolute link http://www.adobe.com/products/dreamweaver/index.html instructs the browser to find a web site named *adobe.com* on the World Wide Web. Then the browser looks for a file named index.html inside a folder named dreamweaver inside a folder named products.

4   Choose _blank from the Target drop-down menu. Choosing the _blank option will
     cause the hyperlink to the Adobe web site to open in a new, blank browser window or
     tab (depending on the browser).

Set the target window for the hyperlink to open in a blank browser window or tab.

5   Press OK to close the Hyperlink dialog box. Choose File > Save, then File > Preview in
     Browser, or press the Preview/Debug in Browser button (●) in the Document toolbar.

6   Click on the *Adobe Dreamweaver* text. Unlike the Events and Products links you created
     earlier, this link causes your browser to open a new tab or window, and it is pointing to
     an external web page on the Internet.

Linking to an e-mail address

Absolute and relative links can be used to access web pages, but it's also possible to link to an
e-mail address. Instead of opening a new web page, an e-mail link opens up the default mail
program on a visitor's computer and populates the address field with the address you specify
when creating the link. As you may imagine, this kind of link can work differently depending
on how your visitors have configured their computers.

In the last part of this lesson, you gave the visitor a link to some information on Dreamweaver.
Now you'll link them to an e-mail address where they can get some information on learning
Dreamweaver from the folks who wrote this book.

1   Place your cursor at the end of the last line, then hold down your Shift key and press
     Enter (Windows) or Return (Mac OS). Instead of creating a new paragraph, this creates a
     line break, or a soft return, and the text begins immediately below the previous line. Type
     Contact info@agitraining.com for classes on using Adobe Dreamweaver CS5.

2   Highlight the text *info@agitrining.com* and click the Email Link button (✉) in the
     Insert panel.

3 The Email Link dialog box opens with both fields automatically populated. Press OK. You may preview this page in your browser if you choose, however be aware that if you click on the link, your email client will begin to launch.

The Email Link dialog box allows you to link to an e-mail address.

Creating lists

Bulleted lists may be familiar to you if you have worked with word processing or desktop publishing applications. Lists are a helpful way to present information to a reader without the formal constraints of a paragraph. They are especially important on the Web. Studies indicate that people typically skim web pages instead of reading them from beginning to end. Creating lists will make it easier for your visitors to get the most from your web site without sifting through many paragraphs of text.

1 On the events.html page, click and drag to highlight the four lines below *Spring Events:*.

2 Click the Unordered List button (≣) in the Property Inspector. The highlighted text becomes indented, and a bullet point is placed at the beginning of each line.

Use the Unordered List button in the Property Inspector to create a bulleted list.

3   Click the Ordered List button (≔) to the right of the Unordered List button. The bullets change to sequential numbers.

4   Choose Format > List > Properties to open the List Properties dialog box. Choose Bulleted List from the List type drop-down menu. The Numbered List and Bulleted List options in the List type drop-down menu also allow you to switch between ordered and unordered lists.

5   From the Style drop-down menu, choose Square. This changes the default circular bullets to square bullets. Press OK to exit the List Properties dialog box.

Change the bullet style to square in the List Properties dialog box.

You may have noticed that the four lines of text in your list have lost their style. They are slightly larger than your paragraphs and colored the default black instead of the dark gray you applied earlier. This is because you have added the unordered list element to your HTML page, and while the appearance of paragraphs has been defined using CSS, the appearance of an unordered list has not. You will now create a new CSS rule for the appearance of all unordered lists in the document.

6   With all four lines still highlighted, click on the CSS button in the Property Inspector. Click on the arrow to the right of the Size field. Choose 14 from the Size drop-down menu in the Property Inspector. The New CSS Rule dialog box appears. This dialog box appears because it is the first time you have attempted to style an unordered list. After you define the properties, all text formatted as an unordered list will appear the same.

7   From the Selector Type drop-down menu, choose Tag. In the Selector Name text field, the selector *ul* has been chosen for you; *ul* is the HTML tag for an unordered list. If *ul* is not chosen for you, type **ul** inside this text field. Press OK to apply the changes; in this case the font size is set to 14 pixels. Now you need to change the color of the unordered list to match the color of your paragraph.

8   In the Property Inspector, if the Targeted Rule drop-down menu does not read ul, choose ul from the menu. Click on the color swatch and in the top-left corner of the Property Inspector, locate the dark gray swatch, which is hexadecimal color #666. Click on the swatch to apply the color.

9   Choose File > Save. Leave this file open for the next part of this lesson.

Using the Text Insert panel

There are a number of ways to format text in Dreamweaver. One method you haven't explored yet is the Text Insert panel. Because most of the options available in the Text Insert panel are also available in the Property Inspector, you may find it more convenient to use the Property Inspector for common tasks. However, you should be aware of the Character menu located in the Text Insert panel. One of the most common items in the Character menu used on the web is the copyright symbol, ©. You will now insert a copyright notification at the bottom of your Events page.

1   Click to the left of the sentence *This page was created with Adobe Dreamweaver* and type **2010**.

2   Click before the text 2010 to insert your cursor.

3   Click on the menu at the top of the Insert panel and choose Text. Scroll all the way to the bottom of the resulting list and click on Characters to open a menu. Choose the Copyright symbol from the list to add it to the beginning of the line.

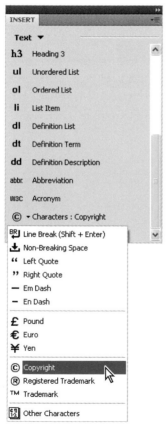

The copyright symbol can be inserted from the Character menu.

4 Highlight the last two lines on your page, beginning with the newly inserted copyright symbol and ending with *Adobe Dreamweaver CS5*. You are going to set these two lines apart from the rest of the page by italicizing them. Layout considerations such as headers and footers will be discussed throughout the following lessons in this book, but for now you can use the Text options in the Insert panel to italicize these two lines.

5 Scroll to the top of the Text options in the Insert panel and click the Italic option.

You could have also used the Italic button in the Property Inspector although you would have to create a new style for it. Additionally, you could have also selected the text and chosen Insert > HTML > Text Objects to accomplish the same thing.

6 Choose File > Save.

Inserting images

Images are an essential part of most web pages. Just as lists make content friendlier and more accessible, images help to give your visitors the rich, immersive experience that they've come to expect on the Web.

Image resolution

While it is possible to resize images with Dreamweaver, it's generally not a good idea. Specifying the width and height of an image in the Property Inspector changes the display size of the image, but it does not resample the image the way a graphic processing application like Photoshop does. The difference may not seem immediately apparent, as a properly resized image may appear identical to an improperly resized image. Unfortunately, visitors to your web site will be the first to notice an oversight in resizing your images.

If you've ever downloaded a large file from the web, you've probably had the experience of waiting impatiently while a progress bar inches its way across the screen like a glacier. This may be an exaggeration, but the fact is that every time you access a page on the Internet, you are downloading all the contents of that page. Images always significantly increase the size of an HTML file, so it's important to properly resize them before including them on your site.

Image formats

The three most common image formats on the web are JPEG, GIF and PNG. While an exhaustive description of how each of these formats compresses data is beyond the scope of this book, a general overview can help you avoid some common pitfalls.

The JPEG format was created by a committee named the Joint Photographic Experts Group. Its express purpose is to compress photographic images. Specifically, it uses lossy compression to reduce the size of a file. This means that it selectively discards information. When you save a JPEG, you decide how much information you are willing to sacrifice by selecting a quality level. A high-quality image preserves more information and results in a larger file size. A low-quality image discards more information, but produces a smaller file size. The goal is to reduce file size as much as possible without creating distortion and artifacts.

Because JPEGs were designed to handle photographic images, they can significantly reduce the size of images containing gradients and soft edges, without producing noticeable degradation. However, reproducing sharp edges and solid areas of color often requires a higher quality setting.

The GIF format was created by CompuServe. GIF is an acronym for Graphics Interchange Format. Unlike the JPEG format, GIFs do not use lossy compression. Instead, GIFs rely on a maximum of 256 colors to reduce the size of images. This means that images with a limited number of colors can be reproduced without degradation. Logos, illustrations, and line drawings are well-suited to this format. Unlike JPEGs, GIFs excel at reproducing sharp edges and solid areas of color. However, because photographic elements such as gradients and soft edges require a large number of colors to appear convincing, GIF images containing these elements look choppy and posterized.

The PNG format has become increasingly popular on the Web in recent years because it incorporates many of the best features of JPEGS and GIFS. The PNG format is closer to GIFS in that it offers lossless compression and comes in two categories 8 bit and 24 bit. This means it can be used quite effectively for simple graphics as well as continuous tone photographic images. The PNG also offers better transparency features than a GIF, most significantly the support of alpha channels. For many years the adoption of PNGs (especially the use of the transparency) was held back because Internet Explorer 6 ignored the transparency. As the number of people using this browser continues to decline, the PNG format is being used more frequently.

Creating a simple gallery page

Now that you have a better understanding of the types of images that are appropriate for using on your web site, it's time to build the products page that you linked to earlier in this lesson.

1   Double-click on products.html in the Files panel or click on the tab, as it's still open. Place your cursor after the word *Produce* and press Enter (Windows) or Return (Mac OS) to create a new line.

2   Choose Insert > Image. The Select Image Source dialog box appears. Navigate to the dw03lessons folder that you chose as your root folder at the beginning of the lesson and open the images folder. Select beets.jpg and press OK (Windows) or Choose (Mac OS).

3   When the Image Tag Accessibility Attributes dialog box appears, type **Beets** in the Alternate text field. Press OK.

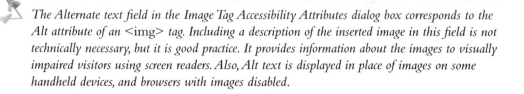

The Alternate text field in the Image Tag Accessibility Attributes dialog box corresponds to the Alt attribute of an <img> tag. Including a description of the inserted image in this field is not technically necessary, but it is good practice. It provides information about the images to visually impaired visitors using screen readers. Also, Alt text is displayed in place of images on some handheld devices, and browsers with images disabled.

4   Click on the Split button in the Document toolbar to view the code that was written by Dreamweaver when you inserted beets.jpg. An *<img>* tag was created, with four attributes. The src attribute is a relative link to the .jpg file in your images folder. The alt attribute is the alternate text you specified in the last step. The width and height attributes are simply the width and height of the image, and these have automatically been added by Dreamweaver. Press the Design button to return to this view.

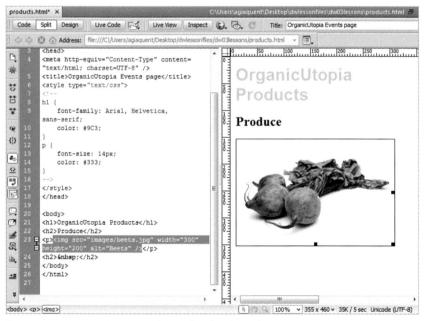

Dreamweaver creates an <img> tag with a number of attributes when you insert an image.

5   Double-click on the images folder in the Files panel to reveal its contents. In the document window, click to the right of the beets image and press Enter (Windows) or Return (Mac OS) to create a new line. Click and drag cucumbers.jpg below the beets image in the Design view. When the Image Tag Accessibility Attributes dialog box appears, type **Cucumbers** into the Alternate text field. Press OK.

6   In the Property Inspector, type **5** into the Border text field and press Enter (Windows) or Return (Mac OS). A border attribute is added to the new *<img>* tag in the Code view and a black, 5-pixel-wide border appears in the Design view.

7   Click on the beets image in the Design view and type **5** in the Border text field in the Property Inspector to give this image a matching border.

Adding a border attribute to an <img> tag with the Property Inspector is a quick way to create a border, but it doesn't give you as much control or flexibility as a CSS-generated border. In Lesson 4, "Styling Your Pages with CSS," you'll learn about the advantages of style sheets.

8   Click to the right of the cucumber image to place your cursor, and press Enter (Windows) or Return (Mac OS) to create a new line. To add the last image, you'll use the Insert panel. Click the menu at the top of the Insert panel and choose Common from the list. Click on the Images:Image option, and the Select Image Source dialog box appears.

Choose Image from the Images drop-down menu in the Common section of the Insert panel.

9   Navigate to the images folder if necessary, select the eggplants.jpg image, and press OK (Windows) or Choose (Mac OS).

10 Type **Eggplants** in the Alternate text field of the Image Tag Accessibility Attributes dialog box, then press OK.

11 In the Property Inspector, type **5** into the Border text field and press Enter (Windows) or Return (Mac OS).

12 Choose File > Save and leave products.html open for the next part of this lesson.

Linking images

Often, gallery pages on the web contain small thumbnail images that are linked to larger, high-resolution images. Like many web conventions, there are practical reasons for this format. Because all the images on a gallery page must be downloaded by visitors in order to view the page, small images are necessary to keep the page from taking too long to load. Additionally, a user's screen isn't large enough to accommodate multiple large pictures at one time. Giving your visitor a way to preview which pictures they would like to see at a larger scale makes the page more usable and more interactive.

1   In products.html, click on the beets.jpg image to select it. In the Property Inspector, type **images/beets_large.jpg** into the Link text field. Press Enter (Windows) or Return (Mac OS). The 5-pixel border around the image turns blue. This border indicates that the image is a link.

2   Click on the cucumber.jpg image to select it. For this image, you'll use Dreamweaver's Point to File feature to create a link. In the Property Inspector, locate the Point to File icon (⊙) next to the Link text field. Click and drag this icon into the Files panel. A blue arrow with a target at the end follows your cursor. As you hover over items in the Files panel, they become highlighted. Release the mouse while hovering over the cucumbers_large.jpg file.

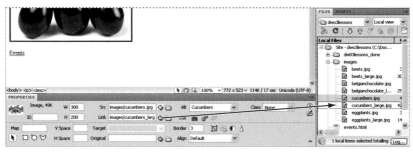

With the Point to File feature, you can simply click and drag to create a link.

3   Select the eggplants.jpg image and use the Point to File icon to link it to eggplants_large.jpg.

4   Choose File > Save, and then File > Preview in Browser. Click on the thumbnails to see the large versions of each image. You'll have to use your browser's back button to get back to the products page, as you didn't select _blank from the Target drop-down menu in the Property Inspector.

Using image placeholders

Often, you will want to start building web pages before you have all the final content available. This happens regularly in professional situations where different people may be responsible for preparing images, writing copy, and creating the site. Next, you'll build a second section in the products.html page that will eventually include a collection of chocolate pictures.

1 In Dreamweaver, on the products.html page, place your cursor to the right of the eggplants.jpg image, and press Enter (Windows) or Return (Mac OS) to create a new line.

2 Type **Chocolate**, then press the HTML button in the Property Inspector and choose Heading 2 from the Format drop-down menu. Press Enter/Return to create a line below the Chocolate heading.

3 Choose Insert > Image Objects > Image Placeholder. When the Image Placeholder dialog box appears, type **belgianchocolate** in the Name text field, **300** in the Width text field, and **200** in the Height text field. Leave the Color set to the default and the Alternative text field blank. Press OK to exit the dialog box.

   A gray box with the name belgianchocolate appears. This box is simply an *<img>* tag with an empty src attribute. If you are new to web design, it's important to note that placeholders are not required, but they are useful in allowing you to visualize a page when you don't have images available. Now you'll insert an image into the placeholder by setting the src attribute in the Property Inspector.

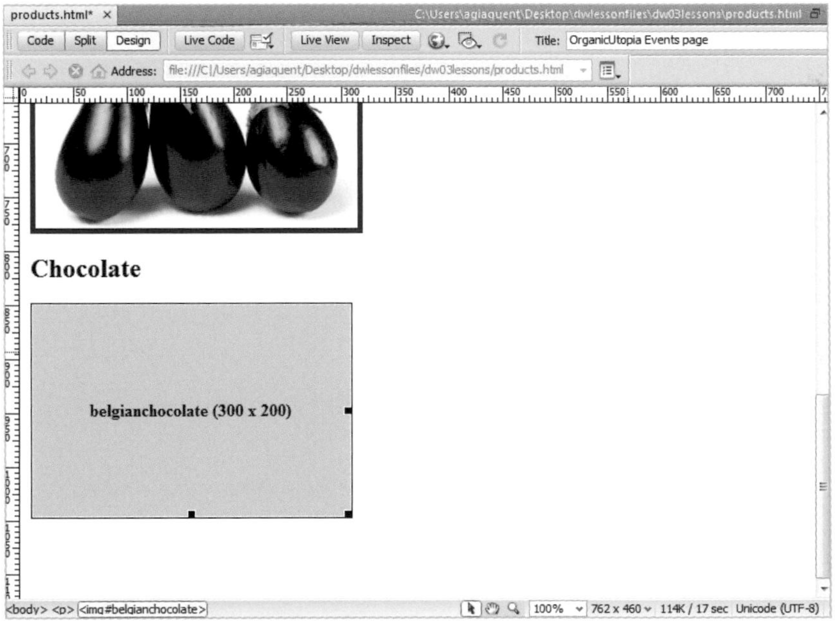

The belgianchocolate image placeholder.

4 With the belgianchocolate image placeholder selected, click and drag the Point to File icon to the right of the Src text field and locate the belgianchocolate.jpg image. The belgianchocolate JPEG replaces the gray box.

5 In the Property Inspector, type **5** into the Border text field and use the Point to File icon (☺) of the Link text field to link belgianchocolate.jpg to belgianchocolate_large.jpg. Choose File > Save and leave this file open for the next part of this lesson.

Editing images

Although it's best to make adjustments to your images using a professional graphics-editing program like Adobe Photoshop, sometimes that's not an option. Dreamweaver offers a number of editing options, including an Edit link that allows you to quickly open a selected image in the graphics editor of your choice.

The Edit button can be customized in the File Types/Editors section of the Preferences dialog box. You can use this section to add or subtract programs from the list of available editors, and set programs as the primary choice for handling specific file extensions.

Adjusting brightness and contrast

Now you'll use Dreamweaver's Brightness and Contrast button to lighten up the eggplants image on your products page.

1 Click on the eggplants.jpg image in products.html to select it, then click on the Brightness and Contrast button (◑) in the Property Inspector.

Select the Brightness and Contrast button in the Property Inspector.

A warning dialog box appears, indicating that you are about to make permanent changes to the selected image. Press OK.

2   When the Brightness/Contrast dialog box appears, drag the Brightness slider to 20 or type **20** in the text field to the right of the slider.

3   Drag the Contrast slider to 10 or type **10** in the text field to the right of the slider.

4   Click the *Preview* checkbox in the lower-right corner to see the original photo. Click the Preview checkbox again to see the changes. Press OK.

While changing the brightness and contrast is very convenient in Dreamweaver, you should be sure you are not performing the corrections on the original, as these changes are destructive.

Resizing images

Next, you'll see how Dreamweaver allows you to quickly optimize images; you'll change the size and quality of the belgianchocolate.jpg image; but before you make any permanent changes, you'll duplicate this image in the Files panel. It's good practice to save copies of your image files before making permanent changes. Later, you'll use this backup copy to undo your changes.

1   In the Files panel, click on the belgianchocolate.jpg file to select it. From the Files panel menu (⋅≡), select Edit > Duplicate. A new file named belgianchocolate - Copy.jpg appears in the list of files inside the images folder.

2   Click on the belgianchocolate.jpg image in the document window to make sure it is selected, then click the Edit Image Settings button (⚙) in the Property Inspector. The Image Preview dialog box opens; it offers many of the features included in the Adobe Photoshop CS5 Save for Web & Devices dialog box.

3   Make sure that the Options tab in the top-left corner is selected. Click on the black
    arrow to the right of the Quality text field and drag the slider down to 30 percent. The
    belgianchocolate.jpg image in the preview window becomes pixelated. As discussed
    earlier, a lower JPEG quality setting reduces file size at the cost of image clarity, and so
    this is not a good setting.

Reducing the quality of the belgianchocolate image causes pixelation.

4   Drag the quality slider back up to 70 percent and click the File tab in the top-left corner
    of the dialog box.

5   In the Scale section, drag the % slider to 60 percent. The belgianchocolate.jpg image in
    the preview window shrinks; its new dimensions are reflected in the W and H text fields.

6 Press OK to exit the Image Preview dialog box. The belgianchocolate.jpg image is reduced to 60 percent of its original size.

The belgianchocolate image has been resized and permanently altered.

Similar to the brightness and contrast features, be careful when resizing images in Dreamweaver. In the workflow of this exercise, if you were to save this file, the source image would have been permanently resized.

Updating images

Assuming you have a backup copy of an image, it is possible to swap one image for another. To swap out the image, you'll simply change the Src attribute, using the Property Inspector. But first, it's a good idea to rename the duplicate image to get rid of the spaces in the filename.

1 Right-click (Windows) or Ctrl+click (Mac OS) the file named belgianchocolate - Copy. jpg in the Files panel and choose Edit > Rename. Type **belgianchocolate_copy.jpg** and press Enter (Windows) or Return (Mac OS).

Although filenames including spaces usually work just fine on your home computer, many web servers aren't designed to handle them. To prevent broken links, it is a common practice to use the underscore or hyphen characters in place of spaces when naming files for the Web.

2   Click on the belgianchocolate.jpg image in the Design view to select it. In the Property Inspector, highlight the text that reads *images/belgianchocolate.jpg* in the Src text field.

3   Click and drag the Point to File icon to the belgianchocolate_copy.jpg image you just renamed. The resized belgianchocolate.jpg image is replaced with the copy you made earlier.

4   Choose File > Save.

Congratulations, you have finished this lesson. In the next lesson, you will dig much deeper into the use of CSS for styling your page.

Self study

To practice styling text with the Property Inspector, create styles for the text in events.html. If you're feeling bold, try copying the CSS styles from the Code view.

To make the thumbnail links in products.html open in a new window, set their target attributes to _blank in the Property Inspector.

Try adding your own photos to the products page. Remember to be careful when resizing them!

Review

Questions

1   Of the two most common image formats used on the web, which is better suited for saving a logo?

2   If an inserted image is too small, can you make it larger by increasing its size in the Property Inspector?

3   How do you insert a copyright symbol (©) in Dreamweaver?

Answers

1   Because logos usually contain a lot of hard edges and solid areas of color, the GIF format is the most appropriate choice.

2   Yes, it is possible to increase the display size of an image; however, doing so reduces image quality.

3   Use the Characters drop-down menu in the Text tab of the Insert bar.

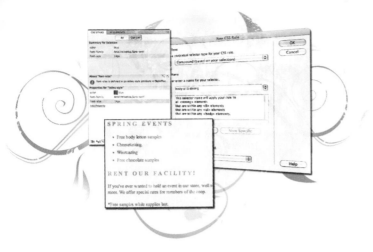

What you'll learn in this lesson:

- Introducing Cascading Style Sheets (CSS)
- Comparing CSS and *<font>* tags
- Using the CSS Styles panel
- Creating Class and Tag styles

Styling Your Pages with CSS

Many years ago, creating a beautiful web page required a lot of work, using the limited capabilities of HTML tags. The introduction of Cascading Style Sheets changed the way pages are created, giving designers an extraordinary amount of control over text and page formatting, as well as the ability to freely position content anywhere on a page. In this lesson, you'll focus on techniques for styling text with Cascading Style Sheets.

Starting up

Before starting, make sure that your tools and panels are consistent by resetting your workspace. See "Resetting the Dreamweaver workspace" on page 3.

You will work with several files from the dw04lessons folder in this lesson. Make sure that you have loaded the dwlessons folder onto your hard drive from the supplied DVD. See "Loading lesson files" on page 3.

Before you begin, you need to create site settings that point to the dw04lessons folder from the included DVD that contains resources you need for these lessons. Go to Site > New Site, or, for details on creating a site, refer to Lesson 2, "Setting Up a New Site."

See Lesson 4 in action!

Use the accompanying video to gain a better understanding of how to use some of the features shown in this lesson. The video tutorial for this lesson can be found on the included DVD.

What are Cascading Style Sheets?

In the last lesson you had a brief introduction to Cascading Style Sheets (CSS); now you will dive in a bit deeper. CSS is a simple language that works alongside HTML to apply formatting to content in web pages, such as text, images, tables, and form elements. Developed by the World Wide Web Consortium (W3C), CSS creates rules, or style instructions, that elements on your page follow. There are three locations for CSS: (1) directly within the *<head>* section of an HTML document, (2) inline (the CSS is located side by side with your HTML tags), or (3) an external file that can be linked to any number of HTML pages. If you completed Lesson 3, you have had experience with the first option.

A style sheet is a collection of CSS rules; typically, rules that belong to a specific project, theme, or section are grouped together, but you can group rules in any way you want. You can place style sheets directly within your page using the *<style>* tag or in an external .css file that is linked to your document with the *<link>* tag. A single page or set of pages can use several style sheets at once.

You can apply CSS rules selectively to any number of elements on a page, or use them to modify the appearance of an existing HTML tag. Whenever or wherever you apply a rule, that rule remains linked to its original definition in the style sheet, so any changes you make to the rule automatically carry over to all items to which the rule has been applied.

Each CSS rule is composed of one or more properties, such as color, style, and font size, which dictate how an item is formatted when the rule is applied. A single CSS rule can include several properties, just as a single style sheet can include multiple CSS rules. Dreamweaver's CSS Styles panel lets you easily view and modify any of these properties and change the appearance of your page in real time.

This sample rule is composed of three properties that control the color, typeface, and size of any text to which it's applied. In the simplest example, the CSS rules define the appearance of an H1 or heading element:

```
H1 {
    color: red;
    font-family: Arial,Helvetica,Sans-serif;
    font-size: 28px;
}
```

Here is the result of the preceding code snippet:

CSS-styled text shown in the Design view.

CSS rules can affect properties as simple as typeface, size, and color; and as complex as positioning and visibility. Dreamweaver uses CSS as the primary method of styling page text and elements, and its detailed CSS Styles panel makes it possible to create and manage styles at any point during a project.

A little bit of ancient history: when *<font>* tags roamed the Earth

Before CSS came along, you styled text on a page using the *<font>* tag in HTML; you could wrap this limited but easy-to-use tag around any paragraph, phrase, or tidbit of text to apply color, or set the font size and typeface. Although it worked well enough most of the time, the *<font>* tag was a one-shot deal. Once applied, that tag's job was done and you had to use a new *<font>* tag to style additional text, even if the color, size, and typeface values were exactly the same. You will now open an HTML document in which the list is styled using the *<font>* tag.

1   In your Files panel, locate and double-click the HTML file named FontTagList.html to open it in the document window.

2   Press the Code View button in the Document toolbar at the top of the document window. Notice that the *<font>* tag is used to style the items in the bulleted list.

Here, a <font> tag is used to format each bullet point. If you add more bullet points, you'll need to use more <font> tags to keep the style of those bullets consistent with the others.

As you can see, there's a lot of repetition in this code.

3   Press the Design View button on the Document toolbar. Position your cursor at the end of the last bulleted item, press Enter (Windows) or Return (Mac OS) to add a new bullet point, and type **Peppers**. You see that the text reverts to the default typeface, size, and color. You would have to add a new *<font>* tag with the same attributes as the others to get it to match. If you wanted to change an attribute such as the color for all the bullet points, you would have to adjust each tag separately. In early versions of Dreamweaver, there were actually ways to perform global changes using HTML; however, these were sometimes tricky to control, and CSS offers a better solution in any case.

Vegetables to plant in May

- Beets
- Cucumbers
- Eggplants
- Peppers

You may lose the formatting between bullet points when using <font> tags.

4   Choose File > Save to save your work, then choose File > Close.

The dawn of CSS

CSS introduces a new level of control and flexibility beyond the *<font>* tags in HTML. A significant benefit of CSS is the ability to apply consistent formatting of elements across one or all pages in a web site. In the following exercises you will learn a few different ways to create CSS rules that affect the style of your text. The first method you will explore involves creating tag- or element-based style rules. If you completed Lesson 3, you saw this method used to format text. This type of rule alters the appearance of an existing HTML tag, so the tag and any content that appears within it always appear formatted in a specific way. Instead of having to add a *<font>* tag around the contents of each new bullet point in a list, it would be easier for you to tell the HTML tags used to create lists, that bullet point items should always be formatted a certain way.

1   Locate and double-click the file named CSSList.html from the Files panel to open it.

2   Press the Design View button in the Document toolbar if necessary. The list that appears onscreen, unlike the one you saw in the previous example, is formatted without the use of *<font>* tags, and uses only CSS.

3   Position your cursor after the last bulleted item and press the Enter (Windows) or Return (Mac OS) key to create a new bullet point. Type in **Peppers**. The new text matches the bullet points above it.

4   Press Enter/Return again to add a fifth bullet point, and type **Okra**.

  No matter how many bullet points you add, the formatting is applied automatically every time.

5   Select Split view at the top of the document window so that you can see both code and design:

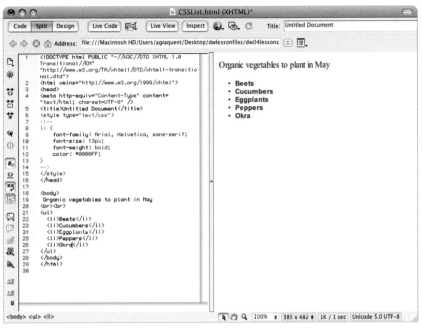

Tags are not used to format this list.

What you'll notice is the absence of any formatting tags like the *<font>* tags you saw in the last exercise. In this example, you have several list items; however, all the styling information, such as the font-family, size, font-weight, and color, is being defined in one place: the CSS rule for the *<li>* tag.

6   If necessary, scroll to the top of the page and you'll see the code that makes this possible:

```
<style type="text/css">
<!--
li {

    font-family: Arial, Helvetica, sans-serif;
    font-size: 13px;
    font-weight: bold;
    color: #0000FF;
}
-->
</style>
```

The formatting rules for color, weight, size, and typeface are assigned directly to the *<li>* tag, which creates new bullet points in an HTML list. It's almost like a dress code for all *<li>* tags; they know that when they are used on the page, they must look a certain way. Best of all, if you need to modify their appearance, you don't have to go through every *<li>* tag in your document and modify *<font>* tags or attributes; just make your changes to that single style rule at the top of the page. You will get a chance to do this shortly; however, let's take a step back and look at how CSS is controlled in Dreamweaver.

7 Choose File > Save to save your work, then choose File > Close.

How do you create CSS rules in Dreamweaver?

In this exercise, you will take a tour of Dreamweaver's CSS controls. If you haven't worked with CSS before, this is a chance to learn a bit more about how it works. If you have worked with CSS previously, this section will help you understand the Dreamweaver interface and how it applies to familiar concepts. Regardless of your comfort level with CSS, you won't be making any changes, merely getting familiar with features that you will be using in later exercises.

You work with CSS rules in a few ways in Dreamweaver:

Using the CSS Styles panel

You can use Dreamweaver's CSS Styles panel to create new rules and/or style sheets that you can place directly within one or more pages in your site. You can easily modify rules directly from the CSS Styles panel. Furthermore, you can selectively apply rules from several places, including the Style or Class menu on the Property Inspector, or the tag selector at the bottom of the document window.

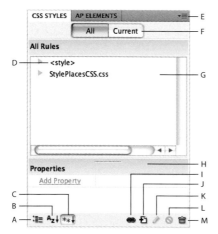

Launch the CSS panel by choosing Window > CSS Styles. **A.** *Show Category View.* **B.** *Show List View.* **C.** *Show Only Set Properties.* **D.** *Internal Style Sheet.* **E.** *CSS panel menu.* **F.** *Switch to Current Selection Mode.* **G.** *Rules pane.* **H.** *Properties pane.* **I.** *Attach Style Sheet.* **J.** *New CSS Rule.* **K.** *Edit Style Sheet.* **L.** *Disable/Enable CSS Property.* **M.** *Delete Embedded Style Sheet.*

1   Choose Window > CSS Styles to open the CSS Styles panel. You'll now free up some screen space by closing the Insert panel: double-click the Insert tab to collapse this panel.

2   Double-click the StylePlaces.html document in your Files panel to open it, and click the Design View button, if necessary.

3   Click in the first line, *Hi there! I'm styled with an INLINE style!*

4   Press the Current button in the CSS Styles panel. A summary pane lists the CSS properties for the current selection. Take a few moments to read through this panel and absorb the summary. Don't worry too much about each detail; you'll have plenty of time to familiarize yourself with this panel. It hopefully makes sense that the properties of the first paragraph are the color blue, the font-family Arial, and the font size of 14 pixels.

Press the Current button to view the rules for a selection.

5   Click on the second paragraph and notice that the color property changes to red. Click on the third paragraph and notice that the color property changes to green. The current selection always lists the properties of the selected text.

You'll now take a look at a new feature in Dreamweaver CS5 called the Enable/Disable CSS Property. This feature allows you to turn any property off (and back on) in order to see how it affects your page appearance.

6   Click on the Color property for the .greenText class. In the bottom right of the CSS Styles panel, click on the Enable/Disable CSS Property button (⊘). This turns off the Color property and your text is now styled with the default black.

Disable a CSS property.

7   To turn the property back on, click the red icon to the left of the color property.

This feature can be extremely useful for understanding what properties are defining your styles as well as for experimenting with styles.

8   Press the All button in the CSS Styles panel to return to this view.

Directly from the Property Inspector

Whenever you format text directly on your page using the Property Inspector, Dreamweaver saves your settings as a new rule, which you have to name, in your document. You can then reapply the rule as many times as you need to by using the Property Inspector or tag selector. Rules that Dreamweaver creates appear in your CSS panel, where you can easily modify or rename them.

1   Click in the second paragraph, *Hi there! I'm styled with an embedded, or INTERNAL style sheet!*

2   In the Property Inspector at the bottom of the screen, press the HTML button, if necessary. This paragraph is styled using a CSS class named red. You'll learn more about classes and how to create and modify them shortly.

3   Press the CSS button in the Property Inspector. You can see the properties of this rule here in the Inspector, and you can also create and modify them here as you did in the previous lesson.

CSS styles are automatically created when you format text with the Property Inspector.

4   Compare the Property Inspector with the CSS Styles panel for a moment: they are displaying the exact same information (as long as you are in the Current mode of the CSS Styles panel).

In the Code view

CSS rules can also be created and modified directly in the Code view. Editing CSS in Dreamweaver's Code view offers a great degree of control and is often called *hand-coding*. Many coders and designers prefer hand-coding because of this control. However, this precise control also has its downsides. For example, when you work in the Code view the potential for error increases dramatically, and misspellings or an incomplete knowledge of CSS syntax can easily break a page.

1   Click in the second paragraph if you are not currently inside it. Press the Code View button to view your page in Code view. If you haven't worked with code previously, see if you can locate the second paragraph. On the left side of the screen, notice the line numbers running from top to bottom; when working with code, each line has its own number, making it easy to refer to and locate objects.

2 On line 10, select the value red in the color property and then delete it. Now type **#CE1A30**. Ignore the Color picker that appears.

```
StylePlaces.html (XHTML)*

Code   Split   Design      Live Code  ⊞⊠   Live View   Inspect   ⊙ ⬚ C    Title: Untitled Document

⬅ ➡ ⊗ ⌂ Address: file:///Macintosh HD/Users/jeremyosborn/Desktop/dw04lessons/StylePlace  [:] ⊞,

Source Code  StylePlacesCSS.css*                                                              ⛀

 4    <meta http-equiv="Content-Type" content="text/html; charset=UTF-8" />
 5    <title>Untitled Document</title>
 6
 7    <style type="text/css">
 8    <!--
 9    .red {
10        color: #CE1A30;
11        font-family: Verdana, Helvetica, sans-serif;
12        font-size: 14px;
13    }
14    -->
15    </style>
16
17    <link href="StylePlacesCSS.css" rel="stylesheet" type="text/css" />
18    </head>
19
20    <body>
21    <p style="color:blue; font-family: Arial,Helvetica,Sans-serif; font-size: 14px;">Hi
      there! I'm styled with an INLINE style</p>
22
23
24    <p class="red">Hi there! I'm styled with an embedded, or INTERNAL style sheet!</p>
25
26
27    <p class="greenText">Oh hello! I'm styled with an EXTERNAL, or attached style sheet!
      </p>

<body> <p>                                              1K / 1 sec   Unicode 5.1 UTF-8
```

Modifying the CSS color property in Code View.

3 Press the Design view button. The text is still red, however it is using a hexadecimal color instead of a keyword. The danger of adding CSS properties by hand of course, is that if you mistype the value you may get a different color or no color at all.

Working with the Code Navigator

The Code Navigator allows you to view the CSS properties directly in the Design view through a small pop-up window. Additionally, it allows you to click on a property and edit it directly in the Split view.

1   Press Ctrl+Alt (Windows) or Command+Option (Mac OS) and click on the third paragraph. A small window appears, listing the properties of the CSS rule applying to this paragraph. The window lists the name of the style sheet, as well as the rule *.greenText*.

2   Place your cursor over the *.greenText* class, and the properties appear in a yellow pop-up window. This feature allows you to quickly view the properties without needing to move to the CSS Styles panel or go into Code view.

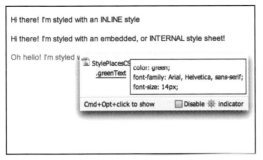

The Code Navigator displays the CSS rules applied to a paragraph.

Understanding Style Sheets

The term "Cascading" in Cascading Style Sheets alludes to the fact that styles can live in three different places, each of which has its strengths and weaknesses. You've actually been working with all three types of styles in the last exercise. The first line is being defined with an inline style, the second with an internal style sheet, and the third with an external style sheet.

Inline style sheets

An inline style is a set of CSS properties defined directly in an HTML tag using the style attribute. These are slightly less common because you can't reuse them, which somewhat defeats the purpose of using style sheets in the first place.

1   Click three times rapidly to select the first paragraph.

2   Press the Split view button, and notice that your selected text is nested inside a paragraph or *<p>* element; however, the CSS style rules for color, font-family, and font-size are contained directly inside the opening paragraph tag. This is called an inline style because the CSS rules are not separated from the HTML.

Although inline styles are part of the CSS language, they are not often used. They present many of the same problems as the older *<font>* tags in HTML. They only apply to one tag at a time and are not easily reusable. So when are they used? Inline styles are useful when an internal or external style sheet may not be available; a good example of this is HTML-based e-mail.

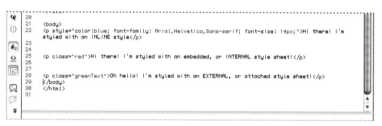

An inline style places the CSS rules inside an opening paragraph tag.

Internal versus external style sheets

Internal style sheets are CSS rules that are contained directly within a document, using the *<style>* tag. The entire style sheet is contained within the opening and closing *<style>* tags. External style sheets are style rules saved in a separate document with the extension ".css". One of the fundamental differences between internal and external style sheets is that with internal style sheets, the CSS rules apply only to the HTML in a single document. For example, if you had a ten-page web site and could only use internal style sheets, you would essentially have ten styles sheets: one per page. If you made a change on one page and then needed to make the other pages look the same, you would have to either copy or redefine internal styles from page to page, not an enjoyable prospect. External style sheets, by contrast, have CSS rules located in one single document. You can attach .css files, or external style sheets, to an unlimited number of HTML pages. This method is extremely flexible: if a style rule such as the font-color for a paragraph is changed in the external style sheet, all paragraphs in the site are instantly modified, whether it be 2 pages, 10 pages or 100 pages.

In Dreamweaver, when you create a new style, the default behavior is to use an internal style sheet. In many ways, a web browser doesn't care which type of style sheet you use; it renders the page exactly the same. There are certain situations when an internal style sheet makes more sense than an external style sheet and vice-versa. You will explore this in more detail in later exercises, but first you need to know how to determine whether a style is internal or external.

1 In the CSS Styles panel, click on the All button. In the top half of the screen you will see a listing for *<style>* and one for StylePlacesCSS.css. The first line is the internal style sheet, and the second is for the external style sheet.

2 If necessary, click on the arrow to the left of the plus sign (Windows) or the arrow (Mac OS) to the left of the *<style>* option, and it expands to show you the rule for the class red. Again, if necessary, click on the arrow to the left of StylePlacesCSS.css to expand this and see the rule for the class .greenText. You may have noticed that the listing for the inline style is not here; only rules for internal and external style sheets are visible in All mode.

In the last exercise, you used the Code Navigator to view the CSS rules applied to a paragraph. You can also use the Code Navigator to quickly determine where the CSS rules are located.

3 Back in Design view, click inside the second paragraph and Ctrl+Alt+click (Windows) or Command+Option+click (Mac OS) to open the Code Navigator. The window reads StylePlaces.html and the class *.red* is indented below it. If a style is located inside an HTML document, as it is in this case, it must be an internal style.

The Code Navigator has located the origin of this CSS rule to be in StylePlaces.html.

4   Place your cursor over the *.red* class, and all the properties appear; this is a quick way to determine the properties.

5   Click on the *.red* rule, and Dreamweaver's Split view opens, sending you directly to the internal style. An experienced hand-coder might use this to directly edit the rule as you did earlier, although you will not be making any changes at this point. Now you will look at the external style sheet again using the Code Navigator.

6   Ctrl+Alt+click (Windows) or Command+Option+click (Mac OS) in the third paragraph to open the Code Navigator.

7   This time, the Code Navigator window lists StylePlacesCSS.css first. If a style is located inside a .css document, as it is in this case, it is an external style. Place your cursor over the *.greenText* class, and all the properties appear.

8   Click on the *.greenText* class, and in the Split view, the external style sheet StylePlacesCSS.css appears. Doing this actually opens the external style sheet, which is a separate document. To return to the original HTML document, press the Source Code button.

Clicking on the Source Code button switches you from the external style sheet back to the original HTML file.

9   Choose File > Save All. Close this document for now. Choosing *Save All* saves not just the HTML document but the external stylesheet at the same time.

Understanding why they're called Cascading

You have defined style sheets and determined that there are three categories of styles. Additionally, you have seen that an HTML document such as the one from the last exercise can contain all three types. Now you'll begin to explore when you might use one type over the other. A good way to look at this is to ask the question, Which one of the style types is most dominant? Consider the following situation: you have a paragraph, or more accurately a *<p>* tag, in your document and you have the three style types (inline, internal, and external). Each one targets the *<p>* tag with the same property (color, for example) but they all have different values, so which one wins? The answer is the inline style is the most dominant because it is closest to the HTML source. The internal style sheet is the next dominant because it is one step farther away from the HTML source, in the head section of the HTML document. Finally there is the external style sheet, which is a separate document and is the least dominant because it is farthest away from the actual source.

We have actually simplified the argument here a bit. The question of which CSS rule "wins" can get even trickier depending on the rules in question. We discuss some of these rules at the end of the lesson.

Creating and modifying styles

You will now get a chance to begin working more deeply with CSS. In this exercise, you'll be picking up where you left off in the last lesson with the events page for the OrganicUtopia web site. In that lesson you covered the creation of new CSS rules; however, you essentially worked with just one category of CSS rules, the element or tag-based rules. In all instances from the last lesson, you defined the properties for a tag, such as *<h1>*, *<p>*, and *<ul>* (unordered lists). You will now explore how to create classes and IDs. First, a brief review of the styles you used in the last lesson tag styles.

A tag style assigns rules directly to a specific HTML tag to alter its appearance. You can attach tag styles to any tag from the *<body>* tag down; as a matter of fact, when you modify page properties (Modify > Page Properties) to change default text formatting and background color, you are using a tag style assigned to the *<body>* tag.

The most basic tag styles are very straightforward. For instance, when you create a rule definition for the *<p>* (paragraph) tag, all paragraphs appear the same. The limitations begin when you want to customize one specific paragraph to appear different from the others. You will explore some solutions to this dilemma; for now, keep in mind that tag styles are a great way to ensure consistency across multiple elements and pages where specific tags are used, such as lists, tables, and paragraphs.

1   Double-click the events.html file in the Files panel to open it. This page has already had its Heading 1, paragraph, and list styled. You will now style the Heading 2.

2   In the Design view, click inside the heading *Spring Events*. This is already formatted as a Heading 2 for you.

3   Click on the CSS button in the left side of the Property Inspector; this allows you to define the properties of the Heading.

4   Choose 18 from the Size drop-down menu on the Property Inspector, and the New CSS Rule dialog box appears. From the Choose a contextual selector type for your CSS rule drop-down menu, choose Tag. In the second field marked *Selector Name*, the selector h2 has been chosen for you. Dreamweaver does this because you placed your cursor inside the text formatted as h2. Press OK. Now you can add additional properties, and Dreamweaver adds them to the definition of the h2 tag.

Defining a Heading 2 for the first time causes the New CSS Rule dialog box to appear.

5   In the Property Inspector, click on the color swatch to choose a color for your text from the Swatches panel that appears. Select a dark green. The color #390, located in the top row, is used in this example. Your heading now changes to green. You have just styled the font-size and color of the *<h2>* tag. At this point, all text formatted as h2 appears this way. You will now format the last heading in the page in order to see this.

6   Click inside the text, *Rent our facility*. In the Property Inspector, click on the HTML button. You need to toggle into this view because you now want to change the HTML formatting, not the CSS.

7   In the Property Inspector, note that the Format for this text is currently set to None. From the Format drop-down menu, choose Heading 2 to see your text change.

Formatting text as a Heading 2 assumes the properties of the CSS rule.

What you have seen in this exercise is an example of HTML and CSS working together with a tag style. In this case, all text tagged in the HTML as a Heading 2 or *<h2>* is defined by the CSS rule as green and 18 pixels. At this point you may be itching to create more complex layouts; if you understand the fundamentals of styling tags, it will pay off as you move to the next level of CSS.

Creating a class style with the Property Inspector

In the last exercise, you created a new CSS rule by defining the properties of the *<h2>* tag. Now you will create another CSS rule, this time using a class. In CSS, class styles have unique names and are not associated with any specific HTML tag. A CSS class can have a specific style that can be applied to one or more elements in your web site. So you might create a class called *holidayText*, for example, and the properties of this class might just be a single rule defining the font-color. Once the class is created, this text could then be applied to a table, paragraph, heading, or form element simultaneously. So on Halloween, if you change the property of the font-color to orange, all text that is defined by the *holidayText* class is orange, and on Valentine's Day, if you change the property of the font-color to red, it all changes to red.

In this exercise, you will create a class using the Property Inspector for the copyright text at the bottom of the page in order to distinguish it from the rest of the page.

1   Click at the end of the paragraph reading *Occasionally we gather personal information at our events* and drag all the way down to the bottom of the page to select the copyright paragraph. Press the CSS button in the Property Inspector if necessary; note that this text has a size of 14 pixels and a dark grey color. This is because these are paragraphs and the CSS rules for paragraphs have these properties. You will now format all this text with a different size and font, and then add a background color.

2   In the Property Inspector, click on the drop-down menu for Size and change the size from 14 pixels to 10 pixels. The New CSS Rule dialog box appears. The default choice for Selector Type is *Class*, which is what you would like to use. Classes, unlike the Tag styles you have been using, must be named; additionally, you must name the class, as Dreamweaver does not do it for you.

Older versions of Dreamweaver automatically assigned generic names to new classes, such as .style1, .style2, and so on. In addition to the New CSS Rule dialog box, this is perhaps one of the most substantial changes in Dreamweaver CS5 (as well as CS4) when it comes to styles: users are now required to name CSS classes. Although this may seem to be an extra step, it is a good one. By being forced to assign names to styles, users are more aware of the code they are generating and make their web pages easier to maintain.

3 In the Selector Name field, type **copyright**. As you type, notice that Dreamweaver adds the text, *This selector name will apply your rule to all HTML elements with class "copyright."* This is Dreamweaver's way of helping you understand how your new class can be applied.

```
┌─────────────────────────────────────────────────────────────┐
│                        New CSS Rule                          │
│ Selector Type:                              ┌─────────────┐   │
│ Choose a contextual selector type for your CSS rule. │  OK  │ │
│   ┌──────────────────────────────────────┐  └─────────────┘   │
│   │ Class (can apply to any HTML element) ▼│ ┌─────────────┐  │
│   └──────────────────────────────────────┘  │   Cancel    │  │
│                                              └─────────────┘   │
│ Selector Name:                                                │
│ Choose or enter a name for your selector.                     │
│   ┌──────────────────────────────────────┐ ┌─┐               │
│   │ copyright                             │ │▼│               │
│   └──────────────────────────────────────┘ └─┘               │
│   ┌──────────────────────────────────────┐                    │
│   │ This selector name will apply your rule to │               │
│   │ all HTML elements with class "copyright".  │               │
│   │                                      │                    │
│   └──────────────────────────────────────┘                    │
│                                                               │
│     ( Less Specific )    ( More Specific )                    │
│                                                               │
│ Rule Definition:                                              │
│ Choose where your rule will be defined.                       │
│   ┌──────────────────────────────────────┐  ┌─────────────┐  │
│   │ (This document only)                 ▼│  │    Help     │  │
│   └──────────────────────────────────────┘  └─────────────┘  │
└─────────────────────────────────────────────────────────────┘
```

Set the rules for the new copyright *class.*

4 Press OK. You now see the text formatted at 10 pixels. Once the class is created, you can add other properties.

5 Click once in the first line of the copyright text. Notice in the Property Inspector that in the Targeted Rule section, the menu is set for .copyright. This is important, as it confirms that you are modifying the class, not the paragraph. In the Property Inspector, choose Verdana, Geneva, sans-serif from the Font menu to add this property to the copyright class. Now you'll add a new line of text and apply the copyright class to it.

6 Place your cursor at the end of the last line of the paragraph and press Enter (Windows) or Return (Mac OS) to add a new line. Type the following text: **All images on this website are the copyright of Bob Underwood.** Notice that the text is using the paragraph style; you need to instruct Dreamweaver to use the copyright class for this line.

7 From the Targeted Rule drop-down menu of the Property Inspector, choose copyright in the Apply Class section, The copyright class is now applied to this paragraph as well.

Use the Targeted Rule menu in the Property Inspector to apply an existing class to an element.

Creating and modifying styles in the CSS Styles panel

Using the Property Inspector is a quick-and-easy way to create and apply styles and make some basic formatting choices; however, the number of style choices in the Property Inspector is very limited. To take advantage of the full power of CSS, you will begin to dive into the CSS Styles panel. In this exercise, you'll explore some of the powerful options that CSS has at its disposal. The first thing you'll do is change the background color of your page by adding a new style to the body tag.

1 At the top of the CSS Styles panel, make sure the All tab is active, and locate *<style>* underneath; if it is not currently expanded, click on the arrow to see the list of current rules in your document. You will now add a new rule for the body tag in order to change the background color.

2 Click on the New CSS Rule icon (✦) at the bottom of the CSS Styles panel. This displays the same dialog box you are accustomed to working with, just accessed from a different location. From the Choose a contextual selector type for your CSS rule drop-down menu, choose Tag. Previously, you have accepted the automatic choices in the Selector Name section, but in this case, you need to instruct Dreamweaver that you would like to create a new rule for the body tag.

3 From the Choose or enter a name for your selector drop-down menu, select body. Press OK. The CSS Rule definition dialog box appears. This dialog box gives you access to the numerous styling options available in CSS.

CSS Rule definition for body

Category: Type, Background, Block, Box, Border, List, Positioning, Extensions

Type
- Font-family:
- Font-size: ____ px   Font-weight:
- Font-style: Font-variant:
- Line-height: ____ px   Text-transform:
- Text-decoration: ☐ underline   Color: ☐
  - ☐ overline
  - ☐ line-through
  - ☐ blink
  - ☐ none

Help   Apply   Cancel   OK

Creating a new rule for the body tag launches the CSS Rule definition dialog box.

4 In the left Category column, select Background to access the Background properties. In the field for Background-color, type in the following hexadecimal number: **#E0F0E4**. The background color does not apply automatically. Press the Apply button in the bottom-right corner to preview the new background color.

5 Press OK to confirm the background color. You will now change the background color for the copyright class at the bottom of the page.

6 In the list of rules in the CSS Styles panel, double-click the *.copyright* class to edit these properties.

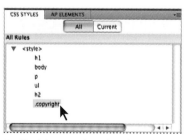

Double-clicking a style in the style window opens the CSS Rule definition dialog box.

7 In the CSS Rule definition dialog box that appears, click on the Background Category, click on the Background-color swatch, and choose whitc (#FFF) from the list. Press OK. The two copyright paragraphs at the bottom of the page are styled with white backgrounds. The gap between the two paragraphs reveals the background color because these are separate paragraphs, and are both block elements. The gap is somewhat visually unappealing and is something you will be fixing a bit later in the lesson.

Advanced text formatting with CSS

Text on the Web is necessarily limited due to the fact that designers cannot assume that fonts they choose in Dreamweaver will be available to the user. There is a small set of fonts that designers can use that are essentially guaranteed to be on all users' systems. Given this limitation, you can use some of the properties in CSS to give your text a distinctive look. In this exercise, you will work with the line spacing of your paragraphs and lists, and the letter spacing of your headings.

1   In the CSS panel, double-click on the rule for p (paragraph) to open the CSS Rule definition dialog box. You will now override the default line-height for your paragraphs. If you have a print background, you may be familiar with leading, which is the amount of space between the lines in a paragraph. Line-height is the same thing as leading.

2   In the Line-height field, type **20**; the value is automatically set for pixels. Press Apply, and you will see the space between your paragraph lines increase. Extra line-height can often make your text more readable, so it is great that you have this option in CSS. However, a problem may arise if you change the font-size. For example, setting the fixed value of 20 pixels looks good with 14-pixel type, but what if you were to later change the font-size of your paragraph? The 20-pixel line-height would look strange. A more flexible way to assign line-height is to use a percentage.

3   From Line-height drop-down menu to the right of the text field, choose percent (%). Change the value from 20 to **120**, and press Apply, you won't actually see a dramatic difference because the end result is similar, but by assigning line-height to 120 percent, your initial font-size isn't as important. There will always be the height of the line plus 20 percent extra, no matter what the font-size is. Press OK.

Changing the line-height value of a paragraph to a percentage is more flexible than using pixels.

Notice that the list under Spring Events did not change. This is because the line-height property applies solely to paragraphs, not lists. If you want to make this list appear the same, you could always apply the same value of line-height. However, you will add extra space between the lines to make the list stand out from the rest of the page.

4 In the CSS Styles panel, double-click on the *ul* rule. The CSS Rule definition dialog box appears. In the field for line-height, type **150**; then from the drop-down menu to the right, select percentage. Press OK, and you now have extra space between your list items. Now you'll style your Heading 2 element.

5 In the CSS Styles panel, double-click the h2 rule. In the Text-transform section, click on the menu, and from the list, choose uppercase. Press Apply, and you will see your two headings, *Spring Events* and *Rent Our Facility!,* transform to uppercase. This helps your headings stand out and is a lot faster than retyping these headings by hand. Now you'll add some space between all the letters.

Transforming your text to uppercase is just a style; in the HTML, your original text still has the standard formatting. One of the few times this might be an issue is if your web page is being viewed without a style sheet; many cell phones and PDAs do not fully support style sheets (or use them at all), and so your text would appear lowercase as it is in the HTML.

6 Select the Block category in the CSS Rule definition dialog box. Block styles generally control the way text is displayed in the browser. In the field for Letter-spacing, type **5**; then choose px from the drop-down menu to the right. Press Apply, and the two headings are extended. Each letter pair has 5 pixels of space between them. Press OK. When used well, letter-spacing can make your headings more readable and unique.

> SPRING EVENTS
>
> - Free body lotion samples
> - Cheesetasting.
> - Winetasting
> - Free chocolate samples
>
> RENT OUR FACILITY!
>
> If you've ever wanted to hold an event in our store, well n
> more. We offer special rates for members of the coop.
>
> *Free samples while supplies last.

Adding letter-spacing and uppercasing to your headings can make them stand out.

Fine-tuning page appearance with contextual and pseudo-class selectors

Earlier in the lesson, you learned that you need more control over your CSS. For example, you will now look at a solution for the following problem. Look at the Spring Events list on your page: lines 1 and 4 both begin with the word Free. Let's say you wanted to emphasize this word slightly to attract your user's attention. You could simply bold the word, but what if you not only wanted to bold it, but change the color as well. It would be possible to create a class to do this, but there is another option that has some useful benefits, with the daunting name of *contextual selectors.*

To make things even more difficult, Dreamweaver actually refers to contextual selectors, which is the official CSS term for them, as *compound selectors*. Despite the terminology, they are very powerful and important to understand.

Contextual selectors apply formatting to tags and classes when they appear in a specific combination. For instance, you usually have rules for the *<p>* (paragraph) and *<strong>* (strong) tag, but then you might have another set of rules for *<strong>* tags inside *<p>* tags. For instance, you can designate that any text inside a *<strong>* tag must be red, unless it is used within a *<p>* tag, in which case it should be blue. This breathes new life into your tag styles by multiplying the number of times you can use them in conjunction with each other.

1   In the first line of the Spring Events list, select the word *Free*. Click on the HTML button in the Property Inspector, then press the Bold button. Using the example from above, let's say that simply bolding this wasn't enough and you wanted to add some color.

2   Press on the CSS button in the Property Inspector; then click on the menu for Targeted Rule and choose <New CSS Rule>. You must do this; otherwise, when you choose a color, you will target the whole list, which is not what you want.

3   Click on the color swatch in the Property Inspector and choose the dark green swatch in the top row, #030. The New CSS Rule dialog box appears.

4   From the Choose a contextual selector type for your CSS rule drop-down menu, choose Compound (based on your selection). In the Selector Name field, the text, *body ul li strong*, appears. This may look strange at first, but it's actually very logical if you read it from left to right. The body tag is the ancestor, or parent, of the ul tag, which is the parent of the li tag, which is the parent of the strong tag. In other words, your style will only apply to strong tags, which are nested in a list item (which is nested in the unordered list, and so on).

Set the Selector Type to Compound to create a contextual selector.

In the official specification of CSS, the concept of ancestor and parent elements is an important one. In fact, the concept is taken even further, in the example above, where the ul tag is referred to as the child of the body element because it is the direct descendant of the body element. There are even sibling elements!

In many ways, including the body element in this rule is overkill. Technically speaking, body is the ancestor of all tags in a document, as it nests virtually everything else, and so you can actually remove it and make your code a little easier to read.

5   Below the Selector Name section, click on the Less Specific button, and the list of rules is shortened to *ul li strong*; this has no effect on the behavior of the rule. Press OK. The word Free is now bolded and dark green. Deselect the text to see the final result. The rule is in place, and anything that is bolded inside a list will have this appearance. You can see this now by bolding the word Free in the fourth line of the list.

6   Press the HTML button in the Property Inspector. Select the word Free in the fourth line and then press the Bold button in the Property Inspector. The word takes on the same appearance. Bolding anything else in the list causes it to have the same appearance, while bolding anything not in a list has only the default effect.

Styling hyperlinks

You're slowly beginning to pull together a page with a color theme to it, even if there is no layout *per se*. A frequently asked question when people are learning to create web pages is how to style the hyperlinks on a page. This can be accomplished with CSS, although there are some precautions. Since the early days of CSS, the default style for unvisited hyperlinks has been a bright blue with an underline for unvisited hyperlinks and a purple color with an underline for visited hyperlinks. An argument is sometimes made that users might be confused by hyperlinks that do not fit this mold. On the other hand, many designers like being able to color their hyperlinks to match the rest of their page. Regardless of the debate, it's important to understand how to do this.

Technically speaking, hyperlinks live in a category called *pseudo-class*. A pseudo-class selector affects a part or state of a selected tag or class. A state often refers to an item's appearance in response to something happening, such as the mouse pointer rolling over it. One of the most common pseudo-class selectors is applied to the *<a>* tag, which is used to create hyperlinks. You'll now create a pseudo-class selector to affect the appearance of hyperlinks on the events. html page in different states:

1   Choose New from the CSS Styles panel menu to create a new rule. The New CSS Rule dialog box appears.

2   From the Choose a contextual selector type for your CSS rule drop-down menu, choose Compound. In the Selector Name section, click to open the drop-down menu to the right of the selector field. You may have different selectors appearing at the top of your menu; this is because Dreamweaver is attempting to create a compound rule, but in fact you are only interested in the last four options, which are a:link, a:visited, a:hover, and a:active. Choose a:link, which affects the appearance of a hyperlink when it hasn't yet been visited. Press OK.

Set the Selector type to Compound and choose a:link from the Selector menu.

3   The CSS Rule definition dialog box appears. Under the Type category, click the color swatch next to Color and choose the green shade you used in the previous exercise (#030). Press OK, and the products link in the first paragraph as well as the two links at the bottom of the page are now green instead of blue. Now you'll set the style for hover links, or a:hover.

4   Once again, choose New from the CSS Styles panel menu and the New CSS Rule dialog box opens. You will leave the state for the visited link alone for now. In this case, the default purple is fine. You will now change the state for a:hover, which defines the color of a hyperlink when a user places their cursor over it.

5   From the Choose a contextual selector type for your CSS rule drop-down menu, choose Compound. In the Selector Name section, choose a:hover from the drop-down menu, then press OK.

6   From the Type category, click the color swatch next to Color and select the bright orange approximately in the center of the Swatches panel (#C60). In the Text-decoration section, mark the last checkbox labeled *none*. This removes the underline from the hyperlink for the hover state only. Press OK.

CSS Rule definition for a:hover	

Category   Type

Type
Background
Block
Box
Border
List
Positioning
Extensions

Font-family:

Font-size: px   Font-weight:

Font-style: Font-variant:

Line-height: px   Text-transform:

Text-decoration: ☐ underline   Color: ■ #c60
☐ overline
☐ line-through
☐ blink
☑ none

Help   Apply   Cancel   OK

Set properties for a:hover, or the appearance of hyperlinks when the mouse pointer rolls over them.

You can preview the appearance of the hyperlinks by clicking on the Live View button in the Application bar or opening your page in a browser.

7   Choose File > Save; then choose File > Preview in Browser and choose a browser from the list to launch it. Place your cursor over the products link, but don't click it. This is the hover link. Click on the products link to bring you to the products page, and then click back to the events page by clicking the Events link at the bottom of the page. The products link is now purple because the browser understands you have visited it.

You will leave off styling the a:active link for now. Setting the a:active property defines the way a link appears when it is being clicked on by a user. Close the web browser.

Div tags and CSS IDs

Your page is coming along nicely on the style front, as you have used quite a bit of CSS, but looking at your page, it's fair to say that it is still lacking a cohesive style. All your various headings and paragraphs, as well as your list, are floating about on the page, and with the exception of the copyright text at the bottom of the page, it's difficult at a single glance to get a sense of where one section ends and another begins. It's time to add more structure to your page through the use of the *<div>* tag and more control of your CSS with ID selectors.

Let's look at the structure first. It would be nice to gather the text on the bottom of your page, starting with the line, *Occasionally we gather...*, and then the two paragraphs below, and put it all into a single section. You could then take this new section and style it separately from the rest of the page. This is possible with the *<div>* tag. In this exercise, you will begin by creating a footer ID.

1   Click and drag to select all the text from the line, *Occasionally we gather...*, down to the bottom of the page. You will be grouping these three paragraphs together.

2   Double-click on the Insert tab to open it; if the drop-down menu is not set to Common, do so now. In the Common section, press the Insert Div Tag (▦) button, and the Insert Div Tag dialog box opens. In the Insert section, the default choice is *Wrap around selection*; this is exactly what you want to do, so leave this option as is.

Press the Insert Div Tag button in the Common section of the Insert panel.

A *<div>* tag by itself doesn't do anything until some CSS properties are attached to it. In other words, unlike other HTML tags, which often have a default visual effect in the browser (think of headings), the *<div>* tag has no effect on your rendered page unless you specifically instruct it to. You will now get to do this.

3   In the field labeled ID, type **footer**. Just like classes, IDs should have good, descriptive names to help identify them. You'll now apply a background color of white to the entire block of text you selected. Notice that there is a field for class as well. Classes and IDs are very similar. The difference between them is that classes can be used multiple times on different elements on a page, whereas an ID can only be used once. In this case, an ID is appropriate because there is only one footer on this page.

4   Click the New CSS Rule button. You needn't change anything here; you are creating an ID with the name footer. The footer name is preceded by the pound sign (#). This is the main difference between ID names and class names. If this were a class named footer, it would be named *.footer*. Press OK, and the CSS Rule definition dialog box appears.

5 Select the Background category, then click on the Background-color swatch. Choose the pure white swatch (#FFF) and press OK. Press OK to close the Insert Div Tag dialog box. In Dreamweaver's Design view, a box has appeared around the text and there is now a white background unifying the footer text.

Set the Background-color to #FFF in the CSS Rule definition dialog box.

If you haven't guessed by now, these are the beginning steps toward page layout with CSS. A footer is a common element on most pages, and there are a few other obvious ones as well: headers, sidebars, and navigation bars to name a few. You'll begin working with these page structures more deeply in upcoming lessons, but first you'll need to have some more control of the CSS rules that you've been working with this lesson.

Internal versus external style sheets

Now that you've seen how to modify a few items in a single page at once, you can only imagine how powerful a style sheet shared by every page in your web site can be. When you create new CSS rules, you have the opportunity to define them in the current document or in a new CSS file. A collection of rules stored in a separate .css file is referred to as an *external style sheet.* You can attach external style sheets to any number of pages in a site so that they all share the same style rules.

So far, you've created internal, or embedded, styles. This means you wrote the style rules directly into the page using the *<style>* tag. Although you can format a page with an internal style sheet, this method is not very portable. To apply the same rules in another page, you have to copy and paste the internal style sheet from one page to another. This can create inconsistency among pages if the same rule is updated in one page and not the other.

To utilize the true power of style sheets, you can create an external style sheet that any and all pages on your site can share. When you change an external style, pages linked to that style sheet are updated. This is especially handy when working with sites containing many pages and sections.

You can create external style sheets in the following ways:

• Move rules from an internal style sheet into a new CSS file.

• Define styles in a page in a new document using the New CSS Rule panel.

• Create a new CSS document from the Start page or File menu.

Now you will export internal styles from your events.html page into a separate CSS file so that other pages may share them.

1   With the events.html document open, expand the style sheet shown in the CSS Styles panel so that you can see all the rules you have created. If you have limited screenspace, double-click on the Insert panel to collapse it.

2   Click on the first rule below the *<style>* tag at the top of the panel and then scroll down if necessary to locate the last rule. Shift+click the last rule in the panel so that all the rules are selected. In the upper-right corner, press the CSS Styles panel menu button (⋅≡) and choose Move CSS Rules.

Select all rules in your style sheet and then choose Move CSS Rules.

3   The Move CSS Rules dialog box appears, asking if you want to move the styles to an existing or a new style sheet. Select A new style sheet and press OK.

4   A Save Style Sheet dialog box appears, asking you to choose a name and location for the new file that is about to be created. Name it **mystyles,** navigate to the root folder of your site (dw04lessons folder), and choose Save.

5   Your CSS Styles panel now shows a new style sheet: mystyles.css. The internal style sheet (shown as <*style*>) is still in your document, but it contains no rules. Click the plus sign (Windows) or arrow (Mac OS) to the left of mystyles.css to expand it and reveal all the rules it contains. There should be no surprises there; the same rules that were in your internal style sheet are now in an external one.

Attaching an external style sheet to your page

Dreamweaver automatically made the new external style sheet available to the current page by attaching it. However, you will have to point other pages to this style sheet in order for them to use it. You can accomplish this with the Attach Style Sheet command in the CSS Styles panel.

1   Double-click on the products.html file from the Files panel. This page contains event information with no formatting applied.

2   If necessary, click the "All" button in the CSS Styles panel, then at the bottom of the CSS Styles panel, click the Attach Style Sheet icon (●). The Attach Style Sheet panel appears.

3   Next to File/URL, click the Browse button to locate a style sheet file to attach. In the dw04lessons folder, select the mystyles.css file from the Select Style Sheet dialog box and press OK (Windows) or Choose (Mac OS). Press OK to close the Attach External Style Sheet dialog box.

Adding an external style sheet.

The page refreshes with the styles defined in the external style sheet. You can also see that the CSS Styles panel shows that mystyles.css and all its rules are now available for use and editing.

Modifying attached style sheets

Because an attached style sheet appears in your CSS Styles panel, you can modify any of its rules just as you would with an internal style sheet. If you modify an external style in one page, the changes apply across other pages that share that style sheet. You'll take one step closer to layout now by modifying the body property in order to add some margins to your page.

1   In the CSS Styles panel, click on the plus sign (Windows) or arrow (Mac OS) to the left of mystyles.css and double-click on the body rule. The CSS Rule definition dialog box opens.

2   Click on the Box category and deselect the checkbox labeled *Same for all* in the Margin column.

Deselect the checkbox in the Margin section of the Box category.

Because CSS is based on a box model, it views every tag as a container. Because the *<body>* tag is the largest container, if you modify its margins, it affects all the content on the page. You'll specifically be changing the left and right margins to create a more centered layout.

3   In the Margin field labeled Right, type **15**, and choose % from the drop-down menu.

4   In the Margin field labeled Left, type **15**, and choose % from the menu. Press OK, and your content shifts toward the center.

Change the left and right margin for body to 15 percent.

5   Choose File > Save All, and then preview your page in the browser. You are able to navigate between the products page and the events page using the hyperlinks in each document. Shorten the width of your browser, and notice that the content adjusts accordingly. There will always be 15 percent space to the left of content in the browser window and 15 percent to the right, thereby centering your content. Open the events.html file in your web browser to see how this page appearance is now being controlled by the external style sheet. When done, close the browser.

Creating a new .css file (external style sheet)

Although it's easy to export styles to a new .css file, you can also create styles in a new .css file from the beginning. The New CSS Rule dialog box gives you this option whenever you create a new rule. By creating styles in an external .css file, you can avoid the extra step of exporting them later, and make the style sheet available to other pages immediately.

1   In the Files panel, double-click on the event1.html file.

2   From the CSS Styles panel menu, choose New; the New CSS Rule dialog box appears.

3 Set the Selector Type as Tag, and choose body from the Tag drop-down menu if it is not automatically selected. At the bottom of the screen, click on the Rule Definition menu and choose (New Style Sheet File); then press OK.

New CSS Rule

Selector Type:
Choose a contextual selector type for your CSS rule.

Tag (redefines an HTML element)

Selector Name:
Choose or enter a name for your selector.

body

This selector name will apply your rule to all <body> elements.

Less Specific   More Specific

Rule Definition:
Choose where your rule will be defined.

✓ (This document only)
(New Style Sheet File)

OK
Cancel
Help

Creating a new external style sheet from scratch.

4 You are prompted to name and save the new .css file. Name it **morestyles.css** and save it in the root folder of your site.

5 When the CSS Rule definition dialog box appears, choose the Background category. Set the background color to light yellow, **#FFC**. Press OK to create the rule.

Your page's background color should be yellow, and the CSS Styles panel reflects that the style was created in a new external style sheet. Now you can attach this style sheet to any other page in your site.

6 Choose File > Save All.

Congratulations! You have finished Lesson 4, "Styling Your Pages with CSS." In the next lesson, you will take a leap into using CSS for layout.

CSS FYI

Inheritance

When you nest one rule inside another, the nested rule inherits properties from the rule in which it's contained. For instance, if you define a font-size and font-family for all <p> tags, it carries over to a class style used within the paragraph that doesn't specify values for either property. It automatically inherits the font-size and font-family from the <p> tag selector.

CSS rule weight

What happens if two classes of the same name exist in the same page? It is possible to have two identically named styles, either in the same style sheet or between internal and external style sheets used by the same page. Along the same lines, it is possible to have two rules that both apply to the same tag. If either of these cases exists, how do you know which rule is followed?

You know which rule is followed based on two factors: weight and placement. If two selectors are the same weight (for instance, two tag selectors for the body tag), then the last defined rule takes precedence.

If a rule of the same name is defined in both an internal and external style sheet in your document, the rule from the last defined style sheet takes precedence. For instance, if an external style sheet is attached to the page anywhere after the internal style sheet, the rule in the attached stylesheet wins.

Adobe Device Central

The widespread use of Internet-ready devices, such as mobile phones and PDAs, makes it more necessary than ever to adapt your work for multiple sizes and platforms. Dreamweaver CS5 is integrated with Adobe Device Central, which displays and simulates the appearance of HTML content in a variety of mobile, PDA, and handheld device skins and environments. Building your pages using the best practices of CSS will help optimize your pages for the small screens of mobile device.

To preview a page in Device Central:

1   With your finished events.html file open, choose File > Preview in Browser > Device Central. Device Central, which is a separate application, launches.

2   The Device Central application shows the page in the default profile which at the time of this writing is Flash Player 10.1 for a multitouch mobile device. You may use the controls on this generic device to preview your page as it would appear on this phone.

   To load the profiles for different mobile devices, you could click on the Browse button and choose a different device to use for emulation.

3   Choose File > Quit (Windows) or Device Central > Quit (Mac OS) to exit Device Central and return to Dreamweaver. Choose File > Close to close the file.

Self study

Create a new document and add some unique content, such as text or images, to it. Afterwards, use the CSS Styles panel to define at least one tag style, two class styles, and one contextual selector (advanced) in a new, external .css file. Create a second document and attach your new external style sheet to it, using the Attach Style Sheet command from the CSS Styles panel. Add content to this page, and style it using the style rules already available from your external style sheet. If desired, make changes to the rules from either document, and watch how both documents are affected by any modifications made to the external style sheet.

Review

Questions

1   What are the four types of selectors that can be chosen when creating a new CSS rule?

2   In what three places can styles be defined?

3   True or false: A style sheet is composed of several CSS rules and their properties.

Answers

1   Tag, Class, ID and Compound (which includes contextual and pseudo–class selectors).

2   Inline (written directly into a tag), internal (embedded inside a specific page using the *<style>* tag), or external (inside a separate .css file).

3   True. A style sheet can contain many CSS rules and their properties.

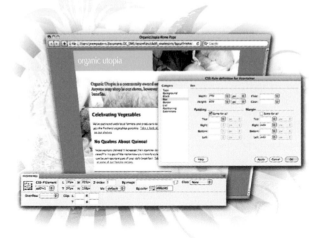

What you'll learn in this lesson:

- Understanding the CSS Box model

- Creating Divs and AP Divs

- Stacking and overlapping elements

- Styling box contents

- Using visual aids to fine-tune positioning.

Creating Page Layouts with CSS

Now that you've used Cascading Style Sheets, you've seen how powerful they can be for styling a page. CSS is equally powerful as a layout tool, allowing you to freely position page content in ways not possible with HTML alone.

Starting up

Before starting, make sure that your tools and panels are consistent by resetting your workspace. See "Resetting the Dreamweaver workspace" on page 3.

You will work with several files from the dw05lessons folder in this lesson. Make sure that you have loaded the dwlessons folder onto your hard drive from the supplied DVD. See "Loading lesson files" on page 3.

Before you begin, you need to create site settings that point to the dw05lessons folder from the included DVD that contains resources you need for these lessons. Go to Site > New Site, or, for details on creating a site, refer to Lesson 2, "Setting Up a New Site."

See Lesson 5 in action!

Use the accompanying video to gain a better understanding of how to use some of the features shown in this lesson. The video tutorial for this lesson can be found on the included DVD.

The CSS Box model

CSS positions elements within a page using the Box model, which refers to rectangular virtual boxes used to hold and place content within a document. Each box can act as a container for text, images, media, and tables and takes up a certain area on the page determined by its width and height. Additionally, each box can have its own optional padding, margin, and border settings (described in detail shortly). In reference to the display of items on a page, CSS regards almost every element on a page as a box.

Toward the end of Lesson 4, "Styling Your Pages with CSS," you began to explore page structure through the use of the HTML *<div>* element. The Box model in CSS applies to all elements in CSS but is often paired with *<div>* tags. The *<div>* element, in conjunction with CSS rules, can be freely positioned, formatted, and even told how to interact with other boxes adjacent to it. You can also stack and overlap *<div>* containers, opening the door to flexible and creative layouts that are not possible with HTML alone.

This lesson dives deeper into the many uses of the *<div>* element. If you have jumped directly to this lesson, it is highly recommended that you understand the basic concepts in Lesson 4, "Styling Your Pages with CSS," before starting this one.

If you've worked with layout applications such as InDesign CS5, the idea of creating and positioning containers for page content should be very familiar to you. Boxes created with the <div> tag can be thought of as analogous to the text and image frames you create in InDesign.

The basics of CSS margins, padding, and borders

The Box model allows each element on a page to have unique margin, padding, and border settings.

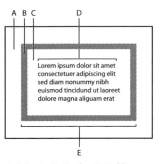

A. *Margin*. *B*. *Border*. *C*. *Padding*.
D. *Content width*. *E*. *Visible width*.

Margins refer to the transparent area surrounding the box, which you set using the margin group of CSS properties. Margins can play an essential role in creating distance between a box and the content surrounding it (such as other boxes), or the boundaries of the page itself. You can set margins for all sides at once or uniquely for each side.

Padding is the distance between the inside edge of the box and its contents; by setting padding, you create space between the box and any text, images, or other content that it contains. You set padding using the padding group of CSS properties, and, like margins, you can set padding for all four sides of a box at once or for each side individually.

The **border** of a box is transparent by default, but you can add width, color, and a border style for decoration or definition around boxes. Borders sit directly between margins and padding, and define the actual boundaries of the box. You set borders using the border group of CSS properties and, like margins and padding, you can define borders for all four sides at once or for each side individually.

You can incorporate each property into any style rule and attach it to a box, similar to the way you've attached classes to paragraphs and tables in previous lessons.

Reviewing the *<div>* element

As mentioned earlier, when exploring and creating page layouts with CSS, you will frequently encounter and use the *<div>* element. The *<div>* element creates areas or divisions within an HTML document; you can place page content such as text and images directly within sets of *<div>* tags. Dreamweaver enables you to create CSS-driven page layouts using the Insert Div Tag and Draw AP Div buttons in the Insert panel; both of which utilize *<div>* tags to create boxes that you can place precisely within your pages and style with CSS rules.

Reviewing the ID selector

In Lesson 4, "Styling Your Pages with CSS," you learned about the different selector types in CSS: classes, tags, pseudo-class selectors, and IDs. In this lesson, IDs take center stage and become an essential part of working with CSS boxes and positioning. An ID is a special selector type created for a unique element using the same name within a page, and it's meant for one-time use only. ID rules appear within a style sheet and are preceded by a pound sign (#), in contrast to classes, which are preceded by a period character (.).

Because IDs can be used only once per page, they are ideal for setting properties that need to be specific to a single element, such as positioning information. In other words, page elements such as headers or columns occupy a specific position on the page, such as top, right, left, and so on. When creating layouts using the Insert Div Tag button, Dreamweaver requires you to create or assign an ID rule for each box created. When drawing boxes with the Draw AP Div button, Dreamweaver automatically creates a unique ID rule that contains positioning, width, and height information for that specific box.

Because the *<div>* element has no display attributes, it is given its properties by either an ID or a class, or both. Think of an ID as a set of instructions that give a *<div>* its unique appearance and behavior (as DNA does to a human being). An ID rule is matched to a *<div>* using the tag's ID attribute.

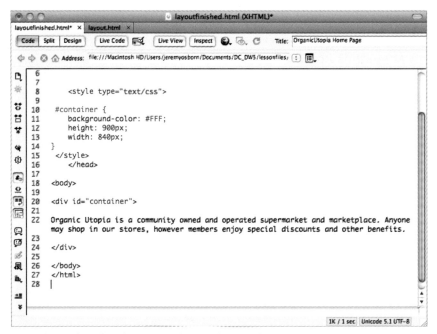

The Code view shows the style sheet and <div> tag that create the container.

Tables or CSS for layout?

A long-standing debate has existed within the web design community about the best approach to creating page layouts. The argument went something like this: Many designers felt like tables were the wrong tool for the job and CSS boxes were adopted as the primary method for positioning page content. Designers in favor of tables asserted that tables are more reliable in older browsers and easier and quicker to build. It's not quite accurate to say that the argument has been completely resolved, but it's clear that layout with CSS is here to stay and more and more people are adopting it every year.

Here is a brief overview of what you need to know:

Tables: Although fewer and fewer sites are being built from scratch in tables these days, there remain countless websites that were built with them and are still on the Web being updated and maintained. Designers who finds themselves having to maintain a tables-based site would do well to understand their behavior. Also, HTML email often relies on the use of tables due to the limited capabilities of email readers.

Tables' limitations include the following: You are restricted to its cell-based structure, and to achieve more complex layouts, you need to nest several levels of tables. Tables also add extraneous code to pages and can present difficulties in accessibility for devices such as screen readers.

Boxes: CSS positioning has been around for many years. However different browsers have chosen to support it at varying and inconsistent levels. At this point, though, most CSS 2.1 positioning properties and practices are supported consistently across the latest browsers. If you need your sites to work reliably in older browsers, testing is still necessary to expose potential inconsistencies.

The CSS Advisor and Browser Compatibility Check features in Dreamweaver CS5 are huge benefits to designers who want to use CSS more extensively. These tools flag and help troubleshoot any CSS-related items that may be incompatible or inconsistent in commonly used browsers. The CSS Advisor and Browser Compatibility Check are discussed in detail in Lesson 14, "Managing Your Web Site: Reports, Optimization, and Maintenance."

Creating a centered container for your page.

The goal of this lesson is to create the home page for the Organic Utopia site. This page will look like the thumbnail below.

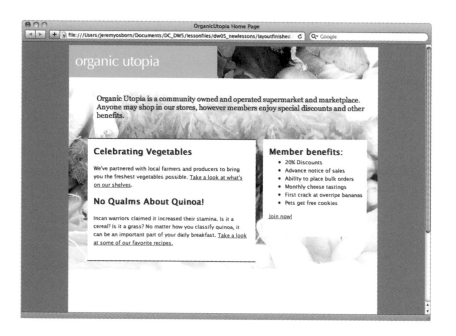

The home page will be a different design and layout than the rest of the site (this layout is covered in more detail in Lesson 6), and you will start by creating a container that will end up nesting the other sections of your page such as the header, sidebar and other elements. This container will have a fixed width of 770 pixels and also be centered within the browser window.

This container will use a combination of relative positioning and automatic margins to achieve the centering effect. Relative positioning allows you to position this box relative to the body of the page, and the automatic margins will force the fixed-width container to stay centered regardless of the browser window's width.

1   In the Files panel, navigate to the dw05lessons folder and double-click the layout.html file to open it. This document has been partially prepared for you, with a background color and a page title added. Additionally, the default font, font color, and font size have been defined as Lucida Sans, grey, and small, respectively. Your first step will be to add a box, which will become your main column of text.

2   If it's not already visible, open the Insert panel by choosing Window > Insert. The Insert panel features a list of objects that can be added to your pages easily.

3   In the bottom-left corner of your document window, click on the *<body>* tag. Remember, the body tag encloses all the other tags within a page. You will now create a new *<div>* element that will function as a container for the other layout elements. In the Insert panel, click on the Insert Div Tag button.

Click the Insert Div Tag to add a container div element.

4   The Insert Div Tag dialog box appears. Click in the ID text field and type **container**, then click on the New CSS Rule button. In the New CSS Rule definition dialog box that appears, make sure that #container is listed as the Selector Name and then click OK. The CSS Rule definition dialog box appears and you can begin to style your container div.

5   Select the Box listing in the Category column on the left side of the dialog box. In the Width text field, type **770** and make sure px (pixels) is selected from the drop-down menu to the right. For Height, type **800** in the text field. In the Margin section, uncheck Same for All, then, from the Right margin drop-down menu, choose auto. Choose auto from the Left margin drop-down menu as well.

Choose the settings for the #container element.

You'll explore using margins soon, but by setting a margin value of auto to the left and right side of the container, you are instructing the browser to put equal amounts of space on the right and left sides. The end result will be a box that is centered within the browser window.

5   Select the Background category on the left side of the dialog box, then click the Background-color swatch and choose the white (#FFF) swatch. This adds a background color of white to your entire container, separating it from the background.

6   Select the Positioning category on the left side of the dialog box and choose relative from the Position drop-down menu. This is key to the success of your next steps. By setting the position of the container to relative you will be able to position the page elements using the container as a frame of reference. Press OK in this dialog box, as well as OK for the Insert Div Tag dialog box that is still open.

7   Choose File > Save, then choose File > Preview in Browser. Your container will be centered in the middle of your browser window and Dreamweaver's default placeholder text is aligned in the top left of your container. (Occasionally, we have noticed Dreamweaver does not add this placeholder text, if this is the case for you, type **content for id "container" Goes Here**.)

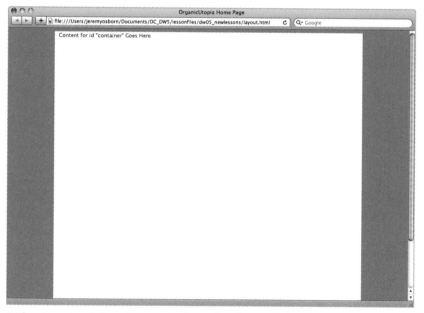

With position set to relative and auto margins the container element will always be centered.

Resize the browser width; the container stays centered until the window is narrower than 770 pixels, at which point the box is cropped. Close your browser. If your container div did not appear centered, it is possible you are using an older browser. Even if your container div is centered, there are a few additional steps you will now add to ensure the page centers in older browsers.

Making layouts cross-browser compatible

If you are new to web design, welcome to the world known as CSS hacks. In an ideal world, all web browsers would render HTML and CSS using the same set of rules, and all web pages would look the same, regardless of the browser. Unfortunately, this is not the case. For a variety of reasons, different web browsers render pages differently. For example, older web browsers such as Netscape 4 and Internet Explorer 4 do not render CSS positioning particularly well. More modern browsers have their own set of quirks as well. In certain cases, additional rules can be added to the CSS that make the page work. These fixes are never ideal because they require additional code and sometimes create more problems than they solve; however, they are necessary if you want your pages to look similar across browsers.

1   Double-click on the body rule in the CSS Styles panel to edit its properties. In the CSS Rule definition dialog box, select the Block category and choose center from the Text-align drop-down menu. Press OK.

This fixes a problem that exists with version 6 (and earlier) of Internet Explorer regarding automatic margins. Although this fixes the bug, it creates another problem in that it will center all text on your page (you can see this currently in your container). So, in order to fix that problem you must create another rule to counteract this one.

2   Double-click the #container rule in the CSS Styles panel. In the CSS Rule definition dialog box, select the Block category on the left, then choose left from the Text-align drop-down menu. This will align your text to the left, and all is back to normal. Press OK to accept these changes.

3   Choose File > Save.

In this exercise you created a centered box named container. In the next exercise, you will place all of your other layout sections as well as your content, into this container. Before doing this, a brief overview of the difference between absolute and relative positioning may help.

Absolute versus relative positioning

Absolute positioning: An element that is set to absolute strictly follows the positioning values given to it, relative only to its containing element. The containing element can be another div or the page itself. Absolutely positioned elements are pulled out of the normal flow of HTML content, and regardless of what surrounds them (for example, text content or neighboring divs), they always appear at the exact coordinates assigned to them.

Here is an example of a div absolutely positioned within another div. The larger div (Box #1) is the containing element, and so any positioning values assigned to Box #2 are relative to the element boundaries of Box #1.

I'm Box #1, and I'm the containing element for Box #2.

I'm Box #2, and I'm positioned within Box #1.

Box #2 is contained, or nested, within Box #1.

Adding additional content to the containing box (#1) has no effect on the nested div. It remains positioned outside the flow of HTML.

I'm Box #1, and I'm the containing element for Box #2.
I'm Box #1, and I'm the containing element for Box #2.
I'm Box #1, and I'm the containing element for Box #2.
I'm Box I'm Box #2, and aining element for Box
#2.I'm B I'm positioned ontaining element for Box
#2. within Box #1.

Box #2 remains in position even with added content in Box #1.

Relative positioning: A relatively positioned element accepts values for position properties such as top and left, but it also takes the normal flow of neighboring HTML content into account. Here are the boxes and values shown in the preceding two figures; the only difference here is that the position property for Box #2 has been set to relative instead of absolute.

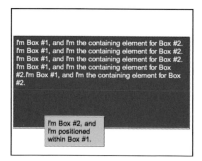

I'm Box #1, and I'm the containing element for Box #2.
I'm Box #1, and I'm the containing element for Box #2.
I'm Box #1, and I'm the containing element for Box #2.
I'm Box #1, and I'm the containing element for Box
#2.I'm Box #1, and I'm the containing element for Box
#2.

I'm Box #2, and I'm positioned within Box #1.

Box #2 is still offset, just as before, but it's being
displaced by the content before it.

Although it appears that the top and left values have changed, they haven't. Unlike absolutely positioned elements, relatively positioned elements stay within the normal flow of HTML content, which means that they can be displaced by the elements (in this case, the text) surrounding them. In this example, Box #2 is still 50 pixels from the top and 50 pixels from the left, but its point of reference is the end of the preceding text content, not Box #1.

Positioning items relatively is useful when you want an item to flow with the items surrounding it. The following image shows five divs nested inside a larger div to create a menu.

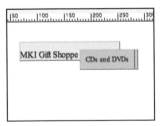

All menu items are positioned relative to one another, and so they fall into place based on each other's position.

The same example is shown in the figure below, with the position set to absolute for all menu items. The result is a collapse of the menu—all the menu items are trying to occupy the same place at the same time, without regard for their neighbors.

When set to absolute, the menu items stack on top of one another, because they all must be at the same place, regardless of the elements that surround them.

The files used for these examples are located in the dw05lessons folder, and are named absolute_relative.html and relative_menu.html. Open them in Dreamweaver and explore the code to further your knowledge.

Any element, or, in this case, any box, can have the position property applied, and one of five possible values can be set: absolute, fixed, relative, static, or inherit. The two most commonly used are absolute and relative, and although both can accept positioning properties such as top and left, they are rendered differently, even with identical positioning values.

Positioning content with AP Divs

Now that your container is centered on the page, you'll need to add boxes to hold content within the container. The easiest and most visual way to place boxes in Dreamweaver is with the Draw AP Div button. An AP or Absolute Positioned Div is placed exactly where you draw it, using the page as its point of reference by default.

For this exercise, you'll want your AP Divs to be positioned using the container as their point of reference. To change the default behavior of AP Divs as you draw them, an additional step is required. This step will ensure that your AP Divs are nested inside the container div.

1   Choose Edit > Preferences (Windows) or Dreamweaver > Preferences (Mac OS) and then choose the AP Elements category. Click the checkbox labeled Nesting. This ensures that the new boxes you create will be nested inside the container. Click OK.

Set your Preferences so that new AP Elements automatically nest when inside your container.

Creating a header section with the Draw AP Div

Now that you've created a container that is centered within your page, you'll add the other layout elements, with the header. The Draw AP Div tool allows you to add boxes within your pages manually. Once a box is added, you can style it with CSS (change the width and height, add background color and more) and you can also add content such as text or images.

1   In the Insert panel, click on the drop-down menu and choose Layout.

The Layout section of the Insert panel displays the available layout icons.

2   In the Insert panel, click the Draw AP Div button (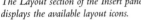). Move back over the page; your cursor is now a crosshair signifying that you can begin to draw.

3   Place your cursor below the placeholder text in the top left corner of the container and then click and drag down and to the right to draw a box. Stop approximately 25% of the way down the screen. The box appears with a handle in the top left corner.

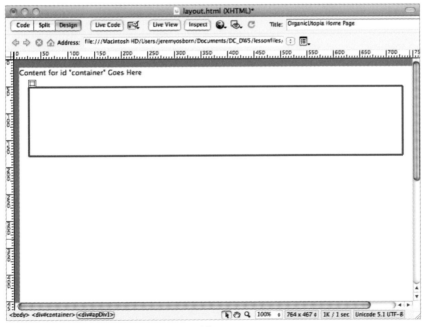

The newly created AP Div has a handle in its top left corner.

5 Click on the selection handle in the top-left corner of the AP Div and click and drag the box around the screen to see how you can position the box manually. Notice in the Property Inspector that the properties for your box are displayed and dynamically change as you move it; currently just the Left and Top position (L and T) will change. Your settings will likely be different than those in the figure.

Click inside the Bg color text field and type **#9fcc41** which is a yellow-green color.

The Property Inspector displays the properties of the AP Div and allows you to set its background color.

You will now position this box to become your header.

6 In the bottom-left corner of the Property Inspector, locate the CSS-P Element text field. It is currently named apDiv1. Select the text within this text field and type **header**.

When Dreamweaver creates new AP Divs, it gives them the default names of apDiv1, apDiv2, and so on. You can, and most often should, rename these, simply because the default name is non-descriptive and unhelpful. Keep in mind that functionally, this is exactly the same step as the previous exercise when you named the div container. In both cases you are creating a CSS ID behind the scenes.

7 Select the placeholder text Content for id "container" Goes Here and delete it. You are about to create your header at the top of the page and you don't need this content.

8 If you currently do not have rulers visible, choose View > Rulers > Show. Click the edge of the header div again, and pay careful attention to the L (Left) and the T (Top) values.

You will now position the header to the top left corner of the container using the Property Inspector.

9 In the Property Inspector, type **0px** into the L (Left) text field and press Enter (Windows) or Return (Mac OS). The box moves and the left side of the box is positioned horizontally at 0 pixels. Type **0px** into the T (Top) text field and the top of the box is positioned vertically at 0 pixels.

Be sure to type the number and the px value (i.e. 100px) together in order for position to be valid.

With Top and Left values both set to 0px the header is aligned to the top-left corner of the container.

9   You also need to set the width of this header. Again, you could do this manually by dragging the edges of the header box, but this is not precise. Better to use number values and match the width of the header to the width of the container.

In the Property Inspector, type **770px** for the W value and **80px** for the H value.

10   You can add content to the box by simply typing in it. Click inside the box on the workspace and type Organic Utopia. You'll be replacing this with the logo a bit later, for now this will serve as a placeholder.

11   Choose File > Save to save your work, and then preview your page by choosing File > Preview in Browser > [Default Browser] or by pressing the Preview/Debug in browser button (●) at the top of the document window. Close the browser when finished.

Adding an introduction section to your page

Now you can add additional sections to your page. The first section you'll add is a box below the header where you'll end up formatting an introductory paragraph to state the mission of the site, and grab the user's attention.

1   Click on the Draw AP Div object and draw a box below your header. Don't worry about the exact size of the box, but make the width smaller than the header and roughly the same height.

A good habit to get into is renaming your AP Divs immediately after they are created. You'll do that now.

2   Click on the edge of the new div and in the CSS-P Element text field, type **intro** and press Enter (Windows) or Return (Mac OS).

3   Click inside the intro box and type the following text: **Organic Utopia is a community owned and operated supermarket and marketplace. Anyone may shop in our stores but members enjoy special discounts and other benefits.**

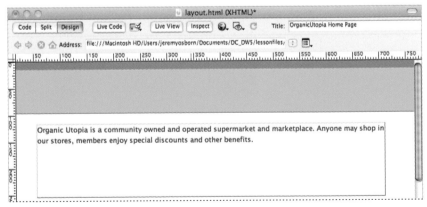

The #intro AP Div with added text

Now you'll format the text in this box using techniques from the last lesson.

4   In the Property Inspector, click on the HTML button if necessary. Select the text you entered and choose Paragraph from the Format drop-down menu.

5   With the text still selected, click on the CSS button in the Property Inspector. Then click on the Font drop-down menu and choose the Georgia, Times New Roman, Times, serif family. The New CSS Rule definition dialog box will open. The Selector Type will be compound. The Selector Name is #container #intro p. Press the Less Specific button to set the selector to #intro p.

Press OK and the change is applied.

6   In the Property Inspector, click on the Text size drop-down menu and choose the keyword large.

Depending on how large you made your intro box, you may need to adjust the width and height of the box.

Set the paragraph text inside the intro box to Georgia and large.

7   Click on the edge of the intro box to activate it and then click on any of the anchor points on the box to adjust the width and height. We used a width of **655px** and a height of **130px**.

Adding images to your layout

Before you add the remaining sections of your page, you'll add images to both the header and container sections of the page. First, you'll add a background image of vegetables to the right side of your header.

1   In the CSS Styles panel double-click the #header rule to open the CSS Rule definition dialog box. Click on the Background category. In addition to the background color, you can also add CSS background images.

2   In the Background image section, press the Browse button. In the select Image Source dialog box, navigate to the images folder within the dw05lessons folder and select veggies.jpg. Press Open (Windows) or Choose (Mac OS). Press Apply and you will see the image tiled across the header.

By default, background images in CSS have this tiled effect, so you will need to add additional properties in order to remove the tiling and position the image to the right.

3   From the Background-repeat drop-down menu, choose no-repeat. From the Background-position (X) drop-down menu, choose right. Press OK and you see the image now aligned to the right side of the header.

Background images can be added and positioned to a <div> element.

A background image is controlled by CSS, and you can only have one background image per element. So in order to have two images inside the header you'll add the Organic Utopia logo as an inline element which means it is being added to the HTML code, not the CSS.

4   Select the Organic Utopia placeholder text in the #header div and delete it. Then choose Insert > Image. In the Select Image Source dialog box, navigate to the images folder within the dw05lessons folder and select ou_logo.gif. Press Open (Windows) or Choose (Mac OS). Type **OrganicUtopia Logo** into the text field when asked to add an Alternative text tag, then press OK. The image appears in the top-left corner of the header. You will position this image away from the sides of the header box a bit later in the lesson.

Photoshop Integration

Often the images used in your web page need to be modified in Photoshop before they integrate well with your design. Photoshop and Dreamweaver are integrated in a few ways. In this exercise you will see how Dreamweaver can optimize .psd files when you insert them into your page.

1   In the CSS Styles panel, double-click the #container rule. Click on the Background category and choose the Browse button in the Background-image section. In your dw05lessons folder, open the artwork folder. Choose the veggiebackground.psd file and press Open (Windows) or Choose (Mac OS) The Image Preview dialog box appears.

This dialog box appears because you have chosen a .psd file to import and this is not a valid file format for the Web. Dreamweaver triggers the Image Preview dialog box, which allows you to optimize the graphic and save it in a more appropriate format.

Importing a .psd file into Dreamweaver will trigger the Image Preview, allowing you to save as a web graphic.

2   Click on the Format menu. The default format is jpeg, but you could also save this as a gif or png. Leave it set to jpeg and slide the Quality slider to 65%.

3   Click on the File button in the top left corner of the Image Preview. This panel below will show you the source dimensions of the image, in this case 800 pixels wide by 600 pixels high. You could choose to resize the image with these controls, however you leave it as is for now. Click OK and the Save Web Image dialog box appears.

4   Navigate to the images folder in the dw05lessons folder and double-click it. In the url section, notice the path images/veggie_background.jpg. It's important to understand that you are saving a copy of the original PSD file as a jpeg in this step. Click save and you now have a link to the new background image.

5   Click on the background-repeat drop-down menu and choose no-repeat, then click OK.

Adding Main and Sidebar content areas

Now you'll add two more sections to your page: a main column which will feature the latest news from our fictional company Organic Utopia and a sidebar column which features incentives for visitors to become members.

1   Click on the Draw AP Div button (▤), then place your cursor below the intro box and click and drag down and to the right. As you are drawing the AP Div notice there are width and height values that are updated in the Status Bar on the bottom right of your document window

The width and height of an AP Div are updated in the Status bar as you draw the div.

Make the AP Div roughly 450px wide by 200px high. Don't try to get the exact dimensions, as it is very difficult to be precise when drawing. You can always fine-tune the width and height in the Property Inspector.

2   Click on the border of the div and in the CSS-P text field rename the div to **main**. Next, click on the Bg color swatch in the Property Inspector and from the color swatches that appear choose white.

3   Click on the Draw AP Div button again and draw another box to the right of the Main div. Make this one approximately the same height, and the width should be about 250. Again don't worry about the exact dimensions for now.

4   Click on the border of the new div and in the CSS-P text field, type **sidebar** to rename the AP Div. Click on the BG color menu and make this background White as well.

You'll now make sure the top edges of the two boxes are lined up.

5   Click on the handle on the top-left of the main div and reposition it to the following left and top values: L (Left) should be **35** and T (Top) should be **260**.

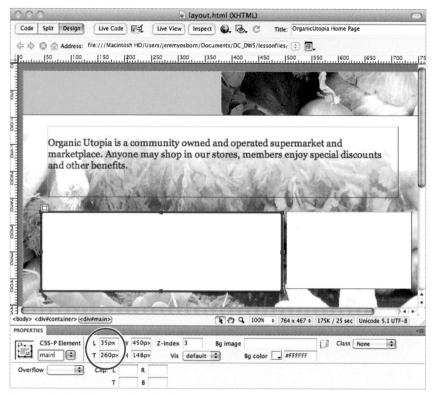

Setting the Left and Top values of an AP Div.

6   Click on the top-left edge of the sidebar div and type **260** for the Top value. You can use the left and right arrows on your keyboard to nudge the div horizontally. We ended up with a Left value of 490.

With the top values the same for both boxes, the top edges line up. Once the boxes are lined up, you can always move them as a unit by selecting and dragging or nudging them.

7   Click on the edge of the main div to select it and then Shift+click the sidebar. With both boxes selected, press your up arrow keys to move both boxes upwards. There is no right value here, use your judgment and push the two boxes closer to the intro text.

Adding additional content and styles

Up to this point, you've been working with the base structure of your layout. Now it's time to add additional content in the form of text so that you can see how your layout works with real content, and make any necessary changes.

1   Double-click the main_content.html file in the Files panel to open it. This is text that has already been formatted; all that is necessary is to copy and paste it into your layout.

2   Choose Edit > Select All and then choose Edit > Copy. Close the main_content.html document. In the layout.html document, click inside the main div and choose Edit > Paste. The content appears styled as Lucida Grande because there is a rule in the body defining the font-family; however, there are no CSS rules yet for headings or paragraphs.

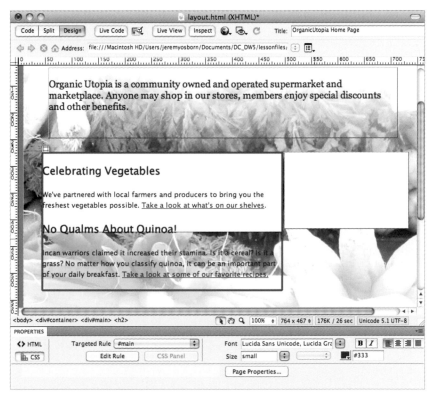

The results of copying and pasting the main_content.html page into your main div element.

You pasted more content than can fit inside this box, which is why the text is flowing outside the boundaries of the container. In fact, what you are seeing are one of the disadvantages of using AP Divs. Defining the width and height of a box in pixels creates an inflexible container. One solution to this is simply to expand the size of the box.

3   Click on bottom of the blue border for the div and drag it down slightly, the box will automatically snap to fit the existing content.

Now you'll add the content to the member benefit section.

4   Double-click the memberbenefits_content.html file in the Files panel. Choose Edit > Select All and then choose Edit > Copy. Close the memberbenefits_content.html document. In the layout.html document, click inside the sidebar and choose Edit > Paste.

5   Click the bottom of the sidebar div and drag it down slightly to expand the box to fit the content.

Setting margins and borders

As you learned earlier, CSS uses the Box model for elements, and as such, each element can be given unique margins, padding, and borders, either for decorative or practical purposes.

Now that you have content inside your columns, it is clear that you need to do some fine-tuning. Your text and logo are crowded against their respective div elements and you should make them more pleasing and readable. Technically, you can start anywhere, but in this exercise, you'll start at the top of your page and work down.

1   Select the Organic Utopia logo in the header. In the CSS Styles panel, press the New CSS Rule button (⊕). The New CSS Rule dialog box appears and the Selector Name, #container #header img is selected. Since the rule gets more specific from left to right, ultimately you are targeting the <img> tag located inside the header div, which is inside the container div. Click OK.

2   In the CSS Rule definition dialog box that appears, select the Box category on the left. If necessary, move the dialog box to see the logo. Uncheck the Same for All checkbox in the Margin section. In the Top text field, type **20** and press Apply. The logo is pushed down 20 pixels from the top of the header div, because there is now a 20-pixel margin applied to the top of the image.

3   In the Left margin text field, type **15** and press OK. Adding a 15-pixel left margin pushes the logo to the right. Now you'll add similar margins in the main column.

4   Click anywhere inside the heading Celebrating Vegetables in the main column. In the CSS Styles panel, press the New CSS Rule button. In the New CSS Rule dialog box, make sure the selector name reads #container #main h2. Press OK.

5   In the CSS Rule definition dialog box, select the Box category, and uncheck the Same for All checkbox in the Margin section. In the Left text field, type **15** and press OK.

Applying a left margin of 15 to the main heading.

6   Click inside the paragraph below the Celebrating Vegetables heading. In the CSS Style panel, press the New CSS Rule button (⊕) and in the New CSS Rule dialog box, make sure that #container #main p is highlighted in the Selector Name text field. Press OK.

7   In the CSS Rule definition dialog box, select the Box category from the left column, and uncheck the Same for All checkbox in the Margin section. In the Left and Right text fields, type **15**. You need to add both left and right padding because the text fills the main container. Press OK.

Overriding default margins in CSS

If you are new to Dreamweaver and/or CSS an important concept is that of default margins. Web browsers will apply default margins to most block elements unless there is a value overriding them. So paragraphs and headings, for example, will have space between them even if you haven't set a value. You can see this space by using Dreamweaver CS5's new Inspect feature.

1   In your document window, click on the Inspect button, which triggers Dreamweaver's Live View mode. Now you can hover over elements on your page and see the normally invisible margins.

2   Place your cursor over the Celebrating Vegetables heading. The yellow highlight shows the margins being applied to this element.

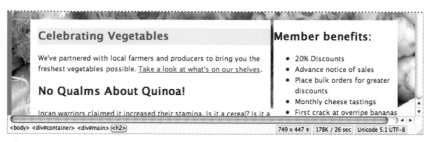

The Inspect feature in Dreamweaver CS5 highlights the margins of an element in yellow

Hover over the paragraph below the heading and note there are margins being applied here as well. In order to reduce the space, you will need to reduce the bottom margin of the heading and the top margin of the paragraph.

3   In the CSS Styles panel, double-click the #container #main h2 style and then select the Box category. Set the bottom margin value to **0 px** and press OK.

4   Click on the Inspect button again and place your cursor over the heading. Note that the bottom margin is gone. You now need to set the top margin of the paragraph to 0 as well.

5   In the CSS Styles panel, double-click the #container #main p style and select the Box category. Set the top margin value to **0 px** and press OK. Now all the paragraphs in the main column shift upwards.

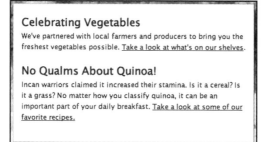

Applying a top and bottom margin of zero reduces space between the paragraph and the heading.

6   Click on the Live View button to de-activate this mode.

Because margins and padding are invisible, many designers resort to applying either background colors or borders to elements at the beginning of the layout process. This helps to understand the relationship between various sections on the page. The Inspect button in Dreamweaver CS5 partially removes the need to do this, but you may still find the original technique useful.

Adding borders to elements

The ability to add borders to elements is a great feature in CSS. Because of the CSS Box model, almost anything can be styled with borders: div elements, headings, lists and more. Additionally, the style, width and color of these borders can be set globally or for any given side.

1 In the CSS Style panel, double-click the #main style and then click on the Border category to begin setting these properties.

2 In the Style category uncheck the Same For All checkbox. Click on the Top menu and choose solid. Then click on the Bottom menu and choose solid.

In the Style menu, note the other options available. Styles such as dotted and dashed are the most reliable styles. For various reasons the other options such as groove, ridge, etc. are not particularly well-supported in older browsers and you should use them sparingly.

3 In the Width category, uncheck the Same For All checkbox and click on the Top menu. Note that you can also choose keywords here for thin, medium or thick. Select (value) and then type **2.** The default value is px.

4 In the Color category, uncheck the Same For All checkbox and in both the Top and Bottom fields type **#063.** This is a dark green color.

Setting border styles for the top and bottom of the Main div element.

Click OK in the CSS Rule definition dialog box.

The borders will be hard to see since the div is still selected.

5 Choose File > Save All and preview the results by choosing File > Preview in Browser.

Take a moment to admire your layout. You're almost done; however the last step is to futureproof your page layout.

6 Close the browser and return to Dreamweaver.

Futureproofing your layout

Absolutely positioning the elements of your page layout is very stable and reliable, but it also has some fundamental limitations. You have already seen what happens when there is more content than can fit inside a box: the box overflows resulting in unattractive content. You have also seen one solution, which is simply to expand the size of the box. Even this is not an ideal solution though. Content on the Web changes constantly; text is added and removed, images are inserted and so on. The designer of the page may have little or no control over this, especially if they are handing a web site off to a client who will eventually be updating and modifying the site.

To help strengthen your layout for future modification you can use a CSS property called overflow. This will help you prevent the worse-case scenario of text that breaks your layout as it overflows its container. For this exercise, you'll apply overflow to the Members Benefits sidebar.

1   Click on the bottom edge of the sidebar and then drag the bottom of the box upwards until half of the list items are overflowing out of the box.

Text that is overflowing over the sidebar

2   Double-click the #sidebar style in the CSS Styles panel and then click on the Positioning category.

3   Click on the Overflow menu and choose auto. This automatically adds scrollbars to any <div> element that has more text than can fit inside. Click OK. You will see in Dreamweaver's design view that the box has snapped to fit the original height.

4   Choose File > Save, then File > Preview in Browser. Your div now has a scrollbar. While it may not be an ideal solution if you do not like scrollbars, at least it doesn't break the layout. Close the browser and return to Dreamweaver.

The pros and cons of Absolutely Positioned CSS layouts

You will now take a look at the limitations and weaknesses of the layout you have just created. Absolutely positioned layouts in Dreamweaver are the quickest and easiest way to get a web page up and working, however, as noted earlier they are not the most flexible.

In this exercise, we hope to point out some of the limitations of Absolutely Positioned layouts so that you can judge for yourself whether they fit all of your needs or you need to be looking at the next step of creating pages using more advanced layout techniques, which are covered in Lesson: 6, "Advanced Page Layout."

To illustrate this, you will take a look at your existing layout as if someone has asked you to make the entire container larger and switch the position of the two columns on your page.

1   In the Design view, click on the edge of your #container div to select it and in the Property Inspector, change the Width from 770 to **840**. The container width expands but when adding this extra 70 pixels of space, your header and the other sections are no longer well-aligned.

Your background image is now also too narrow. This cannot be easily resolved in Dreamweaver. You would have to go back to Photoshop, resize the image, and export it again. For now, you'll simply turn it off temporarily.

2   In the CSS Styles panel, click on the #container style, and click the Current button to see the properties. Now select the background-image property. Click on the Disable/Enable CSS Property button (◌) at the bottom of the panel to turn off this image for now.

Clicking the Disable/Enable CSS Property button removes the style for the background image.

With the background image temporarily removed, it is easier to see the structure of your layout.

3   Click on the right edge of the header and drag it to the right to expand the width. Drag the header beyond the container and notice it is easy to break your layout. This is because absolutely positioned elements don't interact with the other elements on the page

In the CSS Property Inspector, set the W (Width) value of the header to **840**. It must match the width of the container exactly. Although you'll also notice that the background image of the vegetables remains flush right.

4   Click on the edge of the intro box, and, using your arrow keys, nudge it to the right until it is centered within the page.

Now you need to switch the position of the Main and Sidebar divs.

5   Click on the edge of the Main div and use your arrow keys to nudge it to the right. Notice that it overlaps your sidebar. This is due to the behavior of absolutely positioned elements allowing them to occupy the same space on the page.

The property that controls which element is highest in the stacking order is called the z-index. Dreamweaver sets this property automatically when you create AP Divs. Elements with the higher z-index value will always "win" and be visible over elements with a lower z-index. You can also modify z-index values if you choose to adjust this.

6   Click on the edge of the Sidebar div and using your arrow keys nudge to the right until it reaches the original position of the Main div.

You may need to nudge the position of the two boxes until you are satisfied with their position. Additionally, feel free to adjust the width of the boxes if needed.

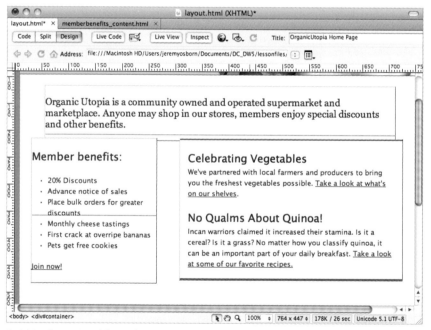

Switching the position of the two boxes requires you to move them manually.

Adjusting the width of the layout and the columns within is not significantly difficult but it's also not very efficient. Wouldn't it be nice if expanding the width of the container automatically readjusted the columns within the new space? In fact, there are techniques you can use to accomplish this. They are called float-based layouts and you will learn these techniques in the next lesson. For now, save your file.

Congratulations, you have finished Lesson 5, "Creating Page Layouts with CSS."

Self study

Get some practice with layout by creating a new div named footer, and bring in the content within the file provided in your assets folder. Style the footer using the techniques learned in this lesson.

Open the style for the sidebar and apply similar margins and borders to those that you applied for the main div.

Experiment with your layout by expanding the width of the container div, changing the background color and adding borders. You will be surprised at how small changes to these properties can have dramatic effects on the appearance of your page.

Review

Questions

1   In what two ways can *<div>* elements be automatically created for the purpose of layout in Dreamweaver?

2   Which one of the following two buttons requires you to assign an ID name: the Draw AP Div button or the Insert AP Div button?

3   What is the overflow property and why would you use it?

Answers

1   By using the Draw AP Div and Insert Div Tag buttons, located in the Layout section of the Insert panel.

2   The Insert AP Div button requires you to assign an ID name if it is a new ID, or choose a pre-existing ID name. The Draw AP Div button creates a generic name for your divs.

3   The overflow property allows you to change the way a box appears if there is too much content. For example, an overflow set to auto creates a scroll bar if there is more content than can fit in the box.

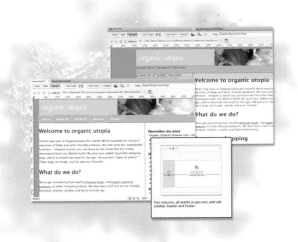

What you'll learn
in this lesson:

- Working with the CSS float property

- Setting different layouts for different pages with CSS

- Using the display:none property

Advanced
Page Layout

The best web layouts account for variable content on a page. As text and images are added and/or removed, your layout can adapt. In this lesson you will create from scratch a two column CSS layout using the float and clear properties in order to create an adaptable page layout.

Starting up

Before starting, make sure that your tools and panels are consistent by resetting your workspace. See "Resetting the Dreamweaver workspace" on page 3.

You will work with several files from the dw06lessons folder in this lesson. Make sure that you have loaded the dwlessons folder onto your hard drive from the supplied DVD. See "Loading lesson files" on page 3.

Before you begin, you need to create site settings that point to the dw06lessons folder from the included DVD that contains resources you need for these lessons. Go to Site > New Site, or, for details on creating a site, refer to Lesson 2, "Setting Up a New Site."

See Lesson 6 in action!

Use the accompanying video to gain a better understanding of how to use some of the features shown in this lesson. The video tutorial for this lesson can be found on the included DVD.

Layout with AP divs versus layout with floats

In this lesson, you'll learn an advanced method of layout in Dreamweaver using CSS boxes that are floated as columns. Unlike the inflexible nature of AP Divs, floated layouts can accommodate additional content more easily, and once you learn how to use them, allow you more creative layout options.

You may be asking: why there are two methods of layout in Dreamweaver, and why am I learning both? To understand this, it helps to keep in mind that historically Dreamweaver has been designed for use in the Design view (in other words, not working in code). As you will soon see, the CSS float property that you will be using to create columns was not designed to be a tool for layout, and requires a good understanding of CSS to be useful.

Floated layouts are trickier to control and understand than AP Divs. Additionally, older web browsers such as Internet Explorer 6 have well-documented bugs and quirks that can prevent floated layouts from rendering correctly. To address these problems, coding techniques known as browser hacks have been developed over the years. The browser hacks involve adding additional code targeted toward one browser in order to make the pages look the same.

Coming back to Dreamweaver, it is likely that the program leans toward using the more reliable and easier to manipulate AP Divs because of its traditional user base. However, as users of Dreamweaver seek to duplicate some of the sophisticated sites they see online, they really have no choice but to work with floats. As you walk through this lesson, it is important to keep in mind that you do not necessarily have to choose between absolutely positioned layouts and floated layouts. Layouts that combine both AP Divs and floated layouts are commonplace and combine the strengths of both.

To get started creating more sophisticated and flexible layouts, you will first need to have a good understanding of the float property.

Creating a floated image

One of the reasons the float property in CSS was created was to allow for the appearance of text to wrap around an image. This concept was borrowed from print design, where the effect is standard practice and often called text wrap or runaround. In CSS, this effect is achieved by allowing elements following a floated element in the HTML markup to surround the element, effectively changing position. This behavior also makes it possible to create columns on a page, although this may not have been the original intent of the rule.

In this exercise, you will learn the basics of using the float property by applying it to an image in order to wrap text.

1   From the dw06lessons site, open the floatimage.html page. You will see a page with a large paragraph block of text. Click in the middle of the paragraph, immediately before the sentence, "We also have added recyclable shopping bags."

2   Now choose Insert > Image and in the Select Image Source dialog box, choose the image recycle_bag.gif from the images folder, and choose OK. In the Alt text field, type **shopping bag** and click OK. The image has width and height dimensions of 81 x 101 pixels and is inserted as a block inside the paragraph.

Set the Alt tag of the inserted image.

The amount of space between the two sentences is determined by the height of the graphic. This is the default flow of HTML when an inline image is inserted into a paragraph.

You'll now wrap the text around the image by applying the float property to the shopping bag graphic.

3   Make sure the image is still selected and then click the New CSS Rule button in the CSS Styles panel. Click on the menu for Selector Type and choose Class. In the Selector Name text field, type **.floatimage** and click OK.

4   In the CSS Rule definition dialog box, click on the Box category, then click on the Float drop-down menu and choose right. Click OK.

5   In the Property Inspector, there is a Class drop-down menu, which by default is set to None.

The default Class is set to None.

From the Class drop-down menu, choose floatimage. With the class applied, the image will now be removed from the flow of the text and be pushed far right to the edge of the container.

Change the Class to floatimage.

6   In the CSS Styles panel, double-click the .floatimage rule. In the Box category, click on the Float drop-down menu and change the value from right to left, then press OK.

The image now floats to the left and the text wraps around it. This wrapping behavior is extremely important to keep in mind as you work with floated elements. You can float elements to the left or right only.

7   In the CSS Styles panel, double-click the .floatimage rule and in the Box category uncheck the Same for All checkbox for the Margin, then type a value of **10** for the Top and **10** for the Right. Make sure the unit is pixels. Press OK. The image now is set off from the text, adding needed space.

Set the Margin for the image.

7   Choose File > Save to save your page. Then choose File > Close to close it.

The above technique is a simple and useful application of the float property. To understand how floated elements are used as layout, it helps to realize that you can float any element (such as a list or a paragraph). In the next exercise you will float div elements in order to create columns.

Creating columns with HTML and CSS

One of the most important aspects of working with floated elements is understanding how they interact with their surrounding elements. This relationship is easy to understand when you have an object with a fixed width and height such as the shopping bag graphic from the last exercise. When floated elements are objects that are not fixed in size, such as a column which is defined by the amount of text inside, things can get interesting.

Creating the HTML Structure with div elements

To begin, you'll start with a page similar to the Organic Utopia layout from Lesson 5, "Creating Page Layouts with CSS." Specifically, the container div is 770 pixels wide and styled to be centered within the browser. The header has one inline image (the Organic Utopia logo) and one background image (the vegetable photo aligned to the right). You will first define the structure of the page by adding div elements for the various sections.

1   In the Files panel, double-click on the layout.html page. Your first step will be to add the navigation section.

2   In the Insert panel, click the Insert Div Tag button, and the Insert Div Tag dialog box opens. Here you can choose where you would like the new div element to be inserted. You need the navigation div element to follow the header.

3   In the Insert Div Tag dialog box, click the Insert drop-down menu. Select the After tag option, then in the drop-dwon menu to the right choose <div id ="header">. Type **navigation** in the ID text field, then press the New CSS Rule button.

Set the properties in the Insert Div Tag dialog box.

The New CSS Rule definition dialog box opens. Click OK. You will now add a few simple styles to the navigation div.

4   In the CSS rule definition dialog box, click on the Background category and type **#88b036** into the Background-color text field to add a green background color. Then click on the Box category and type **100** in the Width text field, then from the drop-down menu to the right and choose **%**. Click in the Height text field and type **36**, and leave the value set to px. Click OK. Click OK again in the Insert Div Tag dialog box. Your navigation section now spans across the width of the container.

You'll now add the two div elements for the main and sidebar columns.

5   Click on the Insert Div Tag button in the Insert panel. Click on the Insert drop-down menu and choose the After Tag option, and then in the drop-down menu to the right choose <div id ="navigation">. Type **main** in the ID text field and then click OK.

6   Click on the Insert Div Tag button in the Insert panel. Click on the Insert drop-down menu and choose the After Tag option, then in the drop-down menu to the right, choose <div id ="main">. Type **sidebar** in the ID text field and then click OK.

The last section you will add will be for the footer at the bottom of the page.

7   Click on the Insert Div Tag button in the Insert panel. Click on the Insert drop-down menu. Select the After Tag option, then in the drop-down menu to the right choose <div id ="sidebar">. Type **footer** in the ID text field, click the New CSS Rule button, then click OK. You will be adding a background-color style now so you can more easily see how the footer interacts with the two columns.

8   In the CSS Rule definition dialog box for the footer, click on the Background category and in the Background-color text field, type **#CCC** to add a light gray. Click OK, and then click OK again in the Insert Div Tag dialog box. You now have the main sections of your page, and you now have to start setting the widths of the columns.

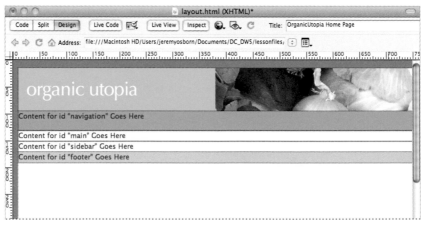

The main sections of your web page are now created.

Setting the width and floating the columns

With the basic structure of your page set up in HTML, you will now set the width of the main and sidebar columns and float them using CSS. You will return to the navigation bar in a later exercise.

1   Click inside the main div, then in the CSS Styles panel, click the New CSS Rule button. When the New CSS Rule definition dialog box opens, click on the Less Specific button, and the Selector Name will read #main. Click OK.

2   In the CSS Rule definition dialog box that appears, click on the Box category, then click type **500** inside the Width text field. From the Float drop-down menu, choose right. Click OK and you will see the main column moves to the right and the sidebar column moves up to fill in the remaining space. Now you'll add some content to see how it fits into the column.

3   In the Files panel, double-click the main_content.html page. Select all the text on this page, then press Ctrl+C (Windows) or Command+C (Mac OS) to copy it. Close the file, then select the placeholder text in the main div and press Ctrl+V (Windows) or Command+V (Mac OS) to paste. The column expands to accommodate all the content. Notice that the footer appears to be behind the main column. This is a result of the floated column. You'll take a look at this shortly, but first you will style the sidebar.

4   Click inside the sidebar div, then in the CSS Styles panel, click the New CSS Rule button. Press the Less Specific button once, and the Selector Name reads #sidebar. Click OK, and in the CSS Rule definition dialog box, click on the Box category. In the Width text field, type **270**. From the Float drop-down menu, choose left. Click OK. Visually not much will change but the two columns now have explicit widths and both are floating.

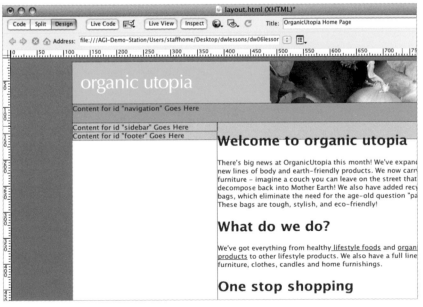

Paste the text into the column.

5 In the Files panel, double-click the sidebar_content.html page. Select all the text on this page and copy it. Close the file, and then click inside the sidebar div and paste, replacing the placeholder text. The sidebar expands to fit this content, which is a definition list.

We have cheated a bit in this exercise and created pre-existing styles for the sidebar content. Many of the techniques for modifying the margins of elements have been covered in earlier lessons. If you're curious, you may look at the styles for the <dl> and <dd> elements to see the details.

What may be most confusing to you is the behavior and appearance of the footer div. As noted earlier, it appears to be behind your two columns. The reason for this has to do with the nature of floated elements. Floated elements are removed from the default flow of HTML and since both columns are floated, the footer ignores them and moves up directly below the navigation section. This is also why the height of the footer has expanded. From the perspective of the footer there are no columns to interact with so it assumes its default behavior.

In order to push the footer below the columns, you need to add another CSS property to the footer called clear.

Using the Clear property

When you apply the clear property to an object, you are essentially adding a rule that says *No floated elements are allowed on either side of me.* In fact, you can specify whether the left, right or both sides can have floated elements. You'll try two different options in order to understand the clear property better.

1 In the CSS Styles panel, double-click the #footer style, and click on the Box category. From the Clear drop-down menu, choose right. Click OK. This puts the footer box on the bottom of the page. You may need to scroll down to see it.

Although this seems to do the trick, there is a potential pitfall. You set the clear property to right, but what would happen if the content in the main column were shorter than the content in the sidebar? Understanding the answer to this question will go a long way toward your understanding of floats and clears, so you'll do a short experiment.

2   In the Main div, select the last three paragraphs and headings and then delete them. With less content in this column now, the footer still behaves the same and stops at the bottom of the main column, but the sidebar is longer now so the footer overlaps it.

Select and delete the last three paragraphs and headings.

Of course, you could fix this by switching the value of the clear property from Right to Left. This would push the footer down in the current layout, but if you are trying to create a consistent layout for your site, you may never know which column will have the most content, so the safest solution is to apply the clear property to both sides.

3   Choose Edit > Undo to bring the content back into the main div.

4   In the CSS Styles panel, double-click the footer style and from the Clear drop-down menu choose both, then click OK. The footer div is now pushed to the bottom because no floated elements are allowed to the left or the right.

Creating a list-based navigation bar

Floats not only can be used for simple image wrapping and creating columns, but also to create navigation. Here you'll start creating a list-based navigation that uses CSS as formatting. This is a great way to create easily editable navigation bars that are search engine friendly because they use text instead of images. Additionally, you can think of navigation as simply a list of links to other pages, so it makes sense to use the list element. The first step is to add the content and then style the list items and the navigation element.

1   Select the placeholder text in the Navigation div and then click the HTML button in the Property Inspector, if necessary. Click the Unordered List button (≡) and the text will become the first bullet in an unordered list.

2   Type **Home**, then press Return. This adds a new list item. Add the following navigation sections pressing Return after each one: **About Us**, **Products**, **Services**, **Contact**. Your layout will begin to break as the list items are added. Don't worry; you will be using float properties to turn this list into a horizontal navigation bar.

Add the list items that will serve as your navigation.

You will now link the 5 items. The pages in this case have not been created so you will use a placeholder link for each item.

3   Select the Home list item, click inside the Link text field in the Property Inspector and type **#** and then press Enter (Windows) or Return (Mac OS). This symbol creates a placeholder hyperlink. Repeat this step for each list item until all five are hyperlinked.

Now you'll apply the float property and turn this vertical list into a horizontal one.

4   Click on the *<li>* element in the tag selector.

Select the <li> element in the tag slector.

Click the New CSS Rule button in the CSS Styles panel and choose Less Specific so the Compound Selector reads #navigation ul li. Click OK.

5   In the Box category, from the Float drop-down menu, choose left. Press the Apply button, and you will see your list items are now stacked horizontally rather than vertically. By applying the float property you have overridden the list items' default behavior.

6   Click on the List category, then from the List-style-type drop-down menu, choose None. This removes the bullet points from each list item. Click OK.

Most of the styling for this navigation bar is done on the <a> tag which defines the appearance of hyperlinks. You'll style the appearance and position of these links now.

7   Click inside any link and then in CSS Styles panel, click the New CSS Rule button. In the New CSS Rule dialog box, click the drop-down menu to the right of the Selector Name text field. This menu lists the possible selectors you could target. You'll be returning to this menu again, but for now choose the #navigation ul li a selector, and then click OK.

New CSS Rule
Selector Type:
Choose a contextual selector type for your CSS rule.
Compound (based on your selection)
Selector Name:
Choose or enter a name for your selector.
#navigation ul li a
This selector name will apply your rule to all <a> elements that are within any <li> elements that are within any <ul> elements that are within any HTML elements with id "navigation".
Less Specific   More Specific
Rule Definition:
Choose where your rule will be defined.
(This document only)
OK   Cancel   Help

Create a new CSS rule for the navigation hyperlinks.

8   In the Type category, check the Text-decoration checkbox labeled none. This will remove the default underline below your hyperlinks. Click on the Color swatch and choose white.

9 Click on the Box category and uncheck the Same for All checkbox for Padding. Type **8px** for the top and bottom values, and **15px** for the left and right values. Press Apply to see the space added between each hyperlink.

Create a new CSS rule for the navigation hyperlinks.

10 Click on the Block category, then from the Display drop-down menu, choose block. This property allows you to define the boundaries of the list item as clickable, not just the text. Click OK.

You're almost finished, however, your navigation links are currently overlapping the boundaries of the green navigation bar. This is because of some default margins, a topic you have run into before. In this case, the default margins of the unordered list are the culprit.

11 Click on the *<ul>* tag in the Tag Selector, then click the New CSS Rule button in the CSS Styles panel. Press the Less Specific button, making sure the selector reads #navigation ul, and then click OK.

12 In the CSS Rule definition dialog box, click on the Box category and type **0** for Margin and Padding. Click OK and the hyperlinks are now centered within the navigation element.

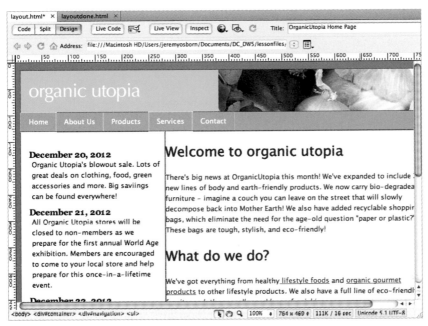

Set the margins for the navigation to give it a more defined look.

The last piece to add is a little interactivity. When the user mouses over any one of the navigation links, you would like it to change color. This improves usability by letting the user know the links are active. You can do this with the hover property for hyperlinks.

13 Click within any link, then click the New CSS Rule button in the CSS Styles panel. In the New CSS Rule dialog box, choose the a:hover property from the drop-down menu to the right of the Selector Name text field.

Select the a:hover property.

Type **#navigation** in front of the a:hover property to create a compound selector. The final selector name should read #navigation a:hover. Click OK.

14 In the Background category of the CSS Rule definition dialog box, click in the Background-color text field, and type **#9FCC41**. This is the same green as the header. Click OK.

15 Save your document and choose File > Preview in Browser to see your list-based CSS menu. Be sure to mouse over the links to see the hover effect.

Changing column layout and size

Another benefit of using floated containers for layout is that they are very easy to change. For example, perhaps you would like to experiment with your sidebar being on the right rather than the left, or perhaps you would like to experiment with changing the width of the entire layout. This can all be accomplished with a few easy modifications of the styles.

1 In the CSS Styles panel, double-click on the #main style. Click on the Box category, change the Float value from right to left, and then click OK. This pushes the main box over to the left of the container and the sidebar slips to the right.

2   In the CSS Styles panel, double-click on the #sidebar style, then click on the Box category and change the Float value from left to right, and then click OK. This ensures the sidebar is flush against the container. That's it! Two simple style changes create a completely different layout.

Change the Float value of the #sidebat style from left to right.

If you'd like to change the overall width of your page layout you can do this by modifying the #container div.

3   In the CSS Styles panel, double-click the #container style and click on the Box category. Change the Width from 770 to **840** and then press Apply. This expands your container, and because your columns are floating, they will both remain aligned to their respective sides. While you are here, select the Height value and delete it, leaving it empty. Having a fixed height is useful at the beginning of the layout progress, but it should be removed at some point in order to accommodate more content.

Click OK. You'll now modify the width of the main id and add some margins.

4   In the CSS Styles panel, double-click on the #main style. Click on the Box category and for Width, type **520**, and then press OK.

Keep in mind that the width of the sidebar and main divs must add up to a number less than the width of the container (840 pixels). In this case, the sidebar is 270 and the main div is 520 which equals 770. This accounts for the 70 pixels of space between the two divs. If the width of the two columns were greater than 840 the layout would break and one of the columns would slip below the other.

Creating the appearance of equal height columns

With the footer cleared to the bottom you now need to focus your attention on another aspect of working with this layout: column height. The height of a div is specified by the amount of content within it. This is why your Main div is longer than the sidebar. Right now this isn't a huge problem because neither column has a background color. You'll add a background color to the sidebar to see the problem first, then we'll take a look at one solution.

1   In the CSS Styles panel, double-click the rule for the sidebar div. Click on the Background category, then, in the Background-color text field, type **#C8D9BC**.

2   Click on the Border category. Uncheck the Same for All checkboxes for Style, Width and Color. In the row labeled Left, choose solid in the Style column's drop-down menu, and type **2** in the Width colum's text field. In the Color column's text field, type **#060**. Click OK.

Set the border for the #sidebar div.

The problem with the column is an aesthetic one. A column generally looks better when it spans to the bottom of the page rather than cutting off abruptly. Additionally, if you are using this layout throughout your site, every page will likely have different amounts of content. As a user moves from page to page, this would create irregular page appearance, as the column height jumps up and down based on the amount of content. To solve this, you'll add a background image to the container div, which simulates the appearance of the column from top to bottom.

3   In the CSS Styles panel, double-click on the rule for the container div. Click on the Background category, and for the Background-image property, press the Browse button and locate the container_bg.gif file in the images folder. Click Choose.

This graphic is 840 pixels wide (which matches the width of your container), but it is only 2 pixels high. Essentially, it is a thin horizontal slice of the page and includes the sidebar color and green border.

4   From the Background-repeat drop-down menu, choose repeat-y. This ensures the graphic will only be tiled from top to bottom. Click OK and you will now see your columns filled in.

Now, the length of the column is irrelevant. The image background will always reach the bottom of the page and maintain a consistent appearance.

Although this technique is useful, it relies on your layout being finalized. If the width of your container or the position any of your columns change, you must then change the background image. Additionally, other changes, such as the color of a column or any padding adjustments, may also require you to modify your background image. For this reason, you should wait until the small changes and adjustments to your layout are complete before making a column background.

How to create a fake column background in Photoshop

The easiest way to make the fake column background is if you happen to have a mockup of your website as an image file or as a Photoshop file with layers. However, if you don't have a mockup, you need to be more creative. Here's how we created our page background.

1   Preview your web page in the browser. Look to make sure you have a clear cross-section of your columns from left to right. If there is any text or images in the column, you may need to go back to Dreamweaver and remove them temporarily.

2   Using your system's screen capture program capture your screen. In the Mac OS, this can be done with the keyboard shortcut, Command+Shift+3. In Windows, use the Print Screen button to capture.

In the case of the Mac OS, this will create a png file that will be saved to your desktop. In the case of Windows, this will copy the screen image to your clipboard.

3   In Photoshop, either open the screen capture image directly (Mac OS) or if in Windows, choose File > New, then press OK and press Ctrl+V.

4   Click on the Rectangular Marquee tool, then in the Options panel, change the style from Normal to Fixed Size. Type in a width of 840 px and a height of 2 px. If your original layout has a different width, you will need to change this width value to match.

5   Click anywhere in the image with the Marquee tool to add a floating selection. Using your arrow keys, you must line up the selection exactly with the edges of the container. If the selection is even 1 pixel off it will result in a mismatch between the image and the real HTML columns.

6   Choose Image > Crop, then choose Save for Web and Devices to save it as a gif, jpg or png. Try to optimize the image in order to make it as small as possible. For example, in our case we saved it as a gif using only 4 colors.

Browser compatibility

Up to this point, the concepts of creating a layout with floats and clears have made sense. There may have been some unusual or unexpected behaviors, but for the most part, once you understand the rules, you can begin to think about how you could apply this to your own designs. That's the good news. The bad news is that the expected behavior of CSS boxes takes a bad turn when we factor older browsers such as Internet Explorer 6 into the equation.

Due to certain rendering bugs in the browser, the behavior of floated elements can be hard to predict, and in some situations can completely "break" a layout. Web designers and developers have addressed this unfortunate behavior over the years by adding code fixes for Internet Explorer 6 to their style sheets, or by coming up with scripting solutions.

Adding code for IE 6

In the layout you have built, there is a code fix you will need to add to make the layout function well in IE 6. The problem is that the footer div that you cleared will not always be pushed below your columns. The bug that causes this can be fixed by "faking" a height for the footer. In general, IE 6 doesn't like floated elements that have no height, so this fix can solve many problems.

1   In the CSS Styles panel, double-click the #footer style, and in the Box category, type **1** for Height. Then click on the drop-down menu and choose %.

Set the Height for the #footer div.

IE 6 needs this height value to prevent the layout from breaking.

2   Click OK and although you will not see any change, the layout is now fixed in IE. This may not have seemed like a big deal, but this is still a relatively simple layout. More complex layouts will reveal other potential problems, especially when floats become involved.

3   Choose File > Save to save your work.

Do I need to optimize for Internet Explorer 6?

As of this writing, Internet Explorer 6 is a 10-year-old browser and Internet Explorer 7 and Internet Explorer 8 have been released, Internet Explorer 9 has been announced for release. Each version has improved on the rendering of CSS. Still, based on percentage, there are still a significant number of users who use Internet Explorer 6 as their primary web browser. Currently, estimates range anywhere from 10-20% of the web browsers.

However, there is also a clear trend in the world of web design to stop optimizing for Internet Explorer 6. The extra code and troubleshooting involved in solving layout and other problems can add time to the development of a site. Additionally, the capabilities of the web have not stood still since 2001 when Internet Explorer 6 was released. Modern browsers are faster and support cool new features that users of Internet Explorer will not see. Still, for many web site builders, it is often a business decision. If a client asks for (and is willing to pay for) a site that works well in Internet Explorer 6, then you will need to deliver.

Applying finishing touches

You'll now tidy up some loose ends with your layout. Specifically you'll add padding to the sidebar to provide some breathing room. You'll also move the rules in your current style sheet to an external style sheet for use in other pages.

1   In the CSS Styles panel, double-click the #main style and then click on the Box category. Uncheck the Same for all checkbox for Padding.

2   Click in the Left text field and type **20**. Press OK, and more space will be added to the inside of the main div.

Be aware that increasing padding values will increase the overall width of a div. This can actually create layout problems. To see this behavior, repeat step 1 and enter a value of 60 pixels for the left padding. The main column will push the sidebar below, effectively breaking the layout. For this reason, many designers prefer adding margins to elements such as paragraphs and lists rather than using padding.

Since the styles you have been creating for this lesson were within an internal style sheet they would only apply to this page. Now you'll move them to an external style sheet so they can be attached to other pages.

3   In the CSS Styles panel, be sure that the All button is selected and then click on the first style (body) and then scroll down and Shift+click the last style (#sidebar). This will select all the styles.

4 Click on the panel menu (·≡) at the top right corner of the CSS Styles panel, and choose Move CSS Rules.

Choose the Move CSS Rules option.

5 Click the radio button labeled A new style sheet and click OK. You'll be prompted to save your style sheet. Type **styles** in the Save As text field and click OK (Windows) or Save (Mac OS). You now have an external style sheet that can be attached to new or existing pages in your site. (If you receive a message saying that duplicate names are being copied, confirm the save, don't cancel.)

6 Choose File > Save. Then choose File > Close to close this page. Save your CSS file, if prompted.

Creating more sophisticated layouts

The two column layout you created represents a good foundation for a web site. You would refer to this as a "Two column fixed-width layout with a header and footer." However, you may be looking for more options. For example, what about a three column layout, or a liquid layout in which the content adjusts to the width of the browser (also referred to as a flexible or fluid layout)? It is beyond the scope of this book to walk through all these options. However, Dreamweaver does offer a way to create different layouts on the fly. You can choose from a gallery of new layouts whenever you create a new page.

1   Choose File > New and make sure HTML is selected as the Page Type. In the Layout column, the None option is the default, but you can also choose from a number of pre-made options.

2   Choose the 2 column liquid, left sidebar, header and footer option. Notice that a small thumbnail with a description of the layout appears. Click Create.

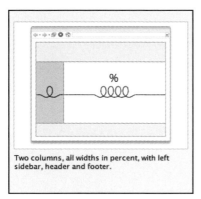

The thumbnail preview of the two column layout.

3   Choose File > Preview in Browser and when prompted, save this file as **2col_liquid.html.** Adjust the width of the browser and you will see that the width of the container page adjusts, as well as the content within. Unlike the layout you created earlier, you might choose this layout because it is more adaptable for different sized monitors.

Take a moment to read the text in this page. It mentions that the code for this page has been commented. You'll take a look at this code now, in order to better understand the pros and cons of using these pre-generated pages.

Close the browser and return to Dreamweaver.

4   Click on the Code View button and scroll to the top if necessary. The code in light gray represents comments that describe virtually every line of the CSS. So why is there a need to comment this file so heavily? To make a long story short, the code in this file is very robust and is optimized for cross-browser display. This means there are styles that address various bugs across different browsers, as well as other relatively advanced CSS code.

This presents a dilemma: You will benefit most from these templates only as long as you know how to modify them. In order to modify them effectively, however, you need to understand the rules of HTML and CSS relatively well. There is a limit to how far a WYSIWYG application can take you in learning these rules.

This should not stop you in exploring these page layouts, however. They are extremely useful, and can be incredible time-savers. Just be aware that reverse-engineering how a page works can also be time consuming, and that the answers may lie in the rules of HTML and CSS, and not in the Dreamweaver application.

5   Choose File > Close All and save any files if prompted.

Congratulations, you have finished this lesson!

Self study

Experiment with the float property by opening the floatimage.html used in the first exercise. Add 5 or 6 instances of the shopping bag graphic in a row and apply the floatimage class to all of them. How could you create a thumbnail photo gallery using this technique?

Review

Questions

1   The float property allows you to float an element to the left, right and center. True or False?

2   What are the three possible values for the clear property? Name a situation where you might use this property.

3   How would you apply padding to a floated column?

Answers

1   False. The float property only has three values: left, right and none. You cannot float an element to center.

2   You can apply the clear property to an element with one of the following values: left, right or both. Elements with a clear property do not allow a floated element to the side specified. A common situation where you might use this would be when you need the footer element on your page to appear below any floated columns.

3   Select the style for the column in the CSS Styles panel and click on the Box category. Then set a value for padding.

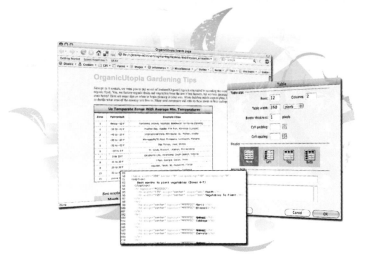

What you'll learn in this lesson:

- Creating and modifying tables
- Styling tables with HTML
- Styling tables with CSS
- Importing table data
- Sorting table data

Working with Tables

Tables have a long and storied history in web design. In this lesson you will learn how to structure and style tabular data using tables. Additionally you will understand the basics of using tables for layout and be able to compare and contrast them with Cascading Style Sheets (CSS) for layout.

Starting up

Before starting, make sure that your tools and panels are consistent by resetting your workspace. See "Resetting the Dreamweaver workspace" on page 3.

You will work with several files from the dw07lessons folder in this lesson. Make sure that you have loaded the dwlessons folder onto your hard drive from the supplied DVD. See "Loading lesson files" on page 3.

Before you begin, you need to create site settings that point to the dw07lessons folder from the included DVD that contains resources you need for these lessons. Go to Site > New Site, or, for details on creating a site, refer to Lesson 2, "Setting Up a New Site."

See Lesson 7 in action!

Use the accompanying video to gain a better understanding of how to use some of the features shown in this lesson. The video tutorial for this lesson can be found on the included DVD.

Using tables in web design

Tables are ideally suited for displaying tabular data. As is discussed in Lesson 5, "Creating Page Layouts with CSS," in the beginning days of the Web, they were the best tools available for designers when it came to layout. Over the years, Dreamweaver has steadily introduced a number of tools and visual aids to help people work with tables. Dreamweaver has mirrored the Web in that it has begun to shift its focus to CSS layout rather than table layout. Slowly, the table is reclaiming its original purpose: displaying tabular data.

In this lesson, you will learn how to automatically import and format existing data into a table. You will also explore how to modify rows and columns, style tables with CSS, and create new tables from scratch.

Importing table data

You'll get a chance right away to see tabular data in action by importing a .csv file into Dreamweaver. A majority of tabular data is exported from spreadsheet programs in the .csv (comma-separated values) and .txt (text) file formats. These are called comma, tab, or other delimited files. Essentially this means that a spreadsheet application converts the data within its rows and columns to an intermediate format that Dreamweaver can read.

Although Dreamweaver can open these files directly, it does not format them directly. With a comma-delimited file, for example, each column value is separated by a comma, and each line break starts a new row. For example, here is how Dreamweaver displays the raw .csv file that you are going to be working with:

The text editor's view of a comma-delimited file.

When imported into Dreamweaver, this file will be translated accordingly into the rows and columns of a new table.

1   In the Files panel, double-click the tips.html file to open it. This is a styled page for the tips section of the OrganicUtopia site. You will be inserting a .csv file with data on the vegetable-growing zones of North America.

2   Click after the last sentence in the main paragraph, and press Enter (Windows) or Return (Mac OS) to make sure your cursor is below the text. Choose File > Import > Tabular Data. The Import Tabular Data dialog box opens.

3   In the Import Tabular Data dialog box, press the Browse button and locate the temperate_zones.csv file in your dw07lessons folder. Press Open.

4   Click on the Delimiter menu to see the various options that are available. In your case, you will be choosing Comma. In the Table width section, leave the Fit to data option selected.

The settings in the Import Tabular Data dialog box affect the way a table is created.

You can either set a specific width for the generated table or let Dreamweaver construct the table automatically, based on the line-length of the incoming data.

5   Press OK, and your table is imported into your document below the text. Your table is imported with 3 columns and 12 rows. A quick way to confirm this is to look in the Property Inspector, where there is a field for columns and rows as well as other useful ways to work with tables.

Zone	Fahrenheit	Example Cities
1	Below -50 F	Fairbanks, Alaska; Resolute, Northwest Territories (Canada)
2	-50 to -40 F	Prudhoe Bay, Alaska; Flin Flon, Manitoba (Canada)
3	-40 to -30 F	International Falls, Minnesota; St. Michael, Alaska
4	-30 to -20 F	Minneapolis/St.Paul, Minnesota; Lewistown, Montana
5	-20 to -10 F	Des Moines, Iowa; Illinois
6	-10 to 0 F	St. Louis, Missouri; Lebanon, Pennsylvania
7	0 to 10 F	Oklahoma City, Oklahoma; South Boston, Virginia
8	10 to 20 F	Tifton, Georgia; Dallas, Texas
9	20 to 30 F	Houston, Texas; St. Augustine, Florida
10	30 to 40 F	Naples, Florida; Victorville, California
11	above 40 F	Honolulu, Hawaii; Mazatlan, Mexico

A 3-column and 12-row table generated by Dreamweaver from a comma-delimited file.

6   Press Dreamweaver's Code view button to see the code that makes up this table. It's safe to say that this is something you would not want to code by hand.

The table is now ready to be formatted according to your specifications. As you can see, you can save yourself a lot of time if your source data is properly formatted, Dreamweaver creates a table for you with all the data properly placed, eliminating the need for you to build a table, and type, or copy and paste, content into each cell.

Selecting table elements

It's worth taking a few moments to learn how to select the various elements of your table. Selecting a specific part of a table can be little tricky until you learn how. In this exercise, you'll look at ways to select a table's rows and columns both by hand and using controls in the Property Inspector. The components of a table include rows, columns, and cells, and other elements such as table headers and footers. The table you created needs some modification. It's rare that a table is created exactly right, and making small tweaks to the column widths and the row heights is the norm.

1   Press the Design view button in the Document toolbar and, without clicking directly, place your cursor over the edges of the table; you see the different sections of the table *light up* with a red border. Also notice that your cursor switches to a black arrow. The red border is Dreamweaver's visual cue for which part of the table you will be selecting, and the black arrow points in the direction of the row or column to be selected.

2   Place your cursor high in the upper-left corner until the entire table is outlined in red. Click once, and the table is selected.

A red border designates which section of the table you are selecting—in this case, the entire table.

3   Place your cursor to the left of the word Zone until you see the top row outlined; click once to select the row.

4   Move your cursor to the top of the word Zone until you see the numbered column outlined in red; click once to select the column.

Selecting a single cell is a little trickier, as the red outlines only appear when your cursor is on the edge of a table, not inside of one.

5   Click inside the cell with the word Zone. In order to select the cell, you use the tag selector at the bottom left of your document window. These tags are an alternative way to select parts of the table.

6   Click on the *<table>* tag first; this selects the table just as you did in step 2. Click on the *<tr>* tag next; this selects the table row. The tr tag appropriately stands for table row. Lastly, click on the *<td>* tag, and the cell itself is selected; *<td>* is defined as a table cell in HTML.

Clicking on the appropriate table tag in the tag selector selects that part of the table.

Some people prefer this method of selecting elements of their tables because it removes the chance that clicking on the table will move or modify it.

7   Click inside any cell in the table again, and choose Modify > Table > Select Table. This is yet another way to select tables. The Modify > Table command is one you'll be returning to. You can also select the table by right-clicking (Windows) or Ctrl+clicking (Mac OS) the table and choosing Table > Select Table from the contextual menu.

Modifying table size

Although importing tabular data from a text file is quick and easy, the data is seldom formatted perfectly. When you first imported the data, there was a choice to *Fit Table Width To Data*. The width of the table when you choose this option isn't always predictable, due to the way Dreamweaver does its calculations. Although it is possible to set the width of the table during the import stage, this isn't always convenient if you don't know what the data looks like. Luckily, it's easy to change the size of tables in Dreamweaver. The first thing you'll do is set a fixed width for the table.

1　If your table is not currently selected, select it now. In the Property Inspector, type **550** in the W text field and make sure the drop-down menu to the right is set to pixels, then press Enter (Windows) or Return (Mac OS). This expands the table to a width of 550 pixels.

Look closely at the top of your table; there is a visual guide outlined in green that displays the width of your table as well as the width of each column. This guide will come in handy when you are trying to create precisely measure tables, although it can also be turned off.

You can turn off this guide by choosing View > Visual Aids > Table Widths.

2　Choose File > Save, then File > Preview in Browser and open this page in your browser; resize the browser window a few times. Because the table has a fixed width of 550 pixels, its width stays constant. Close the browser and return to Dreamweaver.

3　In the Property Inspector, your table should still be selected. In the W (Width) text field, type **75** and choose % from the drop-down menu to the right; notice a change in your table width in the Design View.

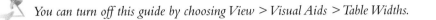

You can set the table width to a percentage of the browser window by using the Property Inspector.

Choose File > Save, then preview the page in your browser again and resize the browser window. The table width now resizes because you set it to be a percentage rather than a fixed width. Close the browser and return to Dreamweaver.

4　Reset your table to the original width by typing **550** in the W text field and choosing pixels from the drop-down menu.

You also have the ability to resize the columns and rows in the Design view. You can do this manually using the Property Inspector

5   Place your cursor inside the table and then over the dividing line between the first column and the second column. Your cursor changes to a double-arrow. Click and drag slowly to the right to expand the width of the first column notice at the top of the two columns that there are blue numbers that update with the width of the columns. This has the effect of reducing the second column's width, although it leaves the third column's width alone.

6   Expand the first column to at least 50 pixels; the content in the second column breaks to the next line. Place your cursor on the dividing line between the second and third column, and click and drag slowly to narrow the width of the third column (thereby expanding the width of the second column). This example uses values of 390 pixels for the third column and 88 pixels for the second.

If you are mathematically inclined, you may have noticed that the three column values don't add up to 550. This is because there are additional factors of cell padding, cell spacing, and borders to consider.

Oftentimes, approximate column widths are not sufficient; Dreamweaver allows you to apply exact column widths in the Property Inspector.

7   Place your cursor above the first column until the red outline appears, and click once to select the column. The bottom half of the Property Inspector expands, allowing you to adjust the properties of only this column. Type **45** into the W text field. The width does not appear to change dramatically, but it is now 45 pixels.

Selecting a column and entering a specific width in the Property Inspector sets the column to that width.

8   Click above the second column to select it. Type 100 into the W text field. Click above the third column and type 400 in the W text field.

You also have the ability to create a fixed height for rows.

9   Click on the left edge of the top row to select the whole row. In the Property Inspector, type **35** in the H text field, and press Enter (Windows) or Return (Mac OS) to apply the change.

Modifying table structure

In addition to modifying the width of columns and rows, the structure of a table often needs to be modified (for example, adding and deleting rows and columns, as well as merging cells in the column). First, you'll add a new row to the top of your table and then convert it to a header row. There are a few ways to add rows and columns in Dreamweaver, you'll begin with the Modify > Table command.

1   Click inside any of the cells within the first row. Dreamweaver needs to have some frame of reference when adding a row.

2   Choose Modify > Table > Insert Rows or Columns. The Insert Rows or Columns dialog box opens.

3   The Insert Rows radio button should be selected. For Number of rows, leave the default value of 1. In the Where section, select *Above the Selection*. Press OK to add the new row to the top of the table.

Use the Insert Rows and Columns dialog box to add new rows or columns to an existing table.

4   Place your cursor on the left side of the new row until the red outline appears. Click once to select it. In the Property Inspector, locate the Header checkbox to designate this row as a Header row. This will help you style your table later on.

Now you'll merge the three cells in this top row in order to add the header text that will span across your columns.

5   With the top row still selected, right-click (Windows) or Ctrl+click (Mac OS) to open a contextual menu. Choose Table > Merge Cells, and the three cells merge into one. This is referred to as columnspan.

6 Click inside this merged cell and type **US temperate zones with average min. temperatures**. Defining a row as a header as you did in step 4 wraps text in a *<th>* element, which in HTML is bold and centered by default.

Us temperate zones with average min. temperatures		
Zone	Fahrenheit	Example Cities
1	Below -50 F	Fairbanks, Alaska; Resolute, Northwest Territories (Canada)
2	-50 to -40 F	Prudhoe Bay, Alaska; Flin Flon, Manitoba (Canada)
3	-40 to -30 F	International Falls, Minnesota; St. Michael, Alaska

Merging cells creates a columnspan, allowing you to add header text.

7 Choose File > Save to save your work.

Creating a table

In addition to creating a table from tabular data, you can also create a table from the ground up using Dreamweaver's Insert Table command.

1 Click to the right of your existing table, and then press Enter (Windows) or Return (Mac OS) two times. You will be placing a second table two lines below the first.

2 Choose Insert > Table, and the Table dialog box opens. Type **12** in the Rows text field, and **2** in the Columns text field. Type **550** in the Table width text field to match the width of your first table and make sure the drop-down menu is set to pixels. Set the Border thickness value to 1 if it is not already.

The Cell padding and Cell spacing values should have no value; you'll return to these properties shortly.

The Insert > Table command creates a new table.

3 In the Header section, select the third option, Top, in order to designate the top row as the header.

4 In the Caption field, type **Best months to plant vegetables (Zones 4–7)**. Table captions are a bit more specific than table headers. A table caption is a short description of the table contents and has its own *<caption>* element; by default, they are displayed centered and at the top of the table.

Table captions are not required, but they are useful, especially from an accessibility perspective, as they supply useful information to screen readers and other devices. Press OK to insert the table.

5 Below the caption, in the first cell of the first column, type **Month**. In the first cell of the second column, type **Vegetables To Plant**. Your columns may shift; in order to adjust them, click on the divider between the two columns, and click and drag it as necessary to visually divide the two columns evenly.

6 In the second row of the *Month* column, type **April**, then five rows below, type **May**.

7 Below the *Vegetables to plant* column, type **Broccoli**. Press the down arrow on your keyboard to move to the next row. Using this technique, first type **Cabbage** and then type each vegetable name in its own row—first **Carrots** and then **Spinach**. Skip one row and, making sure you are beginning in the same row as May, type **Corn**, **Tomatoes**, **Peppers**, **Cucumbers**.

Best months to plant vegetables (Zones 4-7)	
Month	**Vegetables To Plant**
April	Broccoli
	Cabbage
	Carrots
	Spinach
May	Corn
	Tomatoes
	Peppers
	Cucumbers

Press keyboard arrows to quickly move from one cell to another when typing text.

8 To delete the two extra rows at the bottom of the table, click in the first cell of row 11, and then click and drag down and to the right. The four cells are selected. Press Delete to remove the rows.

9 Choose File > Save, and keep this file open for the next exercise.

Formatting and styling tables in HTML

The adoption of CSS for styling web pages has affected tables as well. There are two different paths to take when it comes to styling a table. The first method is to use HTML tag properties to modify attributes such as the cellpadding, border, and background color in a table. However, these same attributes can also be controlled with the second method, CSS. It's fair to say that there are more options for styling a table with CSS, but that styling a table with HTML tags is faster for most people. Which method you choose often depends on the project specifications. You'll be learning both methods here so that you have the option to choose. You'll also get a chance to consider the pros and cons of both methods. First, you'll start off with the *traditional* method of styling tables with HTML tags and properties.

1   In the second table you created (Best months to plant vegetables), click on the edge of the first row to select it. In the Property Inspector, click on the HTML category, if necessary, and then click the BG (Background) color swatch. In the left column of swatches, choose the light gray #CCCCCC. The background color of the header row changes to gray.

Select a row and click the BG color swatch to apply a background color.

2   Click inside the April cell, then drag down and to the right until you reach the cell containing the text Spinach; this selects all the cells in these four rows and two columns.

3   Click in the BG swatch text field and type **#FFFCCC**, a light yellow swatch in the lower-right corner. All four rows now have the same background color.

4   Click on the left edge of the empty row after cell that contains the word Spinach to select it. Click the BG color swatch and choose white for this background color. Then click in the May cell and drag down and to the right to the last cell containing the text *Cucumbers*. Click the BG color swatch and choose the light pink color swatch, #FFCCFF, in the bottom-right corner.

Now, you will center the text in your columns.

5   Click at the top of the first column to select it. In the Property Inspector, from Horz (Horizontal) drop-down menu, select Center. Select the second column and repeat this step to center this text.

Select a column and click the Center *option in the Horizontal menu of the Property Inspector.*

6   Choose File > Save, then File > Preview in Browser. Your text is visually categorized by background color now, but it would be a stretch to say that this is a visually pleasing table. There are a few other properties that you can adjust to make this table look a bit better. Close the browser and return to Dreamweaver.

You'll now examine the properties of cell padding.

7   Click in one of the corners of the table until the entire table is outlined in red. Then click on the table to select it. In the Property Inspector, locate the text field for CellPad and type **10**. Press Enter (Windows) or Return (Mac OS) to apply the change. There are now 10 pixels of space added to the inside of all cells; this has the effect of giving your text a bit more breathing room from the borders around it.

Cellpadding is a property that determines the amount of space, measured in pixels, between the sides of a cell and its contents.

8   With your table still selected, locate the text field for CellSpace in the Property Inspector. Type **10** in the CellSpace text field, then press Enter (Windows) or Return (Mac OS) to commit the change. The table changes appearance again. This time, the width between the cells is increased.

Cellspacing is the property that determines the amount of space between your cells.

A table with cellpadding of 10 pixels and cellspacing of 10 pixels.

The space between the cells (the cellspacing) is taking on the properties of the background color. Unfortunately, you cannot control the color of the cellspacing, and so you will actually remove it completely.

9   In the Property Inspector, type **0** in the CellSpace text field and press Enter (Windows) or Return (Mac OS). This removes cellspacing completely. At this point, you only have properties for cellpadding.

10 With the table still selected, locate the text field for Border; it is currently set for 1 pixel, which is the default setting used when a table is created. Replace this value with 0 and press Enter (Windows) or Return (Mac OS). This removes the border completely.

This trick of removing borders completely is used quite a bit with pure HTML tables. This is because there are few good ways to control the appearance of borders using pure HTML. Increasing the border size creates a thick, beveled look that can detract from the rest of your page. Better control for borders exists in CSS.

11 Place your cursor on the small black square on the lower-right of the table until you see the double-arrow. Click and drag the table to the left to reduce its width. You can use the value at the top of the table if you choose, or just change the width until you're satisfied. This example uses a new width of 350 pixels.

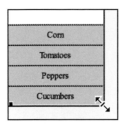

Click and drag the edge of a
table to reduce the width.

12 With the table still selected, press the Split view button in order to see the code generated for this table. In the first line of the table, you see the settings for the border, cellpadding, and cellspacing. In all the *<td>* or cells, you see the properties for alignment and background color repeated for every row. This extra code is part of the tradeoff for the easy application of the color and alignment. Part of the dilemma with this table now is that the alignment and background color settings, as well as the cellspacing, cellpadding, and border settings, are not linked to your CSS in any way.

```
09
90    <table width="350" border="0" cellpadding="10" cellspacing="0">
91  <caption>
92      Best months to plant vegetables (Zones 4-7)
93  </caption>
94    <tr bgcolor="#CCCCCC">
95      <th width="179" align="center" scope="col">Month</th>
96      <th width="195" align="center" scope="col">Vegetables To Plant</th>
97    </tr>
98    <tr>
99      <td align="center" bgcolor="#FFFFCC">April</td>
100     <td align="center" bgcolor="#FFFFCC">Broccoli</td>
101   </tr>
102   <tr>
103     <td align="center" bgcolor="#FFFFCC"> </td>
104     <td align="center" bgcolor="#FFFFCC">Cabbage</td>
105   </tr>
106   <tr>
107     <td align="center" bgcolor="#FFFFCC"> </td>
108     <td align="center" bgcolor="#FFFFCC">Carrots</td>
109   </tr>
110   <tr>
111     <td align="center" bgcolor="#FFFFCC"> </td>
```

The visual styling of the table elements is combined with the structure.

One problem of creating pure HTML tables is the inability to quickly copy the style of one table and apply it to another. Because the content of the table and the style are intertwined, it's hard to separate one from the other. The larger problem is that pure HTML tables have none of the benefits associated with CSS. If your tables are not linked to any CSS, what happens when you redesign your web site? As you saw in the last lesson, a simple change in CSS code can change the background color of your entire site. If the design of your tables clashes with your page, you have a lot of work to do as you locate each table and tweak it to fit.

Formatting and styling tables with CSS

In this exercise, you'll style your initial table using many of the same concepts, such as padding and borders, but this time you'll do it with CSS. There is a little bit more work involved initially, but the result will be a table that not only is more visually appealing than an HTML-based table but also has a reusable style that can be applied to new tables. It's possible to create tag-based styles for all your tables—in other words, to create CSS rules for the various HTML table elements (*<td>*, *<tr>*, and so on). In fact, this is not a bad idea when creating a *default* style for tables in a web site. In this example, however, you will be creating a class style that can readily be applied to different tables. It's not unusual to have three or four different styles of tables in a large web site, each with their own CSS class definitions.

First you'll start by creating general rules for the background color, border, and font appearance of the table; then you'll create more specific rules as you drill down into the table.

1 Press the Design View button to return to this view. Select the first table you created (US Temperate Zones…) by clicking on one of the corners when you see the red outline. If necessary, choose Window > CSS Styles to open the CSS Styles panel. In the CSS Styles panel, click on New; the New CSS Rule dialog box appears.

2 In the Selector Type drop-down menu of the New CSS Rule dialog box, leave the default choice of *Class* selected. In the Selector Name text field, type **styledtable**. Remember that class names are up to you, and choosing a name that is easy to identify and remember is the goal.

3 From the CSS Rule definition drop-down menu, select the mystyles.css external style sheet. This is an important step because you would like to add these styles to your external style sheet rather than writing them to the tips.html page only.

Creating a new class for the style of the table and defining it in the external style sheet.

4   Press OK, and the CSS Rule definition dialog box opens. Select the Background category and click the Background-color swatch. Choose the color white (#FFF) and press OK.

You see no changes onscreen because you need to apply the *.styledtable* class to the table. You'll do that now, and then return to adding rules.

5   Your table should still be selected; if it isn't, do so now. In the Property Inspector, the table properties should be active. (If you are seeing the HTML and CSS properties, you have not selected the table.) On the right side of the Property Inspector, choose styledtable from the Class drop-down menu to apply the class. The background of your table changes to white.

Apply a class to a table by choosing the class name in the Property Inspector.

6   Now you'll return to the styledtable class style and add additional properties. You could have created all your rules first and then applied the styledtable class; however, doing it this way allows you to preview your styling in real-time. Now you'll add some borders and change the font-styling for the entire table.

7   Double-click on *.styledtable* in the CSS Styles panel to reopen the CSS Rule definition dialog box. From the Font-family drop-down menu, choose the Verdana, Geneva, sans-serif. In the Font-size text field, type **10**, and leave the drop down menu to the right set to *px*. In the Color text field, type **#006** (a dark blue), and press Apply to see your changes to the table. Now you'll add a thin border around the entire table.

8   Select the Border category, and choose Solid from the Top drop-down menu. In the Width text field, type **1**. In the Color text field, type **#006**, the same dark blue you used for the font-color. Press OK.

The last property you'll add to the *.styledtable* class is one that is not available in the standard CSS Rule definition dialog box. It's important to realize that the language of CSS is quite large to begin with, and will expand in the future. There are CSS properties that may not be used every day but nonetheless can be very useful. You'll semi-automatically add one such property now called *border-collapse*. This property removes the space between table cells.

9 In the bottom half of the CSS Styles panel in the section labeled *Properties for* "*.styledtable*", click on the blue underlined text, *Add Property*. You may need to click on the Show only set properties icon in the bottom left of the CSS Styles panel in order to add the property. In the resulting text field, type **border-collapse**, then press Enter (Windows) or Return (Mac OS) to commit the change.

Click Add Property *and type* ***border-collapse*** *to add a new CSS property.*

When it is typed correctly, Dreamweaver recognizes this property as part of the CSS language and makes the values available in the next field.

10 Click in the column to the right of the border-collapse property to activate the field. From the drop-down menu, choose *collapse*.

11 Choose File > Save All. Preview your page in your browser to see your styling. Close the browser and return to Dreamweaver.

Advanced CSS styling of tables

You have created a basic style for this table. You will now sharpen up the appearance of this table by adding a background image to the header, setting the text alignment and padding, and finally, creating subtle borders between each of the data cells.

1 Click anywhere inside the header, and in the lower-left corner of your document window, click on the *<th>* tag to select the header. You defined this top row as a table header earlier in the lesson.

2 In the CSS Styles panel, press the New CSS Rule button (⊕) to open the New CSS Rule dialog box. In the Selector Type drop-down menu, the Compound option is listed. This is what you want because you are creating a specific rule for *<th>* tags, but only those found inside the styledtable class.

Create a compound rule to style all header rows within the styledtable class.

3 The Selector name text field has been automatically populated as *.styledtable tr th*. Remember that compound rules are read from left to right. So, within the styledtable class, you are targeting table rows (*tr*) and specifically, table headers (*th*) within table rows.

4 Press OK, and the CSS Rule definition dialog box opens. Select the Background category to access these options.

5 Press the Browse button to the right of the Background-image text field, and in the Select Image Source dialog box, locate the bg_header.jpg image and press OK (Windows) or Choose (Mac OS).

6   From the Background-repeat drop-down menu, choose repeat-x from the list. The source image is a gradient that is designed to tile horizontally. Press Apply to see a preview of this effect on your table. You'll add a few other touches to this header row.

Choose a background image and tile it horizontally in the header row with repeat-x.

7   Select the Border category and uncheck the Style Same for All checkbox. Choose Solid from the Bottom style drop-down menu.

8   Uncheck the Width Same for All checkbox, and then type **2** in the Width text field of the Bottom style. Uncheck the Color Same for All checkbox and type **#006** in the Color text field of the Bottom style; this is the same dark blue color that you've been using for other styling in this table.

Applying a two-pixel-wide, solid, blue border to the bottom of the header row.

9   Select the Type category, and type **14** into the Font-size text field to make the text slightly larger. From the Text-transform drop-down menu, choose capitalize. This property adds a capital letter to the beginning of each word.

10   Press OK to see your styled header.

Controlling cell alignment, padding, and borders with CSS

You'll now make the content within your table a bit more readable by aligning and padding your text as well as creating borders around each cell. Controlling borders and padding is much more flexible in CSS than in HTML; for example, the cellpadding values in HTML are uniform—there is no control over left, right, top, and bottom, as there is in CSS. The same applies to borders. However, before you begin styling padding with CSS, it's a good idea to remove these values from the HTML so that there are no surprises.

1   Click any corner of the table in order to select it. In the Property Inspector, notice the values for CellPad and CellSpace; they are empty, but this stands for default, not zero. You must specifically instruct Dreamweaver to use a value of zero.

2   For all three properties of CellPad, CellSpace, and Border, type **0**. Press Enter (Windows) or Return (Mac OS) when you have added the last value.

Type 0 for CellPad, CellSpace, and Border to make sure they are removed.

3   Click inside any cell of your table, and in the bottom-left corner of your document window, click on the *<td>* tag to select a cell. You could also Ctrl+click (Windows) or Command+click (Mac OS) a cell to select it.

4   Press the New CSS Rule button (*) at the bottom of the CSS Styles panel, and the New CSS Rule dialog box appears. As in the last exercise, you are creating a compound rule that applies only to cells within the *.styledtable* class. Your selector name reads *.styledtable tr td*. Press OK. The CSS Rule definition dialog box appears.

Select the Block category, then from the Text-align drop-down menu, choose center. Press Apply to see this center.

Applying a text-align of center to the <td> element centers all text in your cells.

5   Select the Box category, and in the Padding section, type **5** in the Top text field. Uncheck the Same for All checkbox. In the field for Left, type **2** and press Apply to see your text shift slightly. One of the main differences between HTML cellpadding and CSS cellpadding is the ability in CSS to control all four sides of a cell's padding individually.

6   Select the Border category, and in the Style section, choose Dashed from the Top drop-down menu.

7   Type **1** in the Width text field, and in the Color text field, type **#9AA8BD**, the hexadecimal number for a light blue-gray. Press OK to apply the style.

8   Select the row below the header row, and, if necessary, click on the HTML button in the Property Inspector, then press the Bold button to bold the text for Zone, Fahrenheit, and Example Cities.

9   Choose File > Save All. Then preview your page in your browser to see your table.

The table as rendered in a web browser.

You're nearly finished. Now you'll add some final touches to your table to give it a little extra polish and readability. Close your web browser.

Creating alternate row styling with CSS

A common feature found in many tables is to alternate colors for every other row. Done correctly, this increases the contrast between the rows and allows the user to visually separate the content of the table. This is easily done in CSS by creating a new class solely for background color.

1   Click on the edge of the row labeled 1 to select it. In the CSS Style panel, press the New CSS Rule button (⊕). The New CSS Rule dialog box opens.

Unlike the last few exercises, you will not be using a compound selection. Instead, you will be creating a new class. The reason for this is that you only want to style every other row. There is no automatic way to do this in CSS; after you create the class, it will have to be applied manually.

2   Choose Class from the Selector Type drop-down menu. In the Selector Name text field, type **oddrow** and press OK.

```
                            New CSS Rule

Selector Type:                                    (    OK    )
Choose a contextual selector type for your CSS rule.
                                                  (  Cancel  )
    [ Class (can apply to any HTML element)   ▲▼ ]


Selector Name:
Choose or enter a name for your selector.

    [ oddrow                                 ] [▲▼]

    ┌──────────────────────────────────────┐
    │ This selector name will apply your rule to │
    │ all HTML elements with class "oddrow".     │
    │                                            │
    │                                            │
    │                                            │
    └──────────────────────────────────────┘

        (  Less Specific  )   (  More Specific  )

Rule Definition:
Choose where your rule will be defined.

    [ mystyles.css              ▲▼ ]          (  Help  )
```

Create a new class named oddrow *to style individual rows.*

3   Select the Background category, and type **#EAF1F4**, the hexadecimal color for a light blue, into the Background-color text field. Press OK. Now you will apply the oddrow class to every other row.

4   The row labeled *1* should still be selected; if not, do so now. In the Property Inspector, press the HTML button. From the Class drop-down menu, choose oddrow. The light-blue background color is applied.

5   Starting with the row labeled *3*, apply the oddrow class to all the odd–numbered rows.

\u25cf \u25cb \u25cb	tips.html	

Styling alternating rows with a background color can improve readability.

6   Choose File > Save All. Preview your page in the browser, then close the browser when you are finished.

Reusing CSS for other tables

As you have seen, CSS styling for tables is very powerful and capable of spicing up the appearance of tables without sacrificing their structure. Like CSS for text and layout, the real power is obvious when you apply and link the style to another table.

1   Double-click on the file veggie_names.html. This page is currently linked to the same external style sheet as the tips.html page, and includes an unstyled table. All that needs to be done is to apply the styledtable class you created to this table.

2   Click anywhere in the table, and then click the *<table>* tag in the lower-left corner of the document window to select the table.

3   In the Property Inspector, choose styledtable from the Class drop-down menu on the far right. The style is applied, and the appearance of this table matches the other. The style is flexible enough that, even though the top row has three cells, it has the header style applied.

Applying the styledtable class to a previously unstyled table.

That's it! The hard work of creating the original style pays off when it comes time to creating new tables with identical style. Better yet, if you need to make a global change such as changing the background-color or font color, changing a property in the external sheet will ripple through to all tables.

4   To add the alternating rows of color, click on the third row. In the Property Inspector, press the HTML button, and from the Class drop-down menu, choose oddrow. Repeat this step with every other row to add the style.

The added benefit of having this class handy is that some tables benefit from this style more than others, and so it is your decision whether or not to use it.

5   Choose File > Save All. Keep this file open for the next exercise.

Data sorting tables

There are a few other features relating to managing tables that you may find useful. The structure of tables can be both a blessing and a curse. For example, take a look at the table from the previous exercise. What if you wanted to swap the order of the first two columns? There is no easy way to do this with a static HTML table. Another limitation of tables, especially tables created from tabular data where you may not have control over the order, is the difficulty in sorting the data. Dreamweaver has a feature that allows you to sort your data alphabetically by the column of your choice.

In the first part of the exercise, you will do some copy-and-pasting in order to switch the first two columns.

1   Click the edge of the table to select it. Choose Edit > Copy to copy the table.

2   Click to the right of the table, press Enter (Windows) or Return (Mac OS) twice, and choose Edit > Paste. You can copy and paste tables in Dreamweaver within a page, or from one page to another.

3   In the top table, click at the top of the second column (Common Name) to select it. Choose Edit > Copy to copy the content of the column. Now click at the top of the first column (Latin Name) to select it. Choose Edit > Paste to replace the content of the first column. You now have duplicate columns momentarily, but the next step is to copy content from the second table.

4   In the second table, click on the top of the first column (Latin Name) to select it. Choose Edit > Copy to copy this column's contents. Return to the first table and click on the top of the second column; then choose Edit > Paste.

5   Click on the second table and delete it now, as you no longer need it.

Now you'll sort the first column alphabetically using Dreamweaver's little-known Sort Table feature.

6   Choose Commands > Sort Table to open the Sort Table dialog box. You do not have to make any changes here because the default settings are fine, but take a quick look at the options. The Sort By menu allows you to choose which menu Dreamweaver will use to sort. The Order menu allows you to choose how the table should be sorted, either alphabetically or numerically. Alphabetically is correct for now.

Choose Commands > Sort Table to sort a table alphabetically.

7   Press OK, and the table is sorted, with the first column now in alphabetical order.

8   Choose File > Save All. Congratulations, you have finished this lesson.

Self study

Using your new knowledge of creating tables to display data in Dreamweaver, try some of the following tasks to build on your experience:

Use the Import Tabular Data command to import a tab-delimited .txt file, setting the table's fixed width on import. Select the table using the Tag Selector, and change its width to 50 percent of the page size using the Property Inspector. Preview the table in a browser, noting the way the table changes as the browser window is resized.

Build another table using the Insert Table command, and add a caption to it. Type text into the cells, center the text, and drag the row and column dividers to make them consistent in size. Add a background color and a border to the table using the Property Inspector, and switch to Code View to note the changes to your HTML code.

Create and use an internal CSS rule to change the font used, add padding to the cells, and alternate the colors of your first table's rows. Experiment with applying the class rule to your second table, and note how its appearance changes. Finally, use the Sort Table command to organize both your tables' data alphabetically.

Review

Questions

1 What's the difference between a percentage-based table and a fixed-width table?

2 What is tabular data and how does it relate to tables in Dreamweaver?

3 Name an advantage and a disadvantage of using CSS to style your tables.

Answers

1 A percentage-based table stretches to fit the size of the browser window. A pixel-based table is fixed and does not resize.

2 Tabular data is text often exported from a database or spreadsheet in a delimited format. Dreamweaver creates tables from these files through the Import Tabular Data command found in the File menu. Rows and columns are automatically created in Dreamweaver based on the structure of the text file.

3 One advantage of using CSS to style tables is the ability to link a single style to multiple tables using an external style sheet. A disadvantage might be that the process requires more time in the beginning, and a good understanding of HTML table tags and CSS selectors.

What you'll learn in this lesson:

- Customizing panels and panel groups
- Resizing the document window
- Using guides and grids
- Exploring the tag selector

Fine-Tuning Your Workflow

Once you become familiar with building web pages in Dreamweaver CS5, you'll find yourself using some features more often than others. In this lesson, you'll learn how to save time by customizing the Dreamweaver environment to streamline your workflow.

Starting up

Before starting, make sure that your tools and panels are consistent by resetting your workspace. See "Resetting the Dreamweaver workspace" on page 3.

You will work with several files from the dw08lessons folder in this lesson. Make sure that you have loaded the dwlessons folder onto your hard drive from the supplied DVD. See "Loading lesson files" on page 3.

Before you begin, you need to create site settings that point to the dw08lessons folder from the included DVD that contains resources you need for these lessons. Go to Site > New Site, or, for details on creating a site, refer to Lesson 2, "Setting Up a New Site."

See Lesson 8 in action!

Use the accompanying video to gain a better understanding of how to use some of the features shown in this lesson. The video tutorial for this lesson can be found on the included DVD.

Customizing panels and panel groups

Panels can be moved, grouped, and docked to help keep everything you regularly use at your fingertips. In the next part of this lesson, you'll create a custom workspace for CSS layouts. You'll start by collapsing the Insert panel, and then repositioning the CSS and AP Elements panels.

1   Collapse the Insert panel by double-clicking on the Insert tab at the top of the panel.

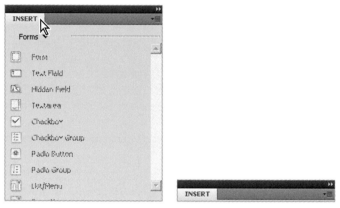

Double-click on the tab at the top of the Insert panel to collapse the panel.

2   Expand the CSS panel group by double-clicking on the CSS Styles tab at the top of the group. This panel group contains two panels: CSS Styles and AP Elements. To see both panels simultaneously, you'll drag the AP Elements panel out of the CSS group.

3 Click and hold the AP Elements tab. Drag this tab into your workspace to detach it from the CSS panel group. The tabs for CSS Styles and AP Elements become title bars.

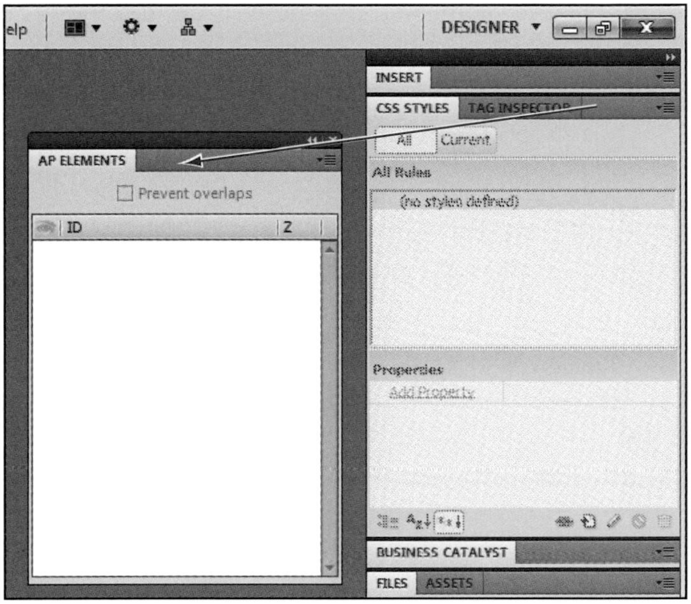

Drag the AP Elements panel out of the CSS panel group.

4 To keep the AP Elements panel from interfering with your workspace, you can dock it with the other panels. Place your cursor over the AP Elements tab at the top of the panel, and click and hold.

5 Drag the AP Elements panel above the title bar of the Files panel group. When a solid line appears above the title bar of the Files panel group, release the AP Elements panel to snap it into place.

6 If your Files panel group was minimized by repositioning the AP Elements panel, expand it by double-clicking on the Files tab at the top of the panel. Move your cursor over the border between the AP Elements panel and the Files panel. When the double-sided arrow appears, drag the border up to make more room for the Files panel group.

7   If necessary, resize the Files panel group further by dragging this border. Right+click (Windows) or Ctrl+click (Mac OS) on the Business Catalyst panel and choose Close. You can always use this command to close panels without having to go to the menus. When you're finished, the panels should look something like the example shown here. This configuration gives you quick access to the panels you'll use the most when creating a CSS-based layout.

The customized panels.

8   To save this workspace, choose Window > Workspace Layout > New Workspace. When the New Workspace Layout dialog box appears, type **CSS Layout** into the Name text field and press OK.

9   Choose Window > Workspace Layout > Designer to switch to the default workspace; then choose Window > Workspace Layout > CSS Layout to switch back to the custom workspace you just created.

Using the Favorites tab on the Insert bar

To help organize the many options available in the Insert bar, Dreamweaver groups similar items into categories. You may have already found yourself using some items more often than others. The Favorites category is a great way to group commonly used items into one place for quick access.

1   Double-click on the index.html file in the Files panel. In this exercise, you'll be inserting a number of images and AP Divs to create two pages in the Sounds of Nature web site. To avoid switching between the Layout and Common tabs, you'll add these items to the Favorites tab.

2   Expand the Insert panel by double-clicking on the Insert tab at the top of the panel. If necessary, adjust the heights of your available panels by dragging the borders between them.

3   Click on the Favorites category in the Insert panel's drop-down menu. Right-click (Windows) or Ctrl+click (Mac OS) in the empty gray area beneath the Favorite category, and choose Customize Favorites from the resulting contextual menu. The Customize Favorite Objects dialog box appears.

Right-click (Windows) or Ctrl+click (Mac OS) in the empty gray area
beneath the Insert panel's Favorite category and choose Customize Favorites.

4   On the right side of the Customize Favorite Objects dialog box, the list of available objects is organized by the tabs, which indicate where each object can be found in the Insert bar. Select Image, then press the Add button (>>) in the middle of the dialog box.

Select Image, and press the Add button.

5   Scroll down and select Draw AP Div from the list of available objects; then press the Add button. Press OK. The Favorites category now features the Image and Draw AP Div elements.

Resizing the document window

If you're familiar with any page layout or graphics programs, adjusting the size of the window in which you're working is probably something that you do regularly. However, when you're working on web pages in Dreamweaver, it's a good idea to think carefully about the size of your document. Because a number of different hardware and software configurations may be used to view your content, it can be tricky to make sure your web site looks good on every user's computer. In the next part of this lesson, you'll resize the document window to make sure the Sounds of Nature web site is being designed with the target audience in mind.

1   Index.html should still be open in your document window. If not, open it now. Also, make sure you're in the Design view. If necessary, press the Design View button in the Document toolbar.

   If you're working on a Windows computer, choose Window > Cascade from the main menu. This step is not necessary if you're working on a Mac OS computer. The Dreamweaver interface for Windows and Mac OS is slightly different, and will be covered in the "Switching between tabs and cascading documents" exercise later in this lesson.

2   Click and drag the bottom-right corner of the document window to resize the window.

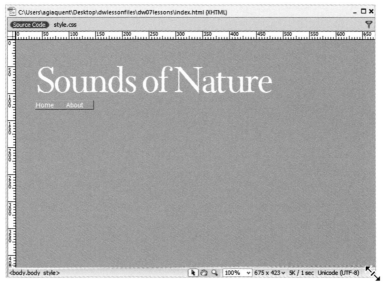

Click and drag the bottom-right corner of the document window to resize it.

If the bottom-right corner of your document window is hidden by the Property Inspector, turn off the Property Inspector temporarily by choosing Window > Property Inspector. Then resize the window and turn the Property Inspector back on.

Resizing the document window like this is flexible and convenient, but you may be tempted to forget about the size of your visitors' screens. An appropriate size on your new, super-deluxe, high-resolution monitor will not be an appropriate size on the ten-year-old monitor you gifted to your uncle when you upgraded.

3   To the left of the corner you used to resize the document window in the last step, there is a Window Size drop-down menu. This menu can be used to select common monitor sizes. From the menu, choose the option that reads 760 x 420 (800 x 600, Maximized).

Choose 760 x 420 (800 x 600, Maximized)
from the Window Size drop-down menu.

The options in the Window Size drop-down menu correspond to a number of common monitor sizes. In this case, an 800 x 600-pixel monitor has been chosen. The size of the page is further reduced to 760 x 420 to accommodate the menu and scroll bars of the user's browser.

4   If the document window switches to Split view, press the Design View button in the Document toolbar.

Using guides

In Lesson 5, "Creating Page Layouts with CSS," you learned how AP Divs can be positioned using guides to easily create precise layouts. Guides are an invaluable tool, and Dreamweaver provides a number of features that make them even more helpful and easy to use. In the next part of this lesson, you'll add an AP Div to index.html and then place an image inside the div. First, you'll draw some guides to help you size and position the div.

1   If your rulers are hidden, choose View > Rulers > Show to turn them on.

Rulers can use inches, centimeters, or pixels in Dreamweaver. Because pixels are the most common unit of measurement on the Web, they are the default. If you prefer inches or centimeters, right-click (Windows) or Ctrl+click (Mac OS) on the rulers to access a context menu where you can choose your preferred unit. In this lesson, you'll be using pixels, so it's a good idea to stick with them for now.

2   Click inside the vertical ruler on the left side of your document window and drag a guide into the center of the page. Double-click on this guide to open the Move Guide dialog box. From this dialog box, you can set an exact location for guides. This feature can be especially helpful when building a web page based on sketches or mockups.

3   Type **38** in the Location text field and press OK. The guide is repositioned 38 pixels from the left side of the document.

4   Create another vertical guide and set its position to 494 pixels. Notice that hovering over either of these guides with the cursor produces a yellow box indicating the guide's position. Now, hold down the Ctrl (Windows) or Command (Mac OS) key and move your cursor over each guide. The blue line with arrows on either end indicates the distance between each of your guides, as well as the distance between guides and the edge of the document window.

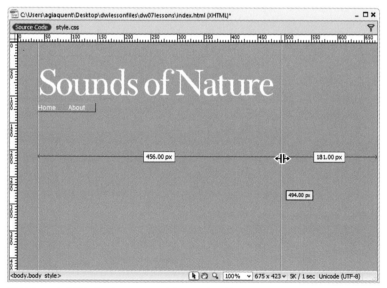

Hold down Ctrl (Windows) or Command (Mac OS) and hover over the guides.

5   Drag two horizontal guides down from the ruler at the top of the document window. Double-click on each of them, then use the Move Guide dialog box to position one of them 152 pixels from the top of the document, and the other 380 pixels from the top of the document.

6   Next, you'll draw an AP Div and start adding some content; but first make sure that Snap to Guides is turned on, by choosing View > Guides > Edit Guides. The Guides dialog box appears, with a number of options for customizing your guides.

If you happen to be using a color in your web page that makes the guides hard to see, you can change their color here. Also, the Lock Guides option can be a helpful way to avoid accidentally repositioning guides. For now, make sure Snap to Guides is checked and press OK.

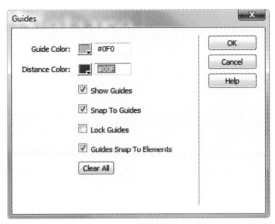

The Guides dialog box allows you to change the color of guides and turn snapping on and off.

7   Now that your guides are set up, you're ready to add some content. With the Favorites category selected in the Insert panel, click the Draw AP Div element you added earlier. Draw an AP Div inside the box created by your four guides.

8   If the edges of the div don't line up with the guides on your first try, select the div by clicking on its name in the AP Elements panel, then drag each edge until it snaps into place.

Readjust the edges of the div by selecting it in the AP Div panel and dragging its edges until they snap in place.

9   Click inside the div to place your cursor, and then select the Image element in the Favorites category of the Insert panel.

10 In the Select Image Source dialog box, select hp_photo.jpg from the images folder inside the dw08lessons folder, and press OK (Windows) or Choose (Mac OS).

11 In the Image Tag Accessibility Attributes dialog box, type **Soothing Lakefront** into the Alternate text field and press OK. The hp_photo.jpg image fits nicely inside the div you created earlier.

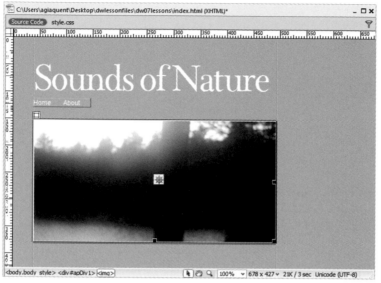

The hp_photo.jpg placed inside of the AP Div.

12 Choose File > Save and leave index.html open.

Using grids

Much like guides, grids are a great way to help keep your layout precise and uniform. In the next part of this lesson, you'll be adding AP Divs and images to the About page of the Sounds of Nature web site. Creating a custom grid will help you align and evenly distribute these new elements on the page.

1 Double-click on the about.html file in your Files panel to open the About page. You may notice that this page has a white background and uses a default typeface. Later on, you'll use the tag selector to change this.

2 Choose View > Grid > Grid Settings to open the Grid Settings dialog box. Much like the Guides dialog box, the Grid Settings dialog box can be used to specify the grid color and turn on snapping. Type **#CCCCCC** in the Color text field and check Show Grid and Snap to Grid to turn the grid on and enable snapping.

3 For this layout, type **38** in the Spacing text field and make sure pixels are selected as the unit of measurement. Choosing a spacing of 38 pixels creates a series of squares that are 38 pixels high by 38 pixels wide. Press OK.

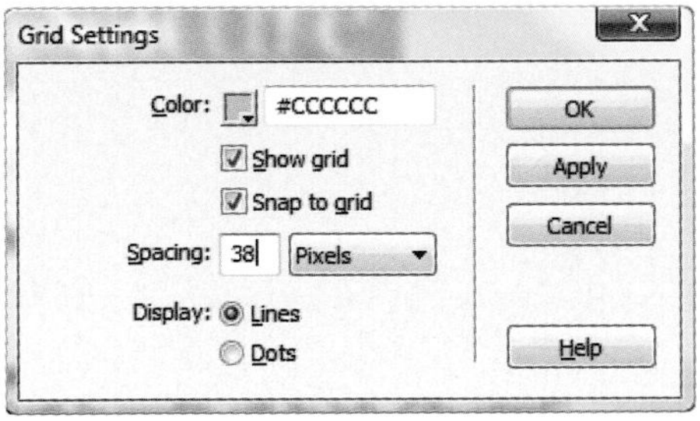

The Grid Settings dialog box.

4 With the grid established, add the AP Divs that will house your images. Press the Draw AP Div element in the Favorites category of the Insert panel. Draw a square div that is 3 grid units wide and 3 grid units high. Use the figure below for reference.

Draw a square AP Div.

5 Press the Draw AP Div element in the Favorites category of the Insert panel again, and draw a second AP Div one grid unit below the first. Use the figure for reference.

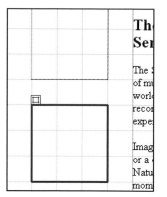

Draw a second AP Div one grid unit below the first.

6 Click inside the first div to place the cursor, and then press the Image element in the Favorites category of the Insert panel.

7 In the Select Image Source dialog box, select tree.jpg from the images folder inside the dw08lessons folder, and press OK (Windows) or Choose (Mac OS).

8 In the Image Tag Accessibility Attributes dialog box, type **tree** into the Alternate text field and press OK. The tree image is positioned inside the AP Div on your page.

9 Repeat steps 7 and 8 to add forest.jpg to the second div. Type **forest** into the Alternate text field of the Image Tag Accessibility Attributes dialog box.

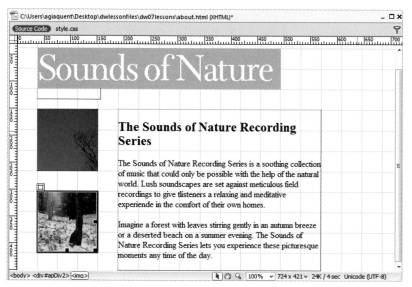

The about.html page after inserting the tree and forest images.

10 Choose File > Save and leave about.html open for the next part of this lesson.

The tag selector

In HTML, the organization of elements takes the form of a family tree. In the previous two exercises, you created AP Divs and then inserted images into them. In HTML terms, all these images are children of the AP Divs within which they reside. It's beyond the scope of this book to explore all the implications of these relationships, but it's important to know that they exist. The tag selector is a feature of Dreamweaver that allows you to select HTML elements based on their relationship to one another. Next, you'll explore the tag selector and then use it to apply a single style that will affect the entire about.html page.

1 With the About page open, click once on the forest image that you inserted at the end of the last exercise. At the bottom-left corner of the document window are a number of HTML tags. This is the tag selector. The *<img>* tag at the end of this line is highlighted to indicate that the forest.jpg image is selected. In addition, the Property Inspector displays information and options related to this image.

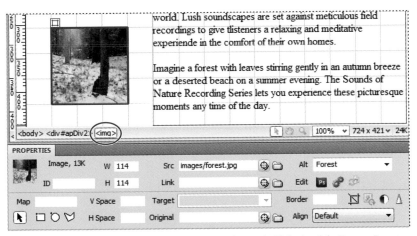

With the forest image selected, the <img> tag in the tag selector is highlighted and the Property Inspector displays information and options related to this image.

2 In the tag selector, click on the *<div#apDiv2>* tag to the left of the *<img>* tag. Notice that the options in the Property Inspector change to reflect the selected div. In this case, you've selected the parent of the forest image.

3 To further illustrate this relationship, choose Edit > Select Child from the main menu. The *<img>* tag becomes highlighted in the tag selector, and the Property Inspector changes to reflect the selected element.

4   Now, select *<body>* on the far-left side of the tag selector. The Property Inspector displays options and information related to the *<body>* tag. Press the CSS button in the Property Inspector. From the Targeted Rule drop-down menu, choose body_style.

With the <body> tag selected in the tag selector, choose body_style from the Targeted Rule drop-down menu.

Because many CSS properties are inherited throughout the document, it is possible to write generalized rules that will be applied to all the elements on a page. In this case, body_style changes the font and text color for the entire document because every element is a descendant of the body.

5   Choose File > Save and leave about.html open for the next part of this lesson.

Switching between tabs and cascading documents

By default, Dreamweaver organizes open documents with a series of tabs in the upper-left corner of the document window. If you'd like to compare documents, or you simply prefer to use separate windows for each document, the cascade option provides an alternative for viewing open files. Next, you'll use this feature to simultaneously view the home page and the About page of the Sounds of Nature web site.

1   Both index.html and about.html should still be open. If they are not, open them now.

2   If you're working on a Windows computer, your documents are already displayed in the cascade view. If you're working on a Macintosh, choose Window > Cascade from the main menu.

The index.html and about.html documents in cascade view.

3   With each document floating in its own window, you can use the bottom-right corner to resize them, as discussed earlier, or use Dreamweaver's tiling feature to display them side by side. Choose Window > Tile Vertically (Windows), or Window > Tile (Mac OS).

With the windows tiled in this fashion, it's possible to see both documents, but unless you have a very large monitor, you won't be able to see either document in its entirety. In the next part of this lesson, you'll use the Zoom tool to fit each document into its window.

Zooming

Because web sites are rarely viewed any smaller or larger than 100 percent of their size by visitors on the web, you'll probably want to use the Zoom tool sparingly. In some cases, it can be helpful for exact positioning or viewing multiple documents at once, but it's a good idea to return to 100 percent when you're finished. Now, you'll use the Zoom and Hand tools to navigate throughout your document, and then you'll choose a magnification setting that will allow you to see the entire About and home pages side by side.

1   At the bottom of the document window on the about.html page, select the Zoom tool (⊕). Click twice inside the document window to zoom to 200 percent.

2   With the Zoom tool still selected, hold down the Alt (Windows) or Option (Mac OS) key and click once inside the document window. The About page zooms out to 150 percent.

3   At the bottom of the document window, select the Hand tool (✋) to the left of the Zoom tool. Click and drag the document in any direction within the document window. The Hand tool allows you to drag a document around in its window like a piece of paper.

Use the Hand tool to drag a document around in its window.

4   Double-click on the Zoom tool at the bottom of the document window to return to 100 percent. Now, choose 66% from the Set magnification drop-down menu to the right of the Zoom tool. Depending on the size of your monitor, this magnification level may allow you to see the entire About page. If not, use the Zoom tool or the Set magnification drop-down menu to find the appropriate size.

5 When you've found the best magnification level for your monitor, click on the title bar of index.html to make this document active. Click and drag to highlight the percentage in the Set magnification text field, and enter in the magnification level you used in the about.html window. Press Enter (Windows) or Return (Mac OS) to commit the new value. When you're finished, your documents should look like the figure shown here.

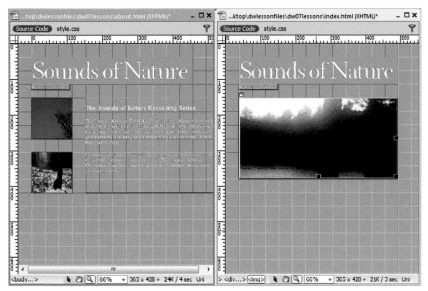

Adjust the magnification level until both pages can be seen in their entirety.

6 To return to the tabbed view, click the Maximize button in the top-right corner of either document window (Windows), or choose Window > Combine as Tabs (Mac OS). As mentioned earlier, you should always remember to return to 100 percent magnification when you're finished using the Zoom tool. Also, you'll want to make sure the Selection tool is active to avoid any surprises when working on later lessons.

7 Click on the Selection tool (⬆) in the bottom of the document window and choose 100% from the Set magnification drop-down menu.

8 Choose File > Save.

Congratulations! You have finished Lesson 8, "Fine-Tuning Your Workflow."

Self study

In this lesson, you followed a predetermined workflow that was tailored toward producing two pages in the Sounds of Nature web site. The key to creating a streamlined workflow is planning ahead. Imagine you were creating a web site for a local bakery. Make some sketches of what the pages would look like. In Dreamweaver, spend some time setting up a workspace that would make building the bakery web site easier. Think about which elements you might use the most. Then, use the guides and the grid to help create a layout that reflects the sketches you made earlier.

Review

Questions

1   Is it possible to resize the document window to preview how a web page will appear on different users' monitors?

2   How can you position guides on the page without dragging them?

3   Are tabs the only way to organize open documents?

Answers

1   Yes. The Window Size drop-down menu at the bottom of the document window contains a number of preset sizes that correspond to common monitor sizes.

2   To more exactly position guides, simply double-click on any guide to open the Move Guide dialog box.

3   No. If you prefer to use floating windows instead of tabs, choose Window > Cascade from the main menu.

What you'll learn in this lesson:

- Inserting Flash content
- Using the Assets panel
- Understanding plug-ins
- Adding video and sound files to a web page

Adding Flash, Video, and Sound Content

As Internet connection speeds increase, people are expecting more dynamic content online. To meet these expectations, designers are increasingly turning to animation, sound, and video to help make web content more compelling and visually engaging.

Starting up

Before starting, make sure that your tools and panels are consistent by resetting your workspace. See "Resetting the Dreamweaver workspace" on page 3.

You will work with several files from the dw09lessons folder in this lesson. Make sure that you have loaded the dwlessons folder onto your hard drive from the supplied DVD. See "Loading lesson files" on page 3.

Before you begin, you need to create a site definition that points to the dw09lessons folder from the included DVD that contains resources you need for these lessons. Go to Site > New Site, or, for details on creating a site definition, refer to Lesson 2, "Setting Up a New Site."

See Lesson 9 in action!

Use the accompanying video to gain a better understanding of how to use some of the features shown in this lesson. The video tutorial for this lesson can be found on the included DVD.

Making web content interesting

Adding video, sound, and animation to a web page is one way to make your pages more interesting and engaging. Video, for example, plays a key role in supplying interesting and varied web content. The barrier to creating original video has decreased dramatically in recent years as has the barrier to distributing this video. Video allows individuals and companies to post commercials, speeches, and other content that otherwise would be difficult to reach an audience.

Sound allows you to enhance web pages by supplementing visual content with music or sound effects. Sound also inspires user interaction (as you'll see later in this lesson), thereby giving the user a more interesting online experience.

Animation gives web pages a whole new life by adding movement and effects to images that still pictures just can't match. Something moving on a web page automatically draws a visitor's eye. Movement is especially effective for banner ads, buttons, and whatever else you'd like your visitors to pay attention to.

Inserting Flash movies

Adobe's Flash CS5 Professional application is used primarily to create animation and interactive projects. In terms of animation, you can use Flash to create animated web banners, buttons, splash pages, slide shows, and more. Inserting Flash animations into your web page is a great way to bring life to an otherwise static environment.

Web banners are a big part of advertising these days. And if a web banner includes moving elements, that movement automatically draws the user's eye right to the banner. In this exercise, you will add a flash banner to place on a web site.

1   In the Files panel, navigate to the dw09lessons folder, and inside the Pages folder, double-click the banner.html page to open it.

2   If the page opens in Split view, click on the Show Design View button.

3   Click in the empty div element at the top of the sidebar on the right. A div element of 220 by 250 has been created for you.

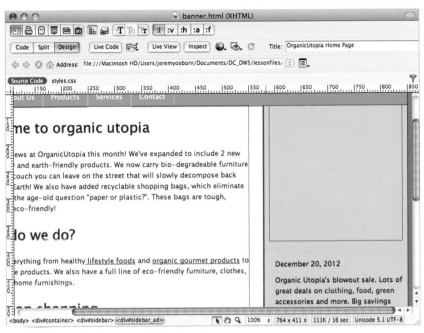

Click in the empty div element named #sidebar_ad.

4   Click on the the Assets tab of the Files panel, and locate the fourth button down, the Flash button (■).

Press the Flash button in the Assets tab of the Files panel.

Click on this button to see the list of .swf files in this site.

Flash movies are labeled with the .swf extension. However, other programs, including After Effects and Dreamweaver, can create .swf files as well.

5   Select the ou_sidebar_ad.swf file and drag it to the sidebar_ad div to insert it.

6   Type **Organic Utopia sidebar ad** in the Title text field when the Object Tag Accessibility Attributes dialog box appears, then press OK.

As you can see, inserting a Flash movie into a web page is much like inserting an image. The width and height of the .swf are automatically established based on the file's physical size, just as they are for images such as .jpeg and .gif files.

The .swf file appears with a generic Flash icon on a gray image. You can preview the image in a number of ways.

7   In the Property Inspector click on the Play button; the banner will appear and play.

Select the Play button in the Property Inspector to make the banner appear.

You must have Flash Player, which is available free from Adobe, installed to view an .swf file. If you don't have the application installed, visit Adobe.com/products/flashplayer to download and install it. Note that visitors to your web site also must have Flash Player installed to view your Flash content. A good rule of thumb when including Flash content on a web site is to let visitors know as soon as they get to your site that they'll need to have Flash Player. Be sure to include the link to the Flash Player web page (the URL provided at the beginning of this paragraph) so that visitors can download the Flash Player, if necessary.

8   After you click the Play button, it automatically turns into a Stop button. This flash file is automatically set to stop after playing once, but with looped animations you could press the stop button to end the playback.

To see the page in the browser choose File > Save, then File > Preview in Browser. If the Copy Dependent Files window appears, press OK. These are files that Dreamweaver automatically adds to the site. Included here is code to help users who may not have the Flash plugin installed.

9   After previewing, close the browser. There are other options in the Properties panel available for Flash files. If you have the Flash authoring program installed you could click on the Edit button, for example, and locate the .FLA authoring file connected with the .swf file. This would allow an easy link if you needed to update or modify your sidebar ad.

When designing web pages, be sure to include space in your design for .swf files, if you're going to incorporate them into the page. The files can vary in size, depending on what you're using them for. To learn more about Flash, visit Adobe.com/products/flash.

Adding video

Adding video to a web page is relatively easy, although the decision to include it should be based on an evaluation of your audience. The large file sizes associated with video will affect the experience of all your users, particularly those who don't have high-speed Internet connections. In this section, you will learn how to integrate video into your web pages using three of the most popular formats: Flash Video, Quicktime and Windows Media.

Flash Video

Flash Video is spreading across the Web, and is the format of choice on a number of sites. One of the primary advantages of Flash Video is that playback is enabled for any browser with the Flash plugin. Because upwards of 95% of all web browsers have some version of the plugin installed, this means your video will find the widest possible audience. Additionally, Flash video can be compressed to a reasonable size while maintaining image quality.

Different programs create Flash Video, including the Adobe Media Encoder, Premiere Pro, and even Photoshop. Creating the video is a separate process, so you'll want to do your homework and learn as much as you can about how it works in order to get the best results. There are essentially two file formats that are used in Flash video: .flv and .f4v. The .flv format is the traditional flash video format and .f4v is a slightly newer format. In this exercise, you'll add a pre-existing .flv video file into your page and add simple player controls to allow users to control the playback of the movie.

1 Double-click the flashvideo.html file. Click below the heading A Look at Our Vegetables.

2 Choose Insert > Media > Flv. The Insert Flv dialog box will appear. Make sure the video type is set to Progressive Download Video and then, to the right of the URL field, click Browse. The Select FLV window opens, browse to your assets folder and select the ou_veggies.flv file and then press Choose.

Insert FLV		
Video type: [Progressive Download Video ▼]		OK
		Cancel
URL: [ ] [Browse...]		Help
(Enter the relative or absolute path of the FLV file)		
Skin: [Clear Skin 1 (min width: 140) ▼]		
▶ ❚❚ ■ ◀》		
Width: [ ] ☑ Constrain (Detect Size)		
Height: [ ] Total with skin:		
☐ Auto play		
☐ Auto rewind		
ⓘ To see the video, preview the page in browser.		

The Insert Flash Video dialog box.

In this example, Progressive Download Video was chosen instead of Streaming Video because the former is the more common method among web developers. Progressive Download Video works by downloading the video to the user's hard drive, and then playing it. Because it's a progressive download, the video starts to play as it downloads, and the user doesn't have to wait for the entire video to download in order to see it. Streaming Video streams video content and plays it on a web page after a short buffer period. The buffer period ensures smooth playback. The catch is that to enable Streaming Video, your videos must be accessible through a web streaming service such as Adobe Flash Media Server. If you want to learn more about the process, click the Help button on the Insert Flash Video dialog box.

Next, you'll want to select a skin. A skin is a control panel that shows up on the bottom of the video, and allows the user to control video playback. In other words, this is where users can play, rewind, and fast-forward their videos.

3   Click on the Skin drop-down menu to examine your choices. You see a preview of the skin just below the menu. In our case, we used Corona Skin 3.

A number of skins are available in the Skin drop-down menu.

If your video is 10 seconds or longer, choose a skin that includes a slider control so that users can scroll through the video at their convenience.

4   Click on the Detect Size button so that Dreamweaver can establish the physical space the video will occupy on the page. The size is based on the size of the actual video.

You can put in your own size, too, although be sure you are aware of the dangers here. Entering a size that's bigger than the original video will either soften or pixelate your video. Additionally, the width and height of a video is called the aspect ratio and if you enter a width and height that do not match the original aspect ratio your viewers will see distorted video. In general, there's no reason not to let Dreamweaver detect the video size.

5   Press OK to insert the video.

You can't see the video in Dreamweaver, so choose File > Save, then File > Preview in Browser to preview it in a web browser. This particular skin will allow you to scrub through your playback as well as mute and change the volume. Close the browser when you are finished previewing.

The Flash Video and player controls on your page.

QuickTime video and Windows Media

QuickTime and Windows Media are also common video formats used on the Web. In many ways they are similar, both offer compressed video with various levels of image and sound quality. When adding either file format to a page the key thing to keep in mind is that viewers must have the necessary plugin to view the video. Unlike Flash video, this is not necessarily a sure thing. Quicktime is traditionally Mac OS-based and Windows Media Video is traditionally Windows-based.

You can download QuickTime from *Apple.com/quicktime/download*. To view Windows Media files, you need Windows Media Player, which you can download at *Microsoft.com/windows/windowsmedia/download*.

QuickTime and Windows Media video are inserted into a page the same way as Flash Video. The difference between the video formats is that users create QuickTime and Windows Media video using different software applications, for example Adobe Premiere Pro and Apple Final Cut Pro.

The process for inserting either Quicktime or Windows Media Video is the same. In this example you may choose either format depending on your platform.

1   In the Files panel, open the insertvideo.html file. Click below the heading, *A look at our vegetables*, if necessary.

2   Go to the Assets panel and select the Movies button to show the videos available in your site.

3   Right-click (Windows) or Ctrl+click (Mac OS) on the veggies.mov file (or the veggies.wmv if in Windows), and choose Insert from the contextual menu to insert it into the page. You'll see a plug-in icon (▦) on the page, indicating that a plug-in is required to see the file.

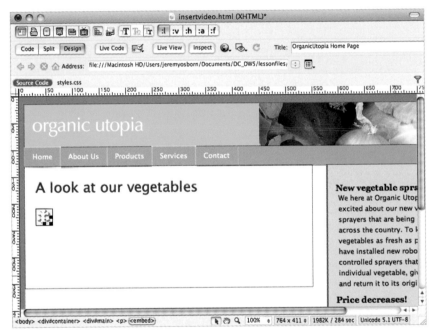

Inserting Quicktime or Windows Media Video files creates a generic plug-in icon.

4   When you insert a plug-in file, you need to manually enter the size of the file and you will also need to add 20 pixels to the height to make room for built-in player controls. The source video here is 320 by 240 so in the Property Inspector, type **320** in the W (width) window and **260** in the H (height) window.

Again, you are using 260 for the height to allow space for the controller. QuickTime and Windows Media files already have a controller built in with the plug-in. You need to allow a little extra space for the video controls when you're entering a size manually.

5 To preview the file, click the Play button in the Property Inspector

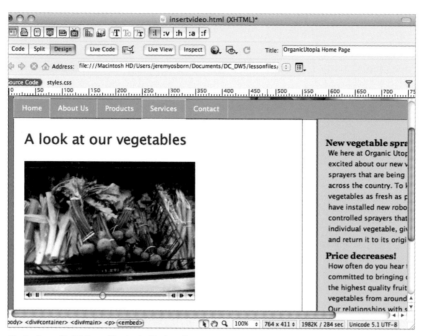

Previewing a Quicktime video in the Design view.

Additionally, you can preview the page in a web browser by pressing the Preview/Debug in Browser button (◉) on the Document toolbar.

If you are having any trouble seeing the video on your page, it may have to do with the lack of a codec on your system. Web video can get a little tricky because there are containers (such as .mov) and there are codecs. The codec does the job of actually compressing the frames of your video and there are hundreds of codecs available. Both Quicktime and Windows Media Player are generally good at identifying which codec you or your users may be missing and then providing links to download and install the necessary codec.

Other web video considerations

In addition to size, consider the following when you're preparing video for the Web:

Length: Unless you'll be offering video through a streaming video service, keep the video length down to keep the file size manageable and the progressive playback smooth.

Audio: Although stereo is nice, using stereo files on the Web is a little iffy, as many home users don't have stereo speakers hooked up to their computers. Stereo creates a larger file size and doesn't add that much to the quality of the sound unless you're doing some tricks with the balance between the speakers, which people without speakers won't hear anyway. Keep your video sound set to mono to help manage the file size a bit more effectively.

Movement, animated graphics, and effects: These things make a video look nice, but increasing the file size can interrupt playback.

Copywritten material: Be careful when choosing material for your video, especially when it comes to music. Pirating is a big issue today. Unless you have the rights to the music or you have permission from the music publisher and are paying royalties, you can't use music for promotional or commercial purposes when it comes to publishing material on the Web.

Inserting sound

Sound is another element you can use to enhance your web site. Sound has the same considerations as video: it can take a while to download and it requires a plug-in, such as QuickTime or Windows Media Player, to hear it.

You can incorporate different types of sound files into a web page. Select a format that will run on any computer, whether the user is on the Windows or Mac OS platform. Three formats are common: .aif, .wav, and .mp3.

Files in the .aif or .wav format are similar; the main difference is where they originate. Windows is generally linked to the .wav format, and Mac OS is associated with the .aif format. The Windows and Mac OS platforms can read both formats. In addition, these files sound similar to one another: both are dynamic and depending on the settings can result in high-quality files.

You can also play .mp3 format files on both the Windows and Mac OS platforms. The big advantage to using an .mp3 file is that it's typically smaller in size than an .aif or .wav file. Depending on the compression settings, the .mp3 format may not reproduce full CD-quality sound, but it downloads faster and takes up less hard drive space. In this exercise, you'll add an mp3 file to your page.

1   In the Files panel, double-click the sound.html file located in the Pages folder. Click in the empty paragraph just below the *What fruit is being eaten in this clip?* paragraph.

2   Choose Insert > Media > Plugin

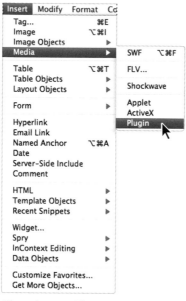

Choose the generic Plugin option to insert sound

3   In the Select File dialog box, go to the Assets folder located in the dw09lessons root folder. Choose the Assets folder and select the crunch.mp3 file.

A plug-in icon ([::]) appears in the table, indicating that a plug-in is required to hear the sound. This plug-in will play in the handler application set for .mp3s in your browser. On the Mac, for example this will be the Quicktime player and in Windows this will be the Windows Media player. Even though there is no visual element to an audio file, by setting the width, you can allow the handler application to display a controller.

4   Click the edge of the plug-in icon and drag it to the right to extend it to approximately 150 pixels wide.

5   Choose File > Save, then preview the page in a browser by pressing the Preview/Debug in Browser button ([○]). The sound plays automatically.

To give users the ability to control the playback of the sound file you will need to change a parameter back in Dreamweaver.

6   Close the browser.

7   With the plugin still selected press the Parameters button in the Property Inspector. This opens the Parameters dialog box.

In the Parameters dialog box, type **autoplay** in the Parameter column and **false** in the Value column. Press OK.

The Parameters dialog box.

8   Choose File> Save, then preview the page in a browser again, and note that you need to press the Play button in the plug-in application in order to hear the sound.

9   Close your browser.

Congratulations! You have finished Lesson 09, "Adding Flash, Video and Sound Content."

Preparing audio for the web

Audio has the same considerations as any other digital file type. You need to pay attention to file size while trying to maintain quality.

Various programs offer audio-editing and format capabilities. This includes programs such as Adobe Soundbooth, Apple Soundtrack Pro, and Audacity (which is available as a free download on the Web).

Once you've edited a sound to your liking, you need to set up certain technical specifications for the final file. This includes the type of file you'll output (.mp3, .aif, and so on), whether the sound is in stereo or mono, and a sample rate. For the Web, a good sample rate is in the 22kHz–32kHz range; 22kHz is at the low end of acceptable quality, and anything higher than 32kHz starts to weigh down the file size.

Stereo is nice, but unnecessary, unless you're moving sound from the left speaker to the right speaker and vice versa. You can save a significant amount of file space by keeping the sound file set to mono.

There are a number of compression choices when it comes to audio. Your best bet is to experiment and see what gives you the results you want. Creating audio files is very much like creating video for the Web: there are no definite answers, and you need to experiment to find the best balance between file size and quality.

Inserting Silverlight content in Dreamweaver

Silverlight is a browser plug-in powered by Microsoft's .NET framework that has support for animation, advanced data integration, web video and interactivity. To insert Silverlight content you need to know the width and height of the content. Additionally, you will need to locate your Silverlight content, which will have the extension .xap, and copy it into your site folder.

1   In a new HTML document, click Insert Div Tag within the Insert panel. In the Insert Div Tag window, click inside the ID text field and type **SL_content**, then press the New CSS Rule button. In the New CSS Rule window, press OK. The CSS Rule definition window appears.

2   Click the Box category and type **640** for width and **480** for height. Press OK, then press OK again to close the Insert Div Tag dialog box. Click on Code view. Select and delete the placeholder text, *Content for id "SL_content" Goes Here.* Keep your cursor between the div tags, you will now paste code here.

3   Choose File > Open and navigate to the sl.html document located in the dw09lessons folder. This file was created using the Silverlight authoring program Expression Blend. In the Code view, locate the <object> tag, then locate this code: <param name="source" value="ClientBin/test.xap"/>. Delete the ClientBin and the forward slash from the code. Select the entire <object> element and press Ctrl+C (Windows) or Command+C (Mac OS) to copy the code for the object.

4   Back in your original HTML document, with your cursor still between the <div> tags, choose Ctrl+V (Windows) or Command+V (Mac OS) to paste the <object> element.

5   Choose File > Save, then Preview in Browser to see your Silverlight content.

Self study

Try inserting and compressing videos using different codecs and file types. You'll find that the results will vary, depending on the file type and codec you choose.

Review

Questions

1   When inserting a Flash animation, what type of file is inserted into the web page?

2   What plug-in is needed to view an .flv file?

3   What is a *skin* when referring to a Flash Video file?

Answers

1   When a Flash animation is inserted into a page in Dreamweaver, an .swf file is used.

2   In order to view an .flv file, a user must have the Flash Player plug-in installed on their computer.

3   A set of controls on the bottom of the video that control video playback.

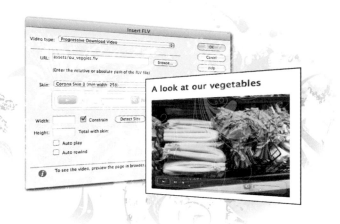

What you'll learn in this lesson:

- Inserting and adding snippets
- Using library items to reuse common items
- Creating and modifying page templates
- Repeating and creating editable regions

Maximizing Site Design

Dreamweaver site definitions allow you to take advantage of extensive management and maintenance tools, including the ability to reuse, repeat, and maintain common items such as menus, logos, code, and even entire page layouts. Dreamweaver's unique snippets, library items, and page templates are indispensable for maintaining a consistent appearance and making sitewide updates a snap.

Starting up

Before starting, make sure that your tools and panels are consistent by resetting your workspace. See "Resetting the Dreamweaver workspace" on page 3.

You will work with several files from the dw10lessons folder in this lesson. Make sure that you have loaded the dwlessons folder onto your hard drive from the supplied DVD. See "Loading lesson files" on page 3.

Before you begin, you need to create a site definition that points to the dw10lessons folder from the included DVD that contains resources you need for these lessons. Go to Site > New Site, or, for details on creating a site definition, refer to Lesson 2, "Setting Up a New Site."

See Lesson 10 in action!

Use the accompanying video to gain a better understanding of how to use some of the features shown in this lesson. The video tutorial for this lesson can be found on the included DVD.

Creating modular page elements

You may have heard the term *modular* before; whether referring to a prebuilt house that you can cart away and place on your property, or a well-built, scalable web site, modular refers to anything you can break down into standardized, reusable components.

Most web sites contain common elements such as headers, footers, and menus that appear consistently across each page. The ability to convert these elements into reusable items is essential for maintaining a consistent look and feel across your pages. Add the ability to make components manageable from a single place and to make sitewide updates, and editing becomes a breeze.

Dreamweaver provides three modular features: snippets, library items, and templates. Each feature offers a different level of reusability, from simple code tidbits to entire pages, complete with navigation, content, and styling.

Introducing snippets

As you build pages and web sites, you'll find yourself creating many similar items several times over. Whether you're creating a two-column layout table or a contact form, snippets make it possible to add any piece of code to a common library, where you can reuse it by simply dragging and dropping it into the page. You can store virtually any item on a page as a snippet.

Dreamweaver comes with an extensive library of common navigation bars, form elements, tables, and even JavaScripts that are available at any time from the Snippets panel. Snippets are stored as part of the Dreamweaver application, and they are not specific to any Dreamweaver site. You can add your own snippets directly within Dreamweaver, and they will be available for you to use at any time on any site.

The Snippets panel is like a super clipboard, and using a snippet is similar to copying and pasting an element onto your page. Changes to a snippet in the Snippets panel do not update snippets you've already used in your pages. For this reason, snippets are a great way to store and place any common page elements that you don't need to manage globally.

The Snippets panel

The Snippets panel displays all available Dreamweaver snippets, broken down by category. You can add and edit snippets and categories directly from the Snippets panel. Using a snippet from the Snippets panel is as simple as locating it and dragging it from the panel to the page.

Dreamweaver provides many ready-to-use snippets that serve as great starting points for forms, lists, and navigation bars (to name a few); many of these require little more than text changes and some basic styling. In the following lesson, you will use some of these snippets to quickly build existing pages for the product display component of the Organic Utopia site.

1   Double-click the home.html file in the Files panel to open it. Choose Window > Snippets to launch the Snippets panel (you can also click on the Snippets tab). In the category list, locate the Text folder and click on the arrow to the left to expand it. You'll use the service mark snippet to add a service mark to this page.

The Snippets panel contains many categories of pre-built snippets for your use.

2   Click to the right of the heading, *welcome to organic utopia*. Inside the Text folder, double-click the service mark snippet, and a superscripted *sm* appears in the heading.

3   At the top of the Snippets panel is a preview of the code that was inserted. In the Snippets panel, click on the panel menu (⋅≡) in the upper-right corner and choose Edit. The Snippets dialog box appears with a name, a description, the snippet type, and then the actual code. This snippet is using the *<sup>*, or superscript, HTML element.

The Snippet dialog box.

4   Press Cancel, as you won't be making any changes at this time.

5   Choose File > Save All.

Creating new snippets

Whenever you have something on a page that you'd like to reuse, creating a new snippet is a good option. You can create new snippets directly from the Snippets panel, and from any selected element(s) on a page.

In this section, you'll convert a pre-existing table to a snippet.

1   Choose File > Open, and choose the gardentips.html page. This page has a pre-styled table. Converting this table to a snippet will allow you to place it anywhere you like.

2   Click anywhere inside the table, and then choose Modify > Table > Select Table. You could also click on the edge of the table to select it.

3   At the bottom of the Snippets panel, click on the New Snippet icon (⊕). The Snippet dialog box opens, and all the code within the table is automatically copied into the *Insert before* window.

4   In the Name field, type **Vege_table**. In the Description field, type **A three column styled table listing the latin and family names of common vegetables**. For the Snippet type, select the *Insert Block* option. For Preview type, select the *Design* option and press OK.

Choosing the *Insert Block* option ensures that the table is inserted as a standalone element. Setting the Preview type to *Design* allows you to see a preview of the table in the Snippets panel, rather than the code.

Setting options in the Snippet dialog box.

In the Snippets panel, you see the new snippet listed. By default, it is located in the last folder you used (Text). Before you do anything else, you'll organize your Snippets panel.

5   In the bottom of the Snippets panel, click on the New Snippet Folder icon (📁). A new folder appears; rename this folder **OU Snippets**, then press Enter (Windows) or Return (Mac OS). Click on the Vege_table snippet and drag it on top of this new folder.

Snippets are actually external files with the extension .csn and are stored deep within your operating system. If someone else has used your current computer to do this lesson, you may see this snippet already present. You may remove it by clicking on the snippet and then clicking the Remove icon (🗑) at the bottom of the Snippets panel.

6   Click once on the *Vege_table* snippet, if necessary. In the top half of the panel, there is a design preview of the table. It is most likely cropped. Depending on how much space you have, it may not be possible to view the entire table; however, you can expand this window by clicking on the dividing line of the panel, and dragging up or down.

Click and drag the dividing line in the Snippets panel to expand or contract the view.

7   Choose File > Open, and choose the latin_names.html file. Click once below the Heading, Latin and Family Names For Common Vegetables. In the Snippets panel, double-click the *Vege_table* snippet, and it is inserted into the new page.

In many ways, a snippet is just a faster way to copy and paste. However, there are a few things to be aware of. Snippets only copy the HTML code and none of the associated CSS. If you look at the preview of the table snippet in the Snippets panel, you will see that it is unstyled. However, when you inserted it into the latin_names page, it appeared styled. This is because the Snippets panel only previews the raw HTML in the design view. The CSS rules for the table are being saved in an external stylesheet and all the pages in this site are already linked to this stylesheet. If you inserted this table into a blank page, it would appear unstyled until you attached the style sheet to the page.

8   In the Snippets panel, click on the panel menu (•≡) in the upper-right corner and choose Edit. The Snippet dialog box appears. In the first line, change the table width value to 350 and press OK. This has no effect on the current table because there is no link between the code in the Snippets panel and the code on your page. However, all future tables will use the new value.

Changing the table width when editing a snippet.

9   Choose File > Save All. Keep this document open for the next exercise.

The Snippets panel lets you modify a snippet only through its HTML code. Here's a shortcut: if you make a change in the Design view, you can recreate the snippet by selecting it and then choosing New Snippet from the Snippets panel. If you select the folder containing the original snippet and save it under the same name, you will be prompted to replace it.

Introducing library items

While snippets are useful, they are perhaps most useful for items that will never change, like a person's name or a logo. However, a more powerful concept is an item that you can add to multiple pages and have linked to an original master item. This is where Dreamweaver library items come in.

With Dreamweaver library items, you can save any common element and manage it from a master copy in your site folder. When you place a library item on a page, the item remains attached to its master; any changes you make to the master automatically update any instances of the item placed throughout your site. Dreamweaver makes sure that any instances of a library item are synchronized.

Library items (unlike snippets) are specific to each Dreamweaver site, and they are stored as separate .lbi files in your site's Library folder.

1   Library items are located in the Assets panel. Choose Window > Assets, if it isn't already open, and then click the Library icon (📖) at the very bottom.

The Library Items category of the Assets panel.

You can add, edit, and manage all library items in your site directly from this panel. You will now convert the Global Navigation menu in your header to a library item.

2   Click on the home.html tab in the top of the document window to open it. Click on the border of the GlobalNav *<div>* element in the upper-right corner to select it. (This is the small box that contains the "Site Map | Login" text)

3   In the Assets panel, click the New Library Item button (✦). You will see a dialog box appear, warning you that this style sheet information will not be copied with this item. Press OK. The selected menu is added as a new library item; name it **GlobalNav**. If you're prompted to update links, choose Update. This ensures that any hyperlinks or references to image files are preserved. The GlobalNav div is now linked to the new library item you created. Note that library items on a page appear highlighted in yellow. Now you're ready to add this library item to other pages.

The GlobalNav <div> element is highlighted yellow because it is now a library item.

4   Click on the gardentips.html tab at the top of your document window (or open it if it is closed). Locate the GlobalNav library item in the Assets panel, and drag it onto the header of the page. An instance of the GlobalNav *<div>* element is placed.

5   Click on the latin_names.html tab (or open it if it is closed) from the Files panel. As you did in step 4, drag a copy of the GlobalNav library item from the Assets panel to the header section. Just as before, an instance of the GlobalNav *<div>* element is placed.

The GlobalNav is now set in the exact location across three pages of your site. You will now modify your library item and all three pages will change.

Modifying and updating library items

The convenience and power of library items are apparent when you need to update a common item across several pages. Because all instances of a library item remain attached to a master copy, when the master item is edited from the library item list, every instance mirrors these changes.

You can edit library items from the Assets panel or by choosing the Open button from the Property Inspector when a library item instance is selected on the page.

1   From the Library Items list in the Assets panel, double-click the GlobalNav library item to open it for editing. A new tab opens because the library item is actually a new file: global_nav.lbi.

The GlobalNav library item opens as a separate document and has no style associated with it.

It's important to realize that there is no style information associated with this file, as Dreamweaver warned you when you created the item. However, this is actually a good thing; it simply takes getting used to the idea that you are modifying the HTML content—all the style information resides in the style sheet.

2   Where it currently reads *Login*, select the text, then type **Your Account**. You will now link the text within the GlobalNav menu to the appropriate HTML pages. Select the text *Your Account*, then in the Property Inspector, click on the HTML button, if necessary, and then click on the Browse for File folder icon. In the Select File window, choose login.html. Press OK (Windows) or Choose (Mac OS).

3   Select the Site Map text. In the Property Inspector, click on the HTML tab if necessary, and click on the Browse for File icon (⊟) to the right of the link field. In the Select File dialog box, choose sitemap.html, then press OK (Windows) or Choose (Mac OS).

4   Choose File > Save. The Update Library Items dialog box appears with a list of the three files. Whenever you modify a library item and save it, a list of all files using the item appears, and you are given the choice to update or not.

When saving library items, any pages affected will appear in the Update Library Items dialog box.

5   Click Update. The files update and the Update Pages dialog box appears.

6   Click on the *Show Log* option in the Update Pages dialog box. A list of the files that were updated appears; this is where you can check to see if there were any problems and how many files were updated. Press Close.

7   Open home.html, gardentips.html, and latin_names.html, and you see that all instances of the menu have been updated in all three pages. Library items are tremendously powerful; the larger the site, the more useful they become. They are tremendously useful with hyperlinked navigation, where they can help prevent broken hyperlinks.

For example, currently you have three documents all using a library item that is linked to the login.html and sitemap.html pages. But what happens if you move those two pages into a new folder? You will do this now so you can see how Dreamweaver keeps track of the move and prompts you to update the links.

8   Click on the Files tab, if necessary, to view the list of files in your site. Click on the root folder at the top of the panel (Site – dw10lessons), and then right-click (Windows) or Ctrl+click (Mac OS) to open a context menu. Choose New Folder. Rename the new folder **GlobalNav** and press Enter (Windows) or Return (Mac OS).

Right-clicking on the root folder allows you to create a new folder.

9   In the Files panel, click and drag the login.html file into this new GlobalNav folder. As soon as you do, the Update Files dialog box appears with the list of all the files that need to be updated. This is a huge time-saver if you need to restructure your site; traditionally, you would have to go to each page and relink everything that pointed to this page. Now click Update, and the links on each page are all updated behind the scenes.

10 Click and drag the sitemap.html file to the GlobalNav folder; press Update, and all the files are updated.

11 Choose File > Save All, update your pages if prompted, and then close all your open files.

Occasionally you may need to detach a library item from its master. In order to do this, you must select the library item and then click Detach from the Property Inspector. Just be aware that once a library item is detached, any future changes must be made manually. Also, it is sometimes easier to select a library item in the Code view rather than in the Design view.

Introducing templates

If you are creating several pages that need to share the same look and layout, Dreamweaver templates are for you. A Dreamweaver template is a master document from which other pages can be created; these pages inherit all the elements from the original template, but you can modify each page to include unique content and elements. As with library items, when you edit a template, all pages based on that template update to reflect your changes.

When you create a template, you specify editable regions, or areas of the page that you can modify. By default, all elements of a page created from a template are locked for editing; you can make changes only from the original master template. You can set sections of a page as editable so that you can add or modify content without accidentally (or intentionally) disturbing the original layout.

Templates are also a great mechanism for controlling access to pages on a site. If you need to provide editing ability to others, you can lock out important page elements and give users access to only certain sections of the page.

Templates are site-specific and are stored in a Templates folder under your site's root folder. You open, edit, or create templates from the Templates list in the Assets panel.

Dreamweaver templates work with Contribute, a basic but powerful web content management tool. You can design and manage templates that can be modified and published by Contribute users.

Creating a new template

For the Organic Utopia site, you need to duplicate category and product detail pages for a number of product types and items. To do this, you'll set up templates for each page so that new pages can be easily created but will remain visually consistent with the master layout.

1   In the Files panel (Window > Files), locate and double-click the product_detail.html page to open it for editing. This page has generic text and a placeholder image that will serve as your template.

2   Click on your Assets panel, and then click on the library item. As you did with the other pages, click and drag the GlobalNav item onto the header. This page will shortly serve as a template, and by including a library item, you are maximizing automation.

3   Save the product_detail.html page as a template by choosing File > Save As Template. The Save As Template dialog box appears.

Naming a new template.

4   Choose Save to save the template. If prompted, allow Dreamweaver to update any links by choosing Yes from the dialog box.

Working with editable regions

Next, you will need to define editable regions that you can modify on any pages created from this template. When new HTML pages are generated from templates, there may be certain sections you would like to be editable and other areas that should remain uneditable.

1   Select the placeholder text in the product_detail template that reads *Product Category*. Choose Insert > Template Objects > Editable Region. The New Editable Region dialog box appears.

2   Name the new editable region **ProductCategory** and press OK. The placeholder text now appears inside a blue box with a tab at the top. This portion of the page and the content within it will now be editable in any pages created from this template.

3   Select the placeholder text in the product_detail template that reads *Product Name*. Choose Insert > Template Objects > Editable Region. The New Editable Region dialog box appears. Name this **ProductName** and press OK.

4   Select the image placeholder, then choose Insert > Template Objects > Editable Region. The New Editable Region window appears. Name this **ProductImage** and press OK.

```
                New Editable Region

    Name:  [ProductImage]              (    OK    )

    This region will be editable in documents
    based on this template.            (   Cancel   )

                                       (    Help    )
```

Naming the Editable Region of the image placeholder.

5   Finally, select the paragraph in the sidebar. Choose Insert > Template Objects > Editable Region. The New Editable Region dialog box appears. Name this **ProductDescription** and press OK.

6   Choose File > Save to save the template. You may see a warning about putting the editable region within a block tag; press OK.

At this point, you can create any number of pages and manage them from this template. The editable regions you created will allow you to add content to any new pages based on this template, but will protect the main layout and page elements from unintended changes.

Creating new pages from templates

Now you're ready to create different product pages that will be based on the new template you have built. You'll create two pages, enough to give you a sense of how templates work.

1   Click on the Assets panel, then click on the templates icon and select the product_detail template. In the upper-right corner, press the Assets panel menu and choose New from Template. This opens a new, untitled document based on the template. Choose File > Save. When prompted, navigate to the Products folder in the dw10lessons folder. Name this file **eggplants.html** and press OK (Windows) or Save (Mac OS).

Don't see that new library item or template you just added? Sometimes the Assets panel needs a little help catching up. If you're sure you added a library item or template, but you don't see it listed, click the Refresh button (C) at the bottom of the Assets panel. This updates the list.

2   Click inside the header of your page and notice that you are unable to select or move anything. This section is uneditable. Notice, in the upper-right corner, the yellow highlighted box that reads Template:product_detail. In a similar fashion to library items, this yellow highlight indicates that the page is based on a template.

3   Select the text inside the ProductCategory editable area and type **Vegetables**. Select the text in the ProductName area and type **Eggplants**. Select the Product_image placeholder, and in the Property Inspector, press the Browse for File button (⌐) to the right of the Src text field.

Click on the Folder icon to locate the eggplant image.

Navigate through your dw10lessons folder and locate the images folder. Select the eggplant.jpg image and press OK (Windows) or Choose (Mac OS).

4   Double-click on the products folder in the Files panel to open it, and then double-click on the eggplants.txt file to open it in Dreamweaver. Select all the text, choose Edit > Copy, and then close the text file.

5   Select the text in the Product Description area of the sidebar, then choose Edit > Paste. Choose File > Save.

Another way to use templates is by using the File > New command.

6   Choose File > New. In the New Document dialog box, click on the *Page from Template* option. The first column lists all the sites you have defined; this option should be the dw10lessons site. In the second column, the product_detail template should be selected. Press Create, and the new page is created.

Choose File > New, and then click the Page *from* Template *option.*

7   Choose File > Save, and save this file as **beets.html**. Select the text inside the ProductCategory editable area and type **Vegetables**. Select the text in the ProductName area and type **Beets**. Select the Product_image placeholder, and in the Property Inspector, press the Browse for File button (⬚) to the right of the Src text field.

Navigate through your dw10lessons folder and locate the images folder. Select the beets.jpg image and press OK (Windows) or Choose (Mac OS).

8   In the Files panel, double-click on the products folder to open it, if it is not already open, and double-click on the beets.txt file to open it in Dreamweaver. Select all the text, choose Edit > Copy, and then close the text file.

9   Select the text in the Product Description area of the sidebar, and choose Edit > Paste. Choose File > Save.

Modifying templates

In a similar fashion to library items, when you make changes to the original template, all linked pages are updated.

1   In the Templates list in the Assets panel, double-click the product_detail template to open it for editing.

2   Place your cursor after the image placeholder, and press Enter (Windows) or Return (Mac OS) twice; then type **This vegetable is in season**.

ProductImage

Product_image (250 x 250)

This vegetable is in season|

Insert text after the placeholder image.

3   If you were to save right now, your text would be updated on your two linked pages; however, you need to convert it to an editable item unless you want the text to be locked on those pages.

4   Select the text and choose Insert > Template Objects > Editable Region. Name this region **inseason** and press OK. Choose File > Save. (If you see the Editable Region warning, press OK.) The Update Files dialog box appears; any files linked to this template will now be changed. Press Update, then close the Update Pages dialog box.

5   Click on the beets.html file; notice that it has automatically been updated. In the inseason editable region, update the text to read **This vegetable not in season**.

6   Choose File > Save All, and then close all your open documents.

Repeating regions

A single region may not be the best way to display the content you add to a template-based page. You may require a template that can handle a number of items, such as a table that displays products in a category. If you need to build a flexible template that can hold any number of uniform items, you can add a repeating region to it.

Repeating regions allow you to define an element on a template as repeatable; when you create a page based on that template, you can increase, or repeat, the number of regions to accommodate the information. You'll also be able to reorder these repeated regions at any time without having to move the content. You can set elements such as a table row, paragraph, or small display table as a repeating region, and then duplicate as many as you need to fit the content at hand.

A repeating region is not automatically editable. You need to set editable regions inside any repeating element in order to add to or edit its content.

In the following steps, you'll add a repeating region to your category.html page and convert it to a template so that you can use it to display any number of products in a specific category.

1   Open the category.html page from the Files panel.

2   The table in the center contains one row with two columns, each containing a placeholder image and product title placeholder.. Click on the edge of the table to select it.

3   Choose Insert > Template Objects > Repeating Region. Because you haven't saved this page as a template yet, a dialog box appears, letting you know that you need to convert the page to a template before you add regions. Press OK.

4 When the Repeating Region dialog box appears, assign the new region the name **Products**, and press OK.

The row is now a repeating region, which you can duplicate in any page created from this template.

5 Choose File > Save As Template, and save the new template as **category_display**. Press Save and Update Links if asked.

6 In the left cell, highlight the Product text. Choose Insert > Template Objects > Editable Region. Name the new region **Product Name**, and press OK.

7 Select the placeholder image below the new editable region, and choose Insert > Template Objects > Editable Region. Name the new region **Product Image**, and press OK.

8 In the right cell, highlight the Product text. Choose Insert > Template Objects > Editable Region. Name the new region **Product Name2**, and press OK.

9 Select the placeholder image below the new editable region, and choose Insert > Template Objects > Editable Region. Name the new region **Product Image2**, and press OK.

10 Choose File > Save to save this template.

Templates can't contain duplicate region names. If you try to set two editable regions with the same name, Dreamweaver gives you an error message.

Putting repeating regions into action

You're now ready to create a page from the new category_display template and see how repeating regions work.

1   Open the Assets panel if necessary, then select the category_display template, and choose New from Template from the Assets panel menu.

2   Save the new document as **category_chocolate.html** in your site's root folder. Notice the new repeating region in the middle of the page—its tab features four buttons that allow you to add, remove, and shift repeating regions up or down in the stacking order.

Use the button set at the top of the repeating region to add a new row with two more product display tables.

3   Click the plus sign button (+) on the top of the repeating region; a new table row with two more product display tables appears. Press the plus sign button two more times to see how it will automatically add new rows. Press the minus sign button to remove a row. In the next step, you'll fill in the first four products with information to complete your page.

4   In the first row, type **Belgian Chocolate** in the Product Name text field and **French Chocolate** in the Product Name2 text field. In the second row, type **German Chocolate** in the Product Name text field and **Swiss Chocolate** in the Product Name 2 text field.

The four products now appear in the category page, and as an added benefit, if you wanted to reorder the rows you could do so using the repeating region toolbar.

5   Click on the up arrow in the repeating region toolbar to push the second row to the top. This feature is especially useful for repeating regions with many rows.

6   Choose File > Save All.

Congratulations! You have finished this lesson.

Detach from Template command

If you want to modify a template-based page beyond what the editable regions allow, you can use the Modify > Templates > Detach from Template command, which breaks the current page away from the master template, allowing you to edit it freely. Keep in mind that a page detached from a template will no longer be updated if you make any changes to the original template.

Self study

Create a new template based off of home.html and then create new pages based off the template for the following pages: about_us.html, products.html, services.html and contact.html. Then return to the template and create links to these pages from the navigation bar. Which sections need to be editable and which do not?

Open one of the product detail pages you created, and use Detach from Template to break it away from the product_display template. You'll then be able to freely edit other elements on the page that you did not include in the original editable regions. Create some variations on the newly detached page by trying a new layout, modifying product and picture positioning, or applying a new style to the product title, price, or description. Use the Templates section of the Assets panel to create a new template from the page.

Review

Questions

1 What are two key differences between snippets and library items?

2 How do you add a new snippet to Dreamweaver?

3 Where are library items and page templates stored? Which panel do you use to manage them?

4 What happens to pages based on a template when you modify the original template?

5 True or false: Repeating regions are automatically editable in pages that use them.

Answers

1 Snippets are stored as part of the Dreamweaver application, and are available, regardless of which site or document you're working on; library items are specific to a site definition. Copies of a snippet never update when the original snippet is edited; a library item updates all instances of itself throughout a local site when a change is applied to it.

2 You can drag a snippet from the Snippets panel onto the page, or position your cursor in the page and double-click the snippet in the Snippets panel.

3 Library items and page templates are stored in the Library and Templates folders (respectively) under your local site. You can manage both, using their specific categories on the Assets panel.

4 Dreamweaver updates all pages based on that template to reflect any changes made to the original template.

5 False: You must first set editable regions within a repeating region to add content.

Lesson 11

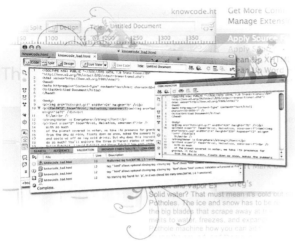

What you'll learn in this lesson:

- Using the Code and Design views
- Taking advantage of the Coding toolbar
- Validating your code
- Formatting your code

Working with Code-editing Features

Dreamweaver provides exceptional code-editing support to complement its powerful visual layout tools and application development features. You can adapt the coding environment so that it fits the way you work. Learn how to change the way you view code, reformat your markup, or use your favorite tag library.

Starting up

Before starting, make sure that your tools and panels are consistent by resetting your workspace. See "Resetting the Dreamweaver workspace" on page 3.

You will work with several files from the dw11lessons folder in this lesson. Make sure that you have loaded the dwlessons folder onto your hard drive from the supplied DVD. See "Loading lesson files" on page 3.

Before you begin, you need to create site settings that point to the dw11lessons folder from the included DVD that contains resources you need for these lessons. Go to Site > New Site, or, for details on creating a site, refer to Lesson 2, "Setting Up a New Site."

See Lesson 11 in action!

Use the accompanying video to gain a better understanding of how to use some of the features shown in this lesson. The video tutorial for this lesson can be found on the included DVD.

Working with code

Although Dreamweaver's traditional audience has been for those who prefer to work in the Design view and not with code, there are many good reasons to dive into the code editing view. In this lesson, you will look at some of the unique functions available in the code view by taking a look at an older web page.

Accessing code with the Quick Tag editor

In this exercise, you will use a feature called the Quick Tag editor. This feature is generally for users who are more familiar with their code. The Quick Tag editor offers an easy way to add CSS class or ID names as well as attributes to your code without having to leave the Design view. The Quick Tag editor works in conjunction with the tag selector. In this exercise, you'll apply a CSS class to the image to float it to the right.

1   Open the oldcode.html file, and click on the image of the beets. In the bottom-left of the document window is the tag selector which now has the *<img>* tag selected.

2   Right-click (Windows) or Ctrl+click (Mac OS) the *<img>* tag in the tag selector. A contextual menu appears with all of the code for the selected image. Choose Quick Tag Editor from the menu. The Quick Tag Editor appears, displaying the code for this tag.

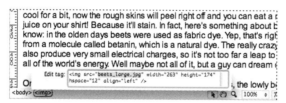

Viewing the attributes and properties of a tag in the Quick Tag Editor.

Instead of switching to the Code view to make changes to this code, you can make changes within the editor.

3   Click once after the align="left" code and press the space bar. A menu is triggered allowing you to choose from a list of possible choices. Double-click the class option and the code will be written for you and the only option floatright is listed, press the Return (or Enter) key to apply this class. Your image now has the class applied and is floating to the right.

You can also use the Quick Tag Editor to remove unnecessary code. For example, this page uses the older *<font>* tag to style text.

4   Click anywhere inside the main paragraph of your document. In the tag selector, click on the *<font>* tag and then right+click (Windows) or Ctrl-click (Mac OS) and from the context menu choose the Remove Tag option.

Quickly remove a tag by right clicking it in the tag selector.

This removes both the opening and closing font tags and the text now reverts to its default unstyled appearance.

Inserting tags with the Tag Chooser

You can use the Tag Chooser to insert any tag into your page with the Dreamweaver tag libraries—these include the Macromedia ColdFusion, ASP.NET, PHP tag libraries among others.

1   Switch to Code view by choosing View > Code or by pressing the Code View button on the Document toolbar.

2   Click in line 5 immediately before the *<style>* tag and press return. Now click back in the empty line 5. You will now add the title tag, which this document does not have.

3   Right-click (Windows) or Ctrl+click (Mac OS) and select Insert Tag. The Tag Chooser appears. The left pane contains a list of supported tag libraries, and the right pane shows the individual tags in the selected library.

4 Expand the *HTML tags* library if necessary and then click on the Page Composition subcategory and click on the *<title></title>* tag. Click on the Tag info button to expand this window. This info gives you a brief synopsis of the function of the tag and is a great way to learn more about HTML tags.

Quickly remove a tag by right clicking it in the tag selector.

5 Click the Insert button to add the tag to your code, then press the Close button. Your cursor is inside the *<title>* tags so type **The Lowly Beet**.

Now let's look at some other features of Dreamweaver CS5 that allow you to work with HTML code.

Inserting and editing comments

Comments are descriptive text that you insert in HTML code to explain the code or provide other information. By default, the text of the comment appears only in the Code view and is not displayed in a browser. You can also modify existing comments. In this exercise, you'll add your own comment to the HTML code, and edit a comment already in the code.

1 Go back into Design view by clicking on the Design view button in the Document toolbar. Click in front of the first character in the first paragraph and choose Insert > Comment.

2 Dreamweaver displays the Comment dialog box. Type **We need to add two or three links to other websites in the text below** and then press OK.

> **Comment**
>
> Comment:
> We need to add two or three links to other websites in the text below.
>
> OK
> Cancel
> Help

Type the comment into the Comment dialog box.

3 A box appears, warning that you will not be able to see comment markers in the Design view unless you select View > Visual Aids > Invisible Elements. Press OK. You will now enable the preference to view Invisible Elements.

4 Choose Edit > Preferences (Windows) or Dreamweaver > Preferences (Mac OS) and click on the Invisible Elements category. Check the box for Comments, and press OK. You now see a small icon with an exclamation point (!)—this is the visual representation of your comment. Click on the icon and the Properties panel will display the comments.

Comments are good way to communicate to members of a team who may be working on the same file. These comments are also visible in the code view.

5 Switch back to the Code view by choosing View > Code or by pressing the Code View button on the Document toolbar.

In the line that corresponds to the location of your comment, Dreamweaver has inserted a comment tag (in gray, by default) that looks like this:

Comments inserted into your code can be seen in both Design and Code view.

To delete a comment, simply select it in Design view and press delete.

6   Choose File > Save to save your work.

Working in the Code view

As you've seen, the Code view is a hand-coding environment for writing and editing HTML, JavaScript, and scripting languages such as PHP and ColdFusion, among others. You can modify your workspace to suit the way you prefer to work with code.

View options

You can set word wrapping, display line numbers for the code, highlight invalid code, set syntax coloring for code elements, set indenting, and show hidden characters from the View > Code View Options menu. The Code View options not available when you are in the Design view, only when in Code or Split view.

- **Word Wrap** wraps the code so that you can view it without scrolling horizontally. This option doesn't insert line breaks; it just makes the code easier to view.

- **Line Numbers** displays line numbers along the side of the code.

- **Hidden Characters** displays special characters in place of white space. For example, a dot replaces each space, a double chevron replaces each tab, and a paragraph marker replaces each line break.

- **Highlight Invalid Code** causes Dreamweaver to highlight in yellow all HTML code that isn't valid. When you select an invalid tag, the Property Inspector displays information on how to correct the error.

- **Syntax Coloring** enables or disables code coloring.

- **Auto Indent** makes your code indent automatically when you press Enter or Return while writing code. The new line of code indents to the same level as the previous line.

- **Syntax Error Alerts** in Info Bar conveniently displays mistakes in your code.

Modifying the Code View Workspace

You can view the source code for Dreamweaver documents in several ways. You can display it in the document window by switching to the Code view, you can split the document window to display both the visual page and its related code in Split view, or you can work in the Code Inspector, a separate coding window. The Code Inspector works like a detachable version of the Code view for the current page.

1   Choose View > Code and Design, to view the code and visually edit the page in the document window at the same time. By default the Code view is split with the Code on the left and Design View on the right.

2   From the view menu choose Design View on Left to swap the views.

Choose Design View on Left to switch the location of the Code and Design views.

The default split view in Dreamweaver CS5 is different than in CS4, if you prefer the CS4 split view(horizontal) you can toggle the Split Vertically option in the View menu.

5   Drag the splitter bar, located between the two panes to the right to adjust the size of the panes in the document window, in this case expanding the Code View.

6   Choose Window > Code Inspector. Working in the Code Inspector is just like working in the Code view, except that it is in a separate window. This might be useful, depending on how you choose to manage your workspace (for example, users who have two monitors could put this window in a separate window).

You can also view your HTML code in the Code Inspector window.

Press the Close button to close the Code Inspector for now.

7 Choose View > Code. You will now look at some of the coding features available in the coding toolbar in Dreamweaver.

The Coding toolbar

The Coding toolbar contains buttons that let you perform many standard coding operations, such as collapsing and expanding code selections, highlighting invalid code, applying and removing comments, indenting code, and inserting recently used code snippets. The Coding toolbar is visible only in the Code view and appears vertically on the left side of the document window. To see what each button does, position the cursor over it until a tooltip appears.

ICON	TOOL NAME	USE
	Open Documents	Lists the documents that are open. When you select a document, it is displayed in the document window.
	Show Code Navigator	Displays a list of code sources related to a particular selection on your page. Use it to navigate to related code sources, such as internal and external CSS rules, server-side includes, external JavaScript files, parent template files, library files, and iframe source files. You can access the Code Navigator from Design, Code, and Split views, as well as from the Code Inspector.
	Collapse Full Tag	Collapses the content between a set of opening and closing tags (for example, the content between *<body>* and *</body>*). You must place the insertion point in the opening or closing tag and then click to collapse it.
	Collapse Selection	Collapses the selected code.
	Expand All	Restores all collapsed code.
	Select Parent Tag	Selects the content and surrounding opening and closing tags of the line in which you've placed the insertion point. If you repeatedly click this button, and your tags are balanced, Dreamweaver will eventually select the outermost *<html>* and *</html>* tags.
	Balance Braces	Selects the content and surrounding parentheses, braces, or square brackets of the line in which you've placed the insertion point. If you repeatedly click this button, and your surrounding symbols are balanced, Dreamweaver will eventually select the outermost braces, parentheses, or brackets in the document.

ICON	TOOL NAME	USE
#	Line Numbers	Hides or shows numbers at the beginning of each line of code.
	Highlight Invalid Code	Highlights invalid code in yellow.
	Syntax Error Alerts in Info Bar	Enables or disables an information bar at the top of the page that alerts you to syntax errors. When Dreamweaver detects a syntax error, the Syntax Error Information bar specifies the line in the code where the error occurs. Additionally, Dreamweaver highlights the error's line number on the left side of the document in Code view. The info bar is enabled by default, but only appears when Dreamweaver detects syntax errors in the page.
	Apply Comment	Wraps comment tags around selected code, or opens new comment tags.
	Remove Comment	Removes comment tags from the selected code. If a selection includes nested comments, only the outer comment tags are removed.
	Wrap Tag	Wraps selected code with the selected tag from the Quick Tag Editor.
	Recent Snippets	Inserts a recently used code snippet from the Snippets panel.
	Move or Convert CSS	Lets you move CSS to another location, or convert inline CSS to CSS rules.
	Indent Code	Shifts the selection to the right.
	Outdent Code	Shifts the selection to the left.
	Format Source Code	Applies previously specified code formats to selected code or to the entire page if no code is selected. You can also quickly set code formatting preferences by selecting Code Formatting Settings from the Format Source Code button, or edit tag libraries by selecting Edit Tag Libraries.

The number of buttons available in the Coding toolbar varies depending on the size of the Code view in the document window. To see all the available buttons, resize the Code view window or click the Show More arrow at the bottom of the Coding toolbar.

Collapsing and expanding tags and code blocks

Dreamweaver lets you collapse and expand code fragments so that you can hide and show various sections of your code. This can help reduce the amount of screen space that is taken up and also prevent mistakes since code that is collapsed cannot be edited. When you select code, Dreamweaver adds a set of collapse buttons next to the selection (minus symbols in Windows; vertical triangles in Mac OS). You can collapse code only in the Code view.

1 Make sure you are in the Code view by pressing the Code View button on the Document toolbar. Scroll to the top of the screen if necessary and click anywhere between lines 6 and 14, which is the *<style>*, tag that contains all your CSS.

2 Click the Collapse Full Tag button in the coding toolbar. You could also choose Edit > Code Collapse > Collapse Full Tag. The *<style>* tag is now collapsed.

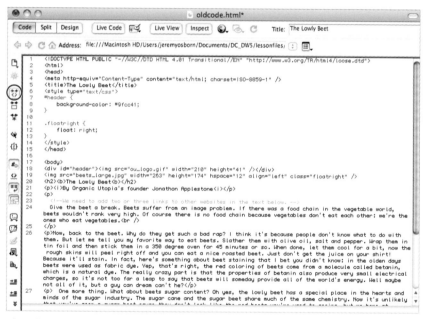

The Collapse Full Tag button collapses the relevant tag.

At any point, you could click on the plus sign (Windows) or arrow (Mac OS) or to the left to expand the code again.

3 In the Coding toolbar click on the Select Parent Tag button. This will select the code that is nesting your existing selection. In this case, the parent is the <head> tag, which is now selected.

The Select Parent Tag button is a great way to replace selecting code by hand. Selecting by hand can often introduce mistakes, the Select Parent Tag will always be more reliable and faster.

4 In the Coding toolbar click on the Collapse Selection button to collapse the *<head>* tag and all its content. You could have also chosen Edit > Code Collapse > Collapse Selection.

5 Click anywhere within your document and note that you could begin to work in your HTML and the *<head>* tag will always remain collapsed until you need to access it.

6 Place your cursor over the collapsed *<head>* section without clicking it and a box will appear, showing you the contents of the collapsed tag.

Double-clicking collapsed code will expand it.

Double-click the collapsed <head> tag to expand it.

To expand all code at once, you can also choose Edit > Code Collapse > Expand All. All your code fragments are now restored to their original view.

Validating your code

In addition to the many options available for formatting your code, you can also use Dreamweaver to find out if your code has tag or syntax errors. Dreamweaver can validate documents in many languages, including HTML, XHTML, PHP, ColdFusion Markup Language (CFML), Java Server Pages (JSP), Wireless Markup Language (WML), and XML. You can validate the current document or a selected tag.

Highlighting and correcting invalid code

You can set Dreamweaver to highlight invalid code (in yellow) in the Code view. When you select a highlighted section, the Property Inspector offers information on how to correct the error. Invalid code is not highlighted by default in Code view. In order to view the invalid code, you must enable this option in the View menu.

1   Select View > Code View Options and turn on the Highlight Invalid Code option by selecting it from the menu.

2   Two tags become highlighted in yellow the <b> and the <i> tags.

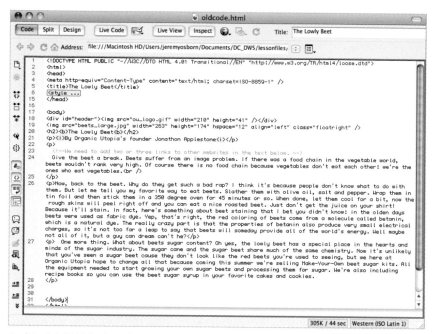

Invalid code is highlighted in yellow in both the Design and Code views.

3   Click once on the highlighted (invalid) code. In the Property Inspector, a this has been identified as invalid markup due to the fact that there is overlapping or an unclosed tag. (In this case, the author used two opening tags and no closing tags)

The Property Inspector identifies the invalid code and suggests how to correct it.

4   Correct the error by simply removing the offending bad markup. Individually select all four tags and delete them. Now you could style them correctly either in the Design view or the Code view.

Running a Report

Site reports allow you to scan your code using a set of criteria. Code which doesn't fit the criteria is identified, allowing you to fix it. In this exercise, you'll run all the reports for HTML.

1   Choose File > Save. Then choose Site > Reports and in the site Report window that appears, check all 5 boxes for HTML reports. Be sure that the Report on menu is set to Current Document. You can also run reports sitewide, for certain files only or an entire folder.

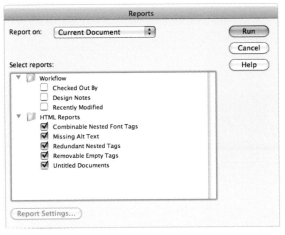

Check the HTML Reports you would like to run.

2   Press Run and the results of the Report appear in a new Site Reports panel below the Properties panel. In this case, there are two warnings that the alt attribute is missing from your images. The alt attribute improves accessibility for images on your page for devices such as screenreaders, and while not technically required, it's a good idea to add them.

3   In the Site Reports panel, double-click the first warning. You will be sent directly to the code and the image will be selected. In the Properties panel, locate the Alt text field and type **Logo** and then press Enter (Windows) or Return (Mac OS) to commit the change.

Clicking on a warning in the Site Reports panel sends you to this code.

4 Repeat this step and double-click on the second warning. This will select your other image. Type **Beets** in the Alt text field, then press Enter or Return to commit the change.

5 Choose File > Save to save your file.

Formatting code

Once you've validated your code, you can further change its look by specifying formatting preferences such as indentation, line length, and the case of tag and attribute names.

1 Select Edit > Preferences (Windows) or Dreamweaver > Preferences (Mac OS).

2 When the Preferences dialog box appears, select Code Format from the Category list on the left. The Code Format preferences appear on the right.

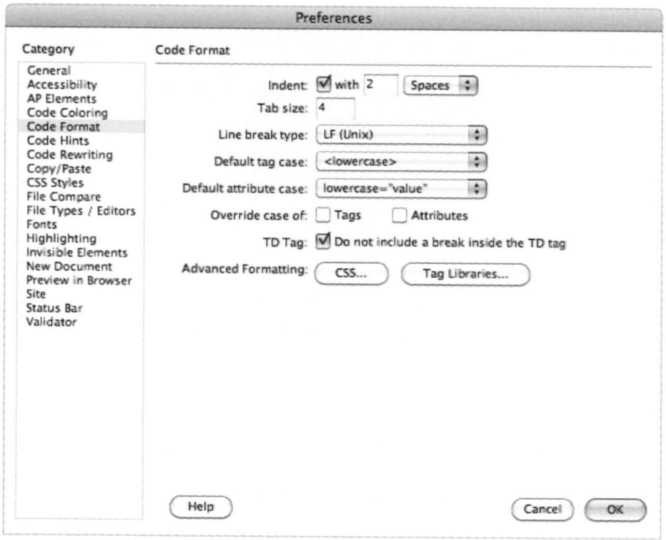

Choose from the Code Format preferences to further change the look of your code.

3 The Code Format preferences allow you to change the way code is written in Dreamweaver. For example, when you press the Tab key, your cursor indents four spaces. Using this preference window, you could increase or decrease the amount of the indent. Press Cancel; you will not be changing any preferences at this point.

If you want to control the way Dreamweaver writes CSS code you may do this by clicking the Advanced Formatting CSS button in the Code Format preferences.

Apply Source Formatting

If you make changes in the Code Format preferences, those options are automatically applied only to new files created in Dreamweaver. To apply new formatting preferences to an existing file, you would need to then select Commands > Apply Source Formatting.

Indenting

Dreamweaver also offers indentation options for you as you write and edit code in the Code view or the Code Inspector. You can change the indentation level of a selected block or line of code, shifting it to the right or left by one tab.

1   In the Code view, click in front of the div element for the header and press the Tab key twice. Alternatively, you can select Edit > Indent Code.

2   To outdent the selected block of code, press Shift+Tab, or you can select Edit > Outdent Code.

 You can also select multiple elements and Indent and Outdent them.

3   Choose File > Save to save your work, then close the file by choosing File > Close.

Congratulations! You've finished Lesson 11, "Working with Code-editing Features."

Self study

Choose File > Save As and make a copy of the oldcode.html page. In the design view experiment with the Quick Tag Editor and try some of the following: Convert a the H2 tag of The Lowly Beet heading to an H3 tag. Use the Quick Tag editor to open the *<img>* tag for the beets and remove the align attribute as it is no longer needed.

In Code View make sure you understand the tools covered in the chapter by clicking on elements and collapsing them. Try clicking within a paragraph and clicking the Select Parent Tag button. Click it again to see what happens. Before you click a third time can you predict what will be selected?

Try formatting the readibility of your code by indenting the nested elements in the file. Selecting multiple elements at once and then pressing the indent (or outdent) buttons will allow you to shift entire blocks of code to the left or right.

Review

Questions

1 What is the purpose of working in the Code view in Dreamweaver?

2 When are the code formatting options that you specify in Code Format preferences applied?

3 What advantages are there in using the tag selector to select, edit, and remove HTML code?

4 How do you know where invalid code exists in your document and how to fix it?

Answers

1 The Code view is a hand-coding environment for writing and editing HTML, JavaScript, server-language code such as PHP and ColdFusion, and any other kind of code.

2 The code formatting options that you specify in Code Format preferences are automatically applied only to new documents that you subsequently create with Dreamweaver. However, you can apply new formatting preferences to existing documents using the Apply Source Formatting command.

3 You can use the tag selector to select, edit, and remove tags without exiting the Design view. The tag selector, situated in the status bar at the bottom of the document window, displays a series of tags that correspond to elements on your page.

4 With the Highlight Invalid Code option selected, Dreamweaver highlights invalid code in yellow in both the Design and Code views. When you select a highlighted section, the Property Inspector offers information on how to correct the error.

What you'll learn in this lesson:

- Creating forms
- Working with the <form> tag
- Adding form elements
- Styling forms with CSS
- Choosing processing options
- Validating forms

Building Web Forms

HTML forms allow you to gather information from visitors to your web site. In this lesson, you'll learn how to add form elements such as text boxes and radio buttons to make your site more interactive.

Starting up

Before starting, make sure that your tools and panels are consistent by resetting your workspace. See "Resetting the Dreamweaver workspace" on page 3.

You will work with several files from the dw12lessons folder in this lesson. Make sure that you have loaded the dwlessons folder onto your hard drive from the supplied DVD. See "Loading lesson files" on page 3.

Before you begin, you need to create a site definition that points to the dw12lessons folder from the included DVD that contains resources you need for these lessons. Go to Site > New Site, or, for details on creating a site definition, refer to Lesson 2, "Setting Up a New Site."

See Lesson 12 in action!

Use the accompanying video to gain a better understanding of how to use some of the features shown in this lesson. The video tutorial for this lesson can be found on the included DVD.

Forms in everyday (web) life

HTML forms are commonly used for questionnaires, hotel reservations, order forms, data entry, and a variety of other applications. Users provide information by entering text, selecting menu items, and so on, and then submit that information to you through a server.

Here's an example of a simple form that includes labels, radio buttons, and push buttons (used to reset the form or submit it):

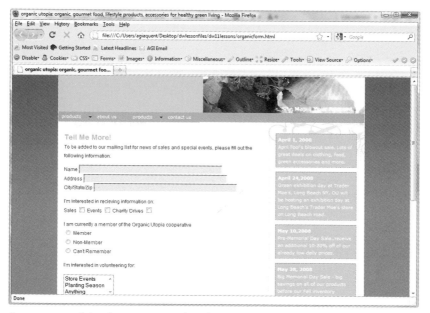

Forms are a great choice when you want to gather information from your audience.

How forms work

An HTML form is a section of a document containing normal content, markup, special elements called controls (checkboxes, radio buttons, and menus, for example), and labels on those controls. The form is completed when a user modifies its controls (by entering text and selecting menu items), and submits the form to an agent for processing.

You can add these controls, commonly called fields, to a page in Dreamweaver, but when the users click the Submit button, their browser won't know what to do with the information they've entered.

Building a contact form

In this lesson, you'll build a contact form for OrganicUtopia. This form allows users to be added to a mailing list for news of sales and special events, and it provides you with relevant data, such as name, email, and which information they would like to receive.

Inserting the *<form>* tag

The first step in building a form in Dreamweaver is to add a form element, which serves as a container for the form fields you'll be adding to it. In hand-coded HTML, you do this by inserting the *<form>* tag into your code. In the Design view, you can add a form element using the Form button.

1   Choose File > Open. When the Open dialog box appears, navigate to the dw12lessons folder. Select the formbase.html file and press Open.

2   Place an insertion cursor where you want your form to appear. Because this is an existing page, click with your mouse in the white area immediately to the left of the word *Name*.

Insert your cursor before the Name text field label.

3   In the Insert panel, choose the Forms category from the drop-down menu to display options for adding form elements to a page.

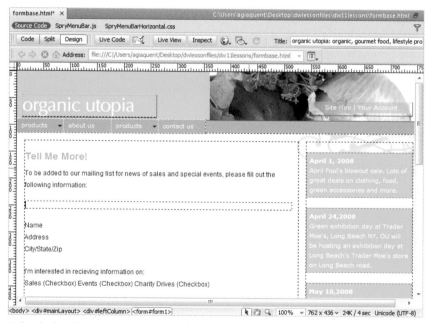

Options for adding form elements to a page are found in the Forms category of the Insert panel.

4   From the Forms category of the Insert panel, select the Form element (▢).

5   You should now see a red outline on your page. This is how a form is displayed in the Design view. If you don't see this outline, choose View > Visual Aids > Invisible Elements to turn on the form element's visibility.

A dotted red outline on your page indicates a placed form element.

Now you'll take a look at the code generated by the steps you just completed in the Design view.

6   In the Document toolbar just above your document window, click on the Code View button to switch to your page's HTML code view.

7 In line 214 of your code, you should see the newly added *<form>* tag. If not, go back to the Design view and click on the form element. When you return to the Code view, it is highlighted in the HTML code for the page.

In HTML code, a form element is added using the <form> *tag.*

Next, you'll move the element labels (Name, Address, and so on) from their current locations on the page to the inside of the form element you just created. This will identify them as fields within the contact form.

8 In the Document toolbar just above your document window, click on the Design View button to switch to your page's visual layout view.

9 Click and drag to select all the text below your form element.

10 Choose Edit > Cut to copy the text to your clipboard and remove it from its current location on the page.

11 Click inside the red outline that represents your form element to place an insertion cursor there.

12 Choose Edit > Paste to place the text from the clipboard into your form element.

All the text for your element labels is now located inside the form element.

Cut and paste existing content from your page into the form element.

Setting form properties

When you were in Code view, you may have noticed that the *<form>* tag includes four different attributes, or descriptors. These attributes are listed as *id*, *name*, *method*, and *action*, and they represent the HTML form element's properties. Rather than type the values for these attributes into the code, you'll switch back to the Design view and add them using the Property Inspector.

1 If necessary, click on the Design View button in the Document toolbar to return to the visual representation of your page.

2 Make sure the form element you added in the previous exercise is selected by clicking on the edge of its red outline. A form field element must be selected before you modify its properties.

3   In the Property Inspector at the bottom of your document window, notice the fields for each form property inside the *<form>* tag.

The fields in the Property Inspector reflect properties found inside the <form> tag in HTML code.

The name in the Form ID text field makes it possible to identify and control the form with a script, as well as to style the form with CSS. It is also very important for form validation, which is discussed later in this lesson.

A form ID is the same ID attribute you have been using to style divs. This form, for example, would have the ID #form1, which is not a descriptive name.

4   In the Form ID text field, type the name **Contact**. Press Enter (Windows) or Return (Mac OS).

The Action field allows you to specify the program, often a Common Gateway Interface (CGI) script, that processes the user's form data. You can type in the path to this program, or use the Browse button to navigate to the desired file. In most cases, you'll need to get this information from your system Administrator or hosting provider.

5   Because you have not yet defined the processing method for this form, leave the Action text field blank.

The Method menu

The Method drop-down menu is where you choose the method used to transmit the data to a server. The Method drop-down menu includes the following choices:

Default uses the browser's default setting to submit the form data to a server. Most browsers use the GET method by default.

GET includes the form data as part of the URL of the request to the server. GET has a length limitation of 8,192 characters in the URL and is less commonly used to send long forms than the POST method.

POST is similar to GET, but it embeds the form data in the header of the server request instead of in the URL. Although the POST method is the most commonly used, be aware that pages sent by this method cannot be bookmarked and are not encrypted for security purposes.

6   Choose the POST method for this exercise.

7   Choose application/x-www-form-urlencoded from the Enctype drop-down menu. The Enctype field defines the encoding type of the data being submitted to a server. Application/x-www-form-urlencoded is used in most situations, unless you're asking the user to upload a file, in which case you would choose multipart/form-data.

The optional Target property specifies the window or frame in which to display the data that is returned. The target value is included in the <form> tag only when you choose to specify it. For more information on target values, see Lesson 15, "Using Legacy Tools: Frames and Tables."

Form properties are set in the Property Inspector.

8   Switch to Code view to see how Dreamweaver creates HTML code for the properties you just defined.

Setting form properties in Design view saves you the effort of writing all this HTML code.

9   Return to Design view to continue with this lesson.

Now that you've defined the properties of the form, you'll use options in the Insert panel's Forms section to add elements to the form.

Adding form elements

A Dreamweaver form is not a form until you add the elements, or fields, that allow the user to provide information to you. Thankfully, the Forms category in the Insert panel contains everything you need to insert any kind of form field into your page.

The Forms category in the Insert panel contains everything you need to add interactive fields to your form.

Common form elements

Of the many form elements you can add using the Insert toolbar, these are the most commonly used ones:

Text fields accept alphanumeric text entries, in single- or multiple-line formats, or in a password (bulleted) format.

Checkboxes allow users to make as many choices as they want from a list of options.

Radio buttons allow only mutually exclusive choices, in that selecting one radio button deselects all others in the group.

List menus permit the selection of single or multiple items from a scrolling list, whereas Jump menus allow you to set each option from a scrolling list to link to a document or file.

Buttons perform actions when clicked. You can assign the default Submit or Reset action to buttons, or define other processing tasks in a script.

A good way to understand all the options available in Dreamweaver for adding elements to a form is to add them to the form you created earlier.

Adding text fields

The simplest and most common type of form field is the text field. Users can enter anything, from their name, to their credit card number, to their dog's name, into a text field. You control the formatting of their responses using the Property Inspector.

1   Click inside the red outline of your form to specify where you want your first text field to appear. For this exercise, it will appear to the right of the word Name.

2   Press the Text Field button (▯) in the Insert panel. The Input Tag Accessibility Attributes dialog box opens, allowing you to set attributes to make your form field more accessible for users as well as whoever is recieving the data after submission.

Make your form more accessible by changing your settings here.

3   In the Image Tag Accessibility Attributes dialog box, specify the following:

   • In the ID section, type **Mailing_list_name**.

   • In the Style section, choose No label tag. The label element in a form provides additonal usabilty for the user. You will take a look at how to use the label tag shortly.

4   Press OK. A new text field appears within the form outline on your page.

The settings you entered define the look of the Name text field as it's added to your form.

5   If it's not already selected, select the text field by clicking on it, and notice the options that become available in the Property Inspector.

6   Type **55** in the Char Width text field to set the text input area to a width of 55 characters.

7   Type **30** in the Max Chars text field to set the maximum number of characters that can be entered. For example, if this were a telephone number field, you probably would have limited it to ten characters.

8   Choose Single Line from the Type options. Choosing Password would cause the user's entry to appear as black dots, even though the correct value would be submitted to the server. The Multi-line option is discussed later, in the "*Adding a text area*" section.

9   Repeat steps 1 to 9 to add Address and City/State/Zip text fields beneath the Name field. When creating the Address text field, give it the ID **Mailing_list_address** and give the last text field the ID **Mailing_list_city_state_zip**. When naming form elements, you should stay away from using spaces between words, use underscores or hyphens instead.

10 Choose File > Save As. In the Save As dialog box, navigate to the dw12lessons folder and type **organicform.html** into the Name text field. Press Save.

Now preview the open page in a browser by pressing the Preview/Debug in Browser button (●) on the Document toolbar. Your form should look like this:

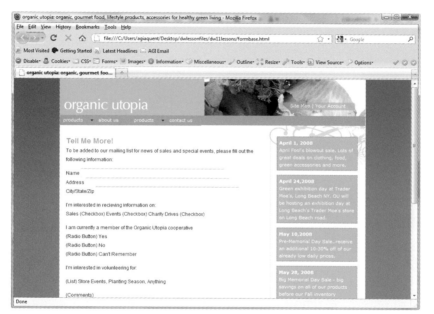

This is what your form should look like with text fields added.

11 Close the browser and return to Dreamweaver.

Adding checkboxes

You'll probably want to have several checkboxes in your forms. They're valuable when you want to get specific responses from your users and you don't want to give them the opportunity to enter incorrect information into text fields. Again, you control the formatting of their responses using the Property Inspector. In this exercise, you will take a look at the use of form labels as well as the importance of setting the names of your form elements.

1   Click and drag both the word Sales and the (Checkbox) placeholder text. Press Delete to remove it from your form and place an insertion cursor.

2   Click on the Checkbox element (☑) in the Insert panel. The Input Tag Accessibility Attributes dialog box opens.

3   In the Input Tag Accessibility Attributes dialog box, type **Sales** for ID, then type **Sales** for the Label. Choose the Wrap with label tag and make sure that Before form item is selected for Position. The label tag is an optional element that adds an extra level of usability to your checkboxes. Users will be now be able to click on the text (in addition to the checkbox) in order to make their selection. The Before and After form item options allow you to change the position of the checkbox.

4   Press OK. A new checkbox appears within the form outline on your page.

5   If it's not already selected, click to select the checkbox, and notice the options that become available in the Property Inspector.

Settings that are specific to the checkbox you've just added to your form appear in the Property Inspector.

6   In the Checkbox name text field on the left side of the Property Inspector, type **Recieve_Info** and press Enter (Windows) or Return (Mac OS). It is important to understand what you are changing here. The *name* of the checkbox is different from the *ID* of a checkbox. An ID is used to style an element, the name is what gets passed when the user presses submit. The problem is that Dreamweaver automatically sets the name based on what you enter for ID back in the Input Tag dialog box, however this is not always a good choice. In the case of checkboxes, you want all the checkboxes to have the same name. To do this you will need to override Dreamweaver's default naming to make this field accessible for scripting and validation.

7   Type **Sales** in the Checked value text field to define the data that's passed to the server when the user checks this checkbox.

8   Choose *Unchecked* in the Initial State section. This setting defines how the checkbox appears when the page is first loaded.

9   Select the word Events and the placeholder (Checkbox) text and delete them. Click on the Checkbox element in the Insert panel. In the Input Tag box, type **Events** and for Label, type **Events**. Additionally, be sure that Before form item is selected for Position and click OK.

10   Click on the checkbox and change the checkbox name to **Recieve_Info**. Because this name is the same as the first checkbox, users will be able to check both and have the values passed. In the Checked Value text field, type **Events** and press Enter or Return.

11   Repeat steps 9 and 10 with different values for the ID and Label to add a third checkbox for Charity Drives. Again, be sure to rename the checkbox, **Recieve_Info**.

Now, preview the open page in a browser. Your form should look like this:

Your form, with checkboxes inserted, should look like this.

12   With the page open in the browser, click on the text for the checkboxes and notice that this selects the box. This is a function of the label tag. Try clicking on the text of your Name and Address text fields. They do not have the same behavior because they do not have labels.

Labels improve accessibility for all users, in particular for those who may be using screenreaders or other devices.

Adding radio buttons

When you add radio buttons to your form, you encounter the same settings in the Property Inspector as you do when you add checkboxes. The only difference between checkboxes and radio buttons is that from a group of radio buttons, only a single option can be selected. Checkboxes allow the selection of multiple options.

To make two or more individual radio buttons mutually exclusive, you select two or more radio buttons and give them the same name in the Property Inspector.

Creating a group of radio buttons by adding buttons one by one is often more time-consuming than it's worth. Thankfully, Dreamweaver offers a more efficient method for creating a list of mutually exclusive options: the radio group.

Adding radio groups

The Radio Group element (▣) in the Insert toolbar provides a quick and easy way to add a list of radio buttons to your form. The same rules regarding naming and values apply, but the Radio Group dialog box allows you to include several entries in a group at once.

1   Click and drag to select the three (Radio Button) placeholders and their labels (Yes, No, and Can't Remember). Press Delete to remove them from your form and place an insertion cursor. You'll create your own labels for this group.

2   Click on the Radio Group button in the Insert panel. The Radio Group dialog box opens, and offers several property options.

Set properties for your radio group in the Radio Group dialog box.

3   In the Name text field of the Radio Group dialog box, type **Membership Status** to give the group a name that associates all the radio buttons together.

    You will now create a unique label for each button.

4   Click on the first entry in this column and type **Member**.

5   In the Value column of the Radio buttons section, you assign a value to each button to be passed back to the server. Click on the first entry in this column and type **Member**. This returns a value of Member when the user clicks on the Member radio button.

6   Select the Line breaks radio button in the Lay out using: section to specify how you want Dreamweaver to express the radio group in the HTML markup. Because radio buttons are usually aligned vertically, this choice is selected by default.

7   Repeat steps 4 to 6 to add *Non-Member* and *Can't Remember* radio buttons. Click the Plus (+) button when you want to add a new radio button to the group.

8   Press OK. Choose File > Save, then preview the open page in a browser. Click on the three radio buttons and note that only one radio button can ever be selected. This is a function of a radio button group: for cases where you want more than one option to be selected and returned, you could use a checkbox.

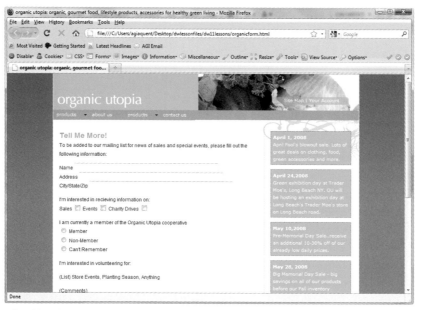

After adding the radio group, your form should look like this.

Adding lists and menus

Lists and menus show choices within a list that permits users to choose single or multiple options. The *List* option displays as a scrolling list, and the *Menu* option displays as a drop-down menu. As is the case with most form fields, you set the properties for lists and menus in the Property Inspector.

1   Click and drag to select the placeholder text—(List) Store Events, Planting Season, Anything—that follows your radio group. Press Delete to remove it from your form and place an insertion cursor. You'll create your own labels for this list.

2 Press Select (List/Menu) button (▣) in the Insert panel. The Input Tag Accessibility Attributes dialog box opens.

3 Type **Volunteer** in the ID text field and leave the additional settings as is and press OK. A new list or menu appears within the form outline on your page.

4 If it's not already selected, click to select the list or menu, and notice the options that are now available in the Property Inspector.

Enter the settings for your newly added list or menu in the Property Inspector.

5 The Type options let you define whether the field is displayed as a scrolling list or a drop-down menu. Click on the *List* radio button to choose this option. Notice that more settings become available on the right side of the Property Inspector.

6 Type **3** in the Height text field to set the number of items to be visible at any given time in the scrolling list.

7 Click in the checkbox to the right of the *Selections* option to allow multiple selections. With this feature activated, users can choose more than one option from your list at a time.

8 Click on the List Values button to enter items for your scrolling list. The structure of the List Values dialog box is identical to that of the Radio Group dialog box. Type **Store Events** as your first Item Label, and **Events** for the first value to be returned.

Now you will add two more items to the list.

9 Click the Plus button (+) in the left corner of the List Values window, and type **Planting Season** as the second Item Label. Then click under the Events value and type **Planting**. Click the Plus button (+) again. Type **Anything** as the third Item Label, and, finally, click under the Planting value and type **Any**. Press OK.

Now the user can choose which activity they want to volunteer for.

10 Choose File > Save to save your work.

Adding a text area

Sometimes within a Dreamweaver form, you want to have a field that simply provides an open area into which users can enter text. For this form, you'll add a Textarea element to provide a region for users to type in their comments about the site.

1   Click and drag to select the placeholder text, (Comments), and retype it without the parentheses, to use as a label for this field.

2   Press Enter (Windows) or Return (Mac OS) to move your cursor to the next line.

3   Click on the Textarea element (▣) in the Insert panel. The Input Tag Accessibility Attributes dialog box opens.

4   In the ID text field, type **Comments**. In the Style section, select Wrap in label tag.

5   Press OK. A new text area appears within the form outline on your page.

6   Click the text area, and notice the options that are now available in the Property Inspector.

7   Type **40** in the Char width text field to set the text input area to a width of 40 characters.

8   Leave the Num lines text field set to 5, and leave Type set to Multi line.

9   Leave the Init Val and Class settings at their defaults and choose File > Save; then preview the open page in a browser. The text area will allow users to type inside, if the amount of text goes below the bottom of the text area, a scrollbar will automatically appear.

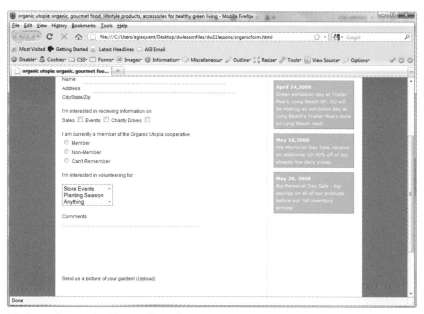

The form so far, as rendered by Mozilla Firefox.

Adding a File Upload field

If you want users to be able to upload a file to your server—for example, a photo for ID purposes—you'll want to add a File Upload field.

1   Click and drag to select the placeholder text in the next line (Upload), and delete it to place an insertion cursor next to your label.

2   Click on the File Field button (🖻) in the Insert panel. The Input Tag Accessibility Attributes dialog box opens.

3   In the Input Tag Accessibility Attributes dialog box, type **filefield** for the ID. Additionally, make sure the Wrap with label tag field is selected.

4   Press OK. A new file field, with the Browse button included, appears within the form outline on your page.

5   If it's not already selected, click to select the file field, and notice the options that become available in the Property Inspector.

6   Type **30** in the Char width text field to set the text input area to a width of 30 characters.

7   Type **30** in the Max chars text field to set the maximum number of filename characters that can be entered.

PROPERTIES				
	FileField name	Char width 30	Class None ▾	
	fileField	Max chars 30		

Set the properties for your File Upload field in the Property Inspector.

8   The Class drop-down menu allows you to apply CSS to style this form field. Using CSS to style form fields is discussed in more detail later in this lesson.

You are now finished with the file field section of your form. Users can now either enter the desired filename or click Browse to navigate to it.

For the file field element to actually upload a user's file to your server, you'll need to ask your server Administrator how the server is configured to accept files.

10 Choose File > Save, then preview the open page in a browser. Your form should look like this:

You're almost finished adding form fields to your form.

11 Close the browser and return to Dreamweaver.

Creating Submit and Reset buttons

As you might expect, none of the field elements you've been adding to your form do any good if the user doesn't have a way to send the information to you. Buttons provide the means for the user to either submit form data, or reset the fields and start over.

1 Place your cursor after the Upload field, then press Enter (Windows) or Return (Mac OS) to specify where you want your button(s) to appear.

2 Click on the Button element (⊟) in the Forms category of the Insert panel. The Input Tag Accessibility Attributes dialog box opens.

3 In the dialog box, specify the following:

• In the ID section, type **Submit**.

• In the Style section, choose No label tag.

4 Press OK. A new button, labeled *Submit* by default, appears within the form outline on your page.

5   If it's not already selected, click to select the button, and notice the options that are now available in the Property Inspector.

Button properties are set in the Property Inspector.

6   The word *Submit* is displayed in the Value field as well. You could change this value to a more user-friendly name if you wanted such as Send, however for now you'll leave it as is.

7   The three options in the Action section specify the action carried out when the user clicks this button. Select the Submit form radio button in the Actions section. Submit and Reset form are self-explanatory, but the None option builds a generic button that you can set to trigger a JavaScript behavior, which is discussed later in this lesson.

8   The Class drop-down menu allows you to apply CSS to style this form field—another technique that is covered later in the lesson.

9   Repeat steps 1 to 9 to add Reset and Validate buttons next to the Submit button. Choose Reset from the Action section in the Property Inspector for the Reset button, and None for the Validate button. Additionally, you will need to type Validate in the Value field to change the default value. Preview the open page in a browser. Your form should look like this:

The Submit, Reset, and Validate button are now placed in the form.

Now that you've finished adding the necessary form fields to your Contact Form page, you'll add style to the form and its elements, using CSS.

Styling forms with CSS

In Lesson 4, "Styling Your Pages with CSS," you explored the many ways you can use CSS to format text and position content on an HTML page in Dreamweaver. The usefulness of CSS is not limited to static page content, however. Dynamic content, such as form fields, can also be successfully and creatively styled using CSS.

The CSS Styles panel.

Attaching external styles

Because you're already familiar with the available CSS options, you will now focus on applying them to the form elements that you've added in this lesson. The styles you apply have been created for you, but you must attach them to your form page in order to access them.

1   If your CSS Styles panel is not currently open, open it now by choosing Window > CSS Styles.

2   In the CSS Styles panel, click on the Attach Style Sheet button (●) in the lower-right corner of the panel. The Attach External Style Sheet dialog box opens.

Select the CSS file you want to attach using The Attach External Style Sheet dialog box.

3   Next to the File/URL field, click the Browse button and select formstyles.css from the dw12lessons folder. Press OK (Windows) or Choose (Mac OS) to exit the Select Style Sheet File dialog box.

4   In the Attach External Style Sheet dialog box, click the Link radio button to create a link *<href>* tag in the code for this page, and reference the location of the published style sheet. Most major web browsers support the link method.

5   In the Media drop-down menu, you can define the target medium for your style sheet. For this exercise, leave this setting at its default.

For more information on media-dependent style sheets, see the World Wide Web Consortium (W3C) web site at W3.org/TR/CSS21/media.html.

6   Press OK to attach the style sheet to this document.

Setting a background color

Once the formstyles CSS is attached, the backgrounds of your form fields change to a light blue color. This happens because formstyles.css contains a tag selector rule, which instructs the *<form>* tag you added earlier in the lesson to include a background color. The rule redefines the *<form>* tag, so the color is applied only to the background of the form fields themselves, and not to the entire body of the page.

The formstyles CSS contains a rule that specifies a background color.

A major benefit of using CSS is that once you complete the initial styling, you can revisit the CSS file and change the included style rules. Because the blue background doesn't fit in with the color scheme of your site, you'll edit the form rule to change the background to a light gray.

1 If it's not already visible, open the CSS Styles panel by choosing Window > CSS Styles.

2 Click on the All button to show all styles attached to this document (as opposed to those applied to a Current selection). Locate formstyles.css in the list of All Rules, and expand it by clicking on the Plus button (+) (Windows) or triangle button (▸) (Mac OS) to its left.

3 From the list of style rules included within formstyles.css, click on the input rule to select it for editing.

CSS can be redefined on-the-fly.

4 Click on the Edit Rule button at the bottom of the CSS Styles panel. The CSS Rule Definition dialog box opens.

5 Select the Background category to the left, and, in the Background color text field to the right, type the hexadecimal code **#d7d7d7**, to replace the current color.

6 To preview the change to the background color, press Apply. Press OK.

You've successfully changed the background color of your form fields by editing an attached CSS.

You've just used a tag selector CSS rule to change the background color of your form. Next, you'll use a class style to change the appearance of the labels on your form fields.

Styling form elements

You probably noticed another CSS rule included in formstyles.css along with the *<form>* definition. It's a class style called *.labels*, and it contains properties that change the font, color, and weight of your form field labels.

The .labels rule can also be edited in the CSS Styles panel.

1   In the CSS Styles panel, click on the *.labels* CSS rule to select it, then click on the Edit Rule button to open its CSS Rule Definition dialog box. You'll just be looking at the properties for this CSS class, not making any changes.

2   Select Type from the Category list on the left, and notice that the following properties have been defined for this rule:

- The Font-family has been changed to Arial, Helvetica, sans-serif.
- The Font-weight is set to bolder.
- The Color has been set to a hexadecimal notation of #9FCC41, or green.

Change the type style of your form field labels in the CSS Rule Definition dialog box.

3   Press Cancel to close the window. You'll now apply this style.

Applying the .label style

The .labels class style will change the font, color, and weight of your form field labels, but you'll have to apply this style to the appropriate text first.

1   In the document window, place your cursor in the Name label, which precedes the first text field in your form. Click to place an insertion cursor there.

2   In the Property Inspector, click on the CSS button if necessary and then click on the Targeted Rule drop-down menu to see a list of available class styles.

3 Choose labels from the Apply Class section to apply the class style.

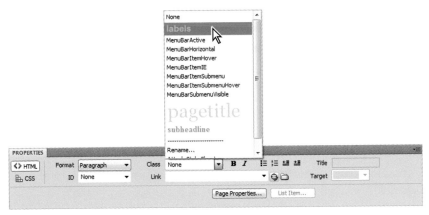

Class styles are applied manually using the Property Inspector.

4 Use the .label style to apply this formatting to the checkboxes, radio buttons, and list. Then save the file and preview it in your browser.

Applying the .label style to all the labels in the form.

These are just a few of the ways you can use CSS to style form elements. Experiment further with different properties to make your form more visually pleasing.

Form processing and validation

As attractive as CSS styling can make your form in Dreamweaver, you can't collect form data without using a server-side script or application (for example, CGI, PHP, ASP) to process the data.

CGI scripts are the most popular form of server-side scripting mechanism used to process form data. Several web sites offer free CGI scripts that you can use. The hosting company for your web site may also provide CGI scripts that perform many common tasks, such as collecting e-mail addresses or allowing visitors to send you comments through a web form.

It's also worth noting that form validation, a method for ensuring that the user has entered the correct type of data in the form's fields, also requires scripting to work correctly. Thankfully, Dreamweaver is capable of adding JavaScript code that checks the contents of specified text fields. This code is added through the use of the Validate Form behavior.

Adding form validation

The Validate Form behavior provides checks and balances for users when they complete forms on your site. You can make certain fields required, make sure a user has entered a value in a required field, or make sure a user has entered the correct type of information in a field. You can run validation on all fields in a form, or on individual fields contained in that form.

The first step, however, is to get to know the Behaviors panel.

A look at the Behaviors panel

Generally speaking, the Behaviors panel provides a means for you to add JavaScript code to your page without actually having to type in the code. The code it inserts adds interactivity to your site, and is usually triggered by some user action. For example, when the user clicks on or hovers over a link, the behavior performs a task. Behaviors are hardly limited to use with forms, as they're commonly used to add rollovers, open new windows, check for plug-ins, and add navigation elements, among other functions.

Specifically, you use the Behaviors panel to add, modify, and remove behaviors. Because you can apply multiple behaviors to the same object, you can also reorder them in the Behaviors panel.

To set behaviors:

1   Access the Behaviors panel by choosing Window > Behaviors. It docks with the Tag Inspector panel on the right side of your screen. If necessary, expand the panel grouping and click on the Behaviors tab to bring it to the front.

The Behaviors panel.

2   In the document window, select the Validate button you created earlier.

3   Click the Plus button (+) at the top of the Behaviors panel to see the list of available objects for the selected object. In this case, the menu displays options associated with a button element. If an option is grayed out, that action is not available for the selected object.

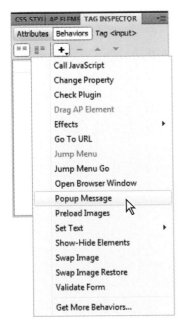

The behaviors displayed are only those associated with a button element.

4   Select the Popup Message action. The Popup Message dialog box appears.

5   Type **Validate this form!** into the Message text field, and press OK.

Popup Message	❌
Message:	Validate this form!

OK
Cancel
Help

Enter text into the Popup Message dialog box to have it appear on the screen.

The behavior is set, but it needs an event, or trigger.

Setting an event or trigger

The popup message needs an event or trigger to know when to appear. In this case, you'll set it to appear when the user clicks on the Validate button.

1   In the top-left corner of the Behaviors panel, click on the Show All Events button (▦).
    The Show All Events button provides a complete (and very long) list of all possible triggers for this behavior.

There are a number of choices for the event that triggers your specific behavior.

2   In this case, the default option "onClick" is the correct choice, but you should know how to change these events for your own projects.

3   Click the onClick event on the left, to access the list of possible events. Choosing an option in this menu would assign the Popup Message event to another trigger. However, you won't be doing that now, make sure that onClick is still selected.

The button behavior you've applied is now ready for previewing.

Previewing the button behavior

Whenever you create interactive features like a popup message, it's important to test them out in a browser to make sure they're working.

1   Use the Browser Preview button to access your web browser, and select it to preview the open page.

2   Press on the Validate button at the bottom of your form. The popup message you set earlier appears.

[JavaScript Application]	✕
⚠ Validate this form!	
OK	

Use this feature to warn your viewers, or to guide them in a certain direction.

Depending on the security configurations of your browser, you may be prompted to allow blocked content. If you'd like to change your preferences to avoid conflicts with scripts created in the Behaviors panel, refer to your browser's documentation for instructions on changing the default settings.

3   Press OK to close the message, and close or minimize your browser window.

To further explore the Behaviors panel and its features, you'll add a Form Validation behavior to the same button.

Validating form fields

Because it's a behavior you usually want performed when a user submits their form data to you, the Validate Form action is most often applied to the Submit button in a form. For this lesson, you'll apply this action to the Validate button you created, change its position in the behavior order, delete it, and reapply it to the correct button.

1   In the document window, select the Validate button at the bottom of your form. The Behaviors panel should display the Popup Message action you added in the last exercise.

2   At the top of the Behaviors panel, click the Plus button (**+**), and select Validate Form from the drop-down menu that appears. The Validate Form dialog box opens.

3   In the Validate Form dialog box, enter the following settings:

- Choose "Mailing_list_name", the first entry in the Fields list. The Fields list is a compilation of all the names you assigned to the form fields you added to the form earlier in this lesson. (This is one reason why it's so important to name your fields.)

- Click in the *Required* checkbox to require data entry into this field before the user can submit the form.

- Click on the *Anything* radio button so the field accepts any alphanumeric entry. For the Name field, leave this button selected.

- To make the behavior require that only numerical data be entered you would select the Number radio button. For the "Mailing_list_name" field, leave this button unchecked.

- To make the behavior check for an @ symbol within the entered data, click on the *Email address* radio button. For the "Mailing_list_name" field, leave this button unselected.

- To make the behavior check for a number within a specific range, enter that range in the Number from fields. Leave this button unchecked and the fields empty.

Specify which form elements get validated, and what is accepted.

4 Press OK to close the Validate Form dialog box.

5 Choose File > Save, then preview the form page in your browser. Leave the Name field blank, and click on the Validate button at the bottom of your form.

Unfortunately, the Popup Message behavior you added earlier runs before the Validate Form behavior, requiring you to close the Popup Message window to see the results of your validation.

Next, you'll adjust the Validate Form behavior to correct these errors.

Changing a form field's behavior order

To keep the popup message from appearing before the results of your validation, you'll need to change the Validate Form behavior's position in the behavior order, delete it, and reapply it to the correct button.

1 In the Dreamweaver document window, click on the Validate button to select it.

2 Click on the Show Set Events button in the Behaviors panel to toggle over to this view. You will now see your two actions, Popup Message and Validate Form, which share the same event, or trigger.

Use the Behaviors panel to reorder behaviors and make them behave differently for the viewer.

3 Click on the Validate Form behavior to select it, and click the up arrow at the top of the panel to move it to a position above the Popup Message behavior. Although this makes the Validate Form action run first, the popup message still appears after the validation window is closed. It actually makes more sense not to have the Validate Form behavior attached to the Validate button at all. You will now remove this behavior and attach it to the Submit button instead.

4 Click on the Minus button (–) to delete it from the behaviors associated with the Validate button.

5 Click on the Submit button at the bottom of your form to select it. Repeat steps 2-4 in the preceding exercise to add the validation action to the Submit button.

Now it's time to see the fruits of your labor.

Verifying field contents

Now that you've adjusted the Validate Form behavior, you'll need to make sure the form functions as you expect it to.

1 Preview the open page in your browser, and click on the Validate button. This should now display only the popup message. Close it.

2 Click on the Submit button. Even though the data is not actually submitted (for lack of a CGI script), the Validate Form warns you that required fields have not been filled.

The Validate Form behavior functions as you originally intended, thanks to some editing in the Behaviors panel.

You've successfully added validation to your form, and completed this lesson in the process.

Self study

Using your new knowledge of building and editing web forms in Dreamweaver, try some of the following tasks to build on your experience:

Edit the Validate Form behavior you applied to the Submit button in the last exercise. Apply validation to the other text fields in your form, providing checks for the specific content to be filled out in each field. Preview the page in your browser to ensure that the validation works.

Create an internal CSS that redefines the *<input>* tag. Set the background color of each form field to light green to match your page's color scheme. Experiment with the other styling options available to you in the CSS Rule Definition dialog box to further style your form elements.

Explore the other form field elements in the Forms category of the Insert toolbar. Add a hidden field to return the creation date of the form when it is submitted, while keeping this information hidden from the user. Add an Image field to turn a placed image into a button with a behavior attached. Group your form fields into labeled sections, using the Fieldset button.

Review

Questions

1   Why is it important to add a form element when building a web form in Dreamweaver?

2   When should you use a radio button group, as opposed to a set of checkboxes, in a form?

3   How does CSS add creativity and efficiency to the form creation process?

4   What do you need in order to collect the form data that a user enters into your form?

5   Where would you access the different JavaScript actions that can be applied to a button in Dreamweaver?

Answers

1   The form element serves as a container for the fields you'll be adding to the form. If you simply add form fields to a page in Dreamweaver, the user's browser won't know what to do with the user's information when they click the Submit button. To identify this information as part of a package, and to specify the route that information should take when submitted, you need to create a Dreamweaver form.

2   The difference between adding checkboxes and radio buttons in a form is that from a group of radio buttons, only a single option can be selected. Checkboxes allow the selection of multiple options.

3   Because CSS allows you to apply several formatting attributes with a single mouse click, both static and dynamic content (such as form fields) can be successfully and creatively styled using CSS. CSS also streamlines your workflow by allowing you to revisit CSS files and change the included style rules once you've completed the initial styling.

4   You can't collect form data without using a server-side script or application such as CGI, JSP, or ASP to process the data. CGI scripts are the most popular form of server-side scripting mechanism to process form data. Several web sites offer free CGI scripts that you can use. Your site's ISP may also provide CGI scripts for you.

5   The Behaviors panel provides a means for you to add JavaScript code to your page without actually having to type in the code. The code it inserts adds interactivity to your site, and is usually triggered by some user action. For example, when the user clicks on or hovers over a link, the behavior performs a task. Behaviors are commonly used to add rollovers, open new windows, check for plug-ins, and add navigation elements. You use the Behaviors panel to add, modify, remove, or reorder behaviors.

What you'll learn in this lesson:

- Spry Framework basics
- Creating a Spry menu bar
- Working with the Spry support files
- Customizing Spry Widgets with CSS
- Building a Spry Tabbed panel

Working with the Spry Framework

The average user's expectations of how a web site looks and feels has changed significantly over the years. The birth of the Rich Internet Application (RIA) has resulted in highly interactive web sites that function more like traditional desktop applications. Dreamweaver CS5 includes Spry Widgets and Data Objects—a library of interactive menus, animated user interfaces, and XML-driven containers that can be added to your projects and customized to take your pages to the next level.

Starting up

Before starting, make sure that your tools and panels are consistent by resetting your workspace. See "Resetting the Dreamweaver workspace" on page 3.

You will work with several files from the dw13lessons folder in this lesson. Make sure that you have loaded the dwlessons folder onto your hard drive from the supplied DVD. See "Loading lesson files" on page 3.

Before you begin, you need to create site settings that point to the dw13lessons folder from the included DVD that contains resources you need for these lessons. Go to Site > New Site, or, for details on creating a site, refer to Lesson 2, "Setting Up a New Site."

See Lesson 13 in action!

Use the accompanying video to gain a better understanding of how to use some of the features shown in this lesson. The video tutorial for this lesson can be found on the included DVD.

Introducing the Spry Widgets

Introduced in Dreamweaver CS3, Spry Widgets give you the ability to create powerful, interactive navigation and content presentation with easy-to-use insert bar elements. Spry Widgets include drop-down and accordion menus, expanding panels, and tabbed containers, all of which harness the power of CSS for easy customization and styling to match any project. They are a great way to enhance navigation, organize content, and add dynamic style to your web pages.

In addition, Spry features a set of data elements and display items that allow you to create dynamic page content that can read from an XML file. You can find the Spry Widgets in their own category on the Insert panel, and within the Layout category as well.

The Spry framework for AJAX

Developed by Adobe, Spry is a JavaScript library for AJAX developers, and features data-driven and interface elements that can be easily added to a page and customized; many of these elements can incorporate real-time data from XML or HTML files. These can be integrated into your existing pages to add features not available with HTML alone.

What is AJAX?

AJAX is an acronym for Asynchronous JavaScript and XML, and represents a combination of technologies: JavaScript, XML, and DHTML (more commonly referred to as DOM Scripting). AJAX is used to develop what is sometimes referred to as Rich Internet Applications (RIAs). RIAs are a great example of how the Web continues to evolve and progress beyond the static web page. RIAs exchange data behind the scenes and can easily update the appearance and display of the web page without the need to reload the page over and over again.

A great example of an RIA is Google's Gmail, which has the ability to update messages, create online chats, and retrieve address book contacts in real-time without the need to go to another page or even reload the existing one. Here, AJAX is used to send and retrieve XML-based data behind the scenes, and updates the appearance and information on the page in real-time.

A look at the project

In this lesson, you'll be completing the OrganicUtopia home page by using and customizing different Spry Widgets. Before you get started, take a look at the completed version of the page to get an idea of what you'll be working toward.

If you haven't already created a site definition for this lesson in Dreamweaver, follow the instructions in Lesson 2, "Setting Up a New Site," to do so before moving ahead.

1 In the Files panel, locate the index_done.html page, and double-click it to open it.

2 To view the Spry Widgets in action, choose File > Preview in Browser, and select a browser to preview the page.

3 With the page open in a browser, move over the Navigation bar at the top. Notice that hovering over each menu item expands it to reveal more menu items.

4 On the right, click on the accordion-style menu to expand and contract different categories of products.

5 In the center of the page, locate the three tabs labeled *featured*, *what's new*, and *testimonials*. Click on each one to reveal a different content area—notice that the page doesn't refresh when you do this.

6 In the lower-right corner, click the Sign Up For Our Newsletter bar to reveal a signup box.

7 Close the browser and return to Dreamweaver. Choose File > Close to close the current file.

The Spry Menu bar

In Lesson 06, "Advanced Page Layout," you created your navigation bar from scratch using an HTML list styled with CSS. However, imagine that you are asked to create a more interactive menu, one which activates a drop-down menu of the sub-categories of your site. Although this is possible to do using CSS with perhaps some help from Javascript, it is not necessarily easy or fast. The Spry Menu bar creates a multi-tiered horizontal or vertical menu that can be easily added as a master navigation element in your page(s). These menus are easy to add, and the Spry Menu bar is a great alternative.

The Spry Menu bar can be added from the Insert panel, and customized using the Property Inspector and CSS Styles panel.

1 From the Files panel, locate and open the index_start.html file for editing.

2 Choose File > Save As, and save the page as **index_work.html** into your site's root folder.

If you can't locate your current site folder, click the Site Root button at the bottom of the Save As dialog box to automatically locate and set it as your save location.

3   At the top of the page, locate the div with the placeholder text that reads {*menu bar here*}.

Locate the placeholder text where the menu bar will go.

Select and delete the placeholder text, but leave your cursor in its place.

4   In the Insert panel, select the Spry category from the drop-down menu at the top, to display the Spry data objects and widgets.

5   Click the Spry Menu bar icon to insert a new menu bar at your cursor position. Choose Horizontal from the dialog box that appears, and click OK to add the menu bar to your page. The bar will be added with four generic navigation items as well as the default Spry Menu bar style which is a light grey background and black text. You will be restyling the appearance of the menu a bit later, first you need to add new menu items.

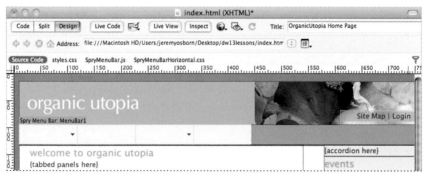

The inserted Spry Menu bar.

To select an entire widget and make it active in the Property Inspector, click the blue tab that appears above its top-left corner.

6   The Property Inspector now displays all the options for the new widget, this includes three columns, each of which represents a new level of navigation for a drop-down menu. Locate the leftmost column, which lets you add and customize the top level links on the menu bar. Select the first item titled *Item 1*.

7   Locate the Text type-in box on the right side of the Property Inspector. Type the name **Home** to rename the item. Press Enter (Windows) or Return (Mac OS).

Use the Property Inspector to modify and rearrange menu bar items and links.

8   Repeat steps 6 and 7 for Item 2, Item 3, and Item 4, renaming them **Products**, **Services**, and **Contact Us**, respectively.

At this point, the structure of the menu is identical to the one created by scratch. However, now you will quickly add two more levels to your navigation. For each top-level menu item, you can add up to two more tiers of menus using the two remaining columns shown on the Property Inspector.

9   Select the Products link in the leftmost column on the Property Inspector.

Locate the plus sign above the second column, and click it to add a new submenu item. Locate the Text type-in field on the right, and rename the new item **Gourmet Foods**. Press Enter/Return.

Add a second level to the menu by clicking the plus icon in the second column.

10   Click the plus sign above the second column twice more to add two new submenu items. Rename them **Lifestyle** and **Beauty**. Next, you'll add a third tier by creating a submenu for the Lifestyle link you just added.

11   Select the Lifestyle link in the center column. Locate the plus sign above the rightmost column, and click it twice to add two new submenu items to the Lifestyle link.

12   Select each of the new items and use the Text type-in field on the right side of the Property Inspector to rename them **Furniture** and **Accessories**, respectively. Press Enter/Return. In addition to adding levels, you can delete them as well. Your first link to Home has three sub-items that Dreamweaver added by default. You will delete them as they don't reflect your site structure.

13 In the leftmost column, select the top-level link named Home. Click on Item 1.1 and then press the minus icon to remove this link. Repeat this step for Item 1.2 and Item 1.3 so there are no sub-items.

If you decide at any point that you would like to rearrange the order of your navigation, you can do so easily.

14 In the Property Inspector, click on the Services link and then press the up arrow. This moves the item up one level and Services is now the second category.

Use the up and down arrows above the first list to re-order the top-level links to set the final order (shown here).

15 Choose File > Save to save your page. The Copy Dependent Files dialog box appears to let you know that files will be copied to your site directory to support the new menu. Press OK to save the page.

After you add a new Spry Widget, the Copy Dependent Files dialog box appears when you save a page.

16 Press the Live View button on the Document toolbar to test your new menu. Mouse over each menu item to see the rollover effects and submenus you created. Press the Live View button again to return to your editing view.

Spry Support Files

The first time you save a page that includes a Spry widget, you are prompted to save some new and necessary files to your site. If you take a peek at your Files panel, you notice a new Spry Assets folder has been added to your site files. This folder contains essential JavaScript, CSS, and image files that style your new widget and make it work. *Be sure to copy this folder to your web server when publishing your site—your widgets will not work without it!*

Customizing Spry Widgets with CSS

Now that you've added a new Spry Menu bar and customized its contents, you're ready to start giving it some style. Each new widget added to your page includes its own, attached CSS file that you can easily modify to have your new menu match the look and feel of your site. All CSS rules can be managed from the CSS Styles panel just like your existing page styles.

1   Locate and, if necessary, expand the CSS Styles panel. Double-click the Insert panel to collapse it and give yourself more screen space. Click the All tab to locate the attached SpryMenuBarHorizontal.css style sheet, and expand it to view all its rules. You have three groups of CSS styles in this page: styles.css is the external style sheet that contains the majority of the styles for the page, the <style> tag represents the internal styles for just this page and SpryMenuBarHorizontal.css is the external style sheet for just the menu bar.

Click on the plus sign (Windows) or arrow (Mac OS) to the left of styles.css as well as <style> to collapse these and view only the Spry menu styles.

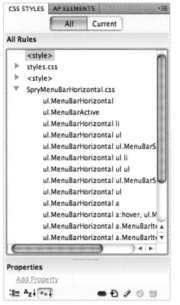

A new style sheet has been attached to your page that controls the formatting of the Spry Menu bar.

There are more than a dozen style rules for this menu, you will now restyle these to fit your page design. A word of warning: the style names for these menu items are very similar and long, so you will need to pay careful attention to which style you are modifying. It may help you to expand the width of the CSS Styles panel in order to see the style names.

2   Select the *ul.MenuBarHorizontal* rule to view its properties. This rule controls the overall appearance and size settings for the menu bar. Click Add Property below the property listing. An empty field appears with a menu to the right.

Click Add property to add a new CSS rule.

Note that depending on your workspace you may need to expand the Properties section of the CSS Styles panel to see the properties.

3   Click on the menu and scroll down the resulting list to select the font-family property. This triggers a new field to the right. Click on this menu and choose the Verdana, Geneva, sans-serif family.

4   Locate the font-size property, which is set to 100%, and click on it to change its value. Type **11**, then click on the rightmost drop-down menu and choose px for the unit value.

5 Select the *ul.MenuBarHorizontal a* rule to view its properties. In the Properties section, click on the value for background-color (#EEE) and type **#88B036** (green) as the new color and press Enter (Window) or Return (Mac OS). This sets the background color of the menu bar which happens to be the same shade as the navigation div.

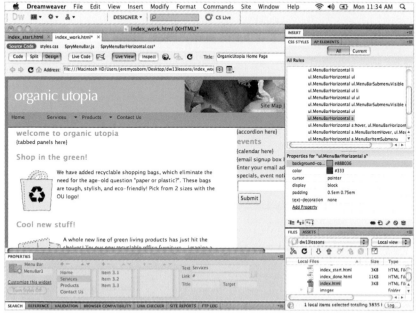

Modify the background-color and color properties of the rule to change the appearance of the menu bar items.

6 Click the color swatch (currently set to black) under the color property and change the color to #FFFFFF (white) and press Enter (Window) or Return (Mac OS). This changes the color of the hyperlinked text on each menu item.

7 In the list of rules, select the *ul.MenuBarHorizontal a.MenuBarItemHover, ul.MenuBarHorizontal a.MenuBarItemSubmenuHover, ul.MenuBarHorizontal a.MenuBarSubmenuVisible* rule to view its properties. This rule controls the appearance of linked menu items as you roll over them in the menu.

Because this long CSS rule will be difficult to locate in the panel, you can count upwards from the bottom of the rules. It is the seventh the from the bottom and the default background color is #33C (blue).

8 Click the color swatch under the background-color property and type **#9FCC41** (light green) as the new color.

9 Click the Live View button on the Document toolbar to test your page and see the new style changes you've made.

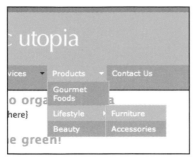

Use Live View to preview the style changes and interactivity on your new menu.

10 Click Live View again to return to the standard view. Choose File > Save to save your project. You'll now take a look at another navigation element: the tabbed panel.

The Spry Tabbed panel

The Spry Tabbed panel widget organizes content into several panels that you can toggle between by clicking on tabs. This is a great way to organize items on a page: it saves space and can improve usability when used correctly.

Editing the content of the tabbed panels is a bit easier to edit than the Spry Menu bar, instead of using the Property Inspector to add and modify content, you can type directly within the tabs or containers in the document window. Tabbed panels can contain almost any type of content, including text, images, video, and Flash movies.

You'll now add a Spry Tabbed panel to your page to display three pieces of featured content.

1 Near the top of your page, select the placeholder text that reads {*tabbed panels here*}, and delete it. Leave your cursor at this position.

2   Double-click the Insert panel if necessary to expand it. Locate and click the Spry Tabbed Panels button and click it to add a new tabbed panel set.

Add a new Spry Tabbed panel at the top of the page, as shown. As with the Spry Menu bar, the Property Inspector allows you to modify and add tab and panel sets.

3   Locate the Panels column in the center of the Property Inspector below. This shows you the current panels (and tabs) in your panel set, and lets you add new ones. Click the plus sign at the top of the column to add a third tab to your panel set.

Press the down arrow in the Panels section to move Tab 3 to the bottom of the list.

4   On the page, click inside the first tab that reads *Tab 1*, then delete the text and type **What's New** in its place. Repeat this for the remaining two tabs, renaming them **Featured** and **Customer Testimonials**, respectively.

Modify tab contents by typing directly on the page. You can bring a specific panel forward by hovering over a tab and clicking the eye icon that appears.

5   Below the tabbed panel, you'll see three paragraphs of content that you'll move and organize into the new panel group. Highlight the entire first paragraph, beginning with the headline *Shop In the Green* and be sure to include the recycle bag image. Choose Edit > Cut.

6   Select the placeholder text Content 1, then choose Edit > Paste to paste the content directly into the What's New panel. You will now place content into the Featured panel.

7   Place your cursor over the Featured tab but don't click yet. Wait for the eye icon (👁) to appear and then click once to bring the tab to the front.

Your new Spry Tabbed panels set after moving the page contents to each of the three tabs (shown in Live View).

8   Select the Featured Stuff! Heading, paragraph and the image of the couch and choose Edit>Cut. Select the placeholder text Content 2 and then choose Edit > Paste.

9   Repeat steps 7 and 8 and cut the remaining content (Our loyal customers) into the third panel (Customer Testimonials).

10   Click the Live View button on the Document toolbar to preview the tabbed panel so far. You should be able to click and flip between each tab's contents. Click the Live View button again to return to Design view. Now it's time to style this panel to match your page theme.

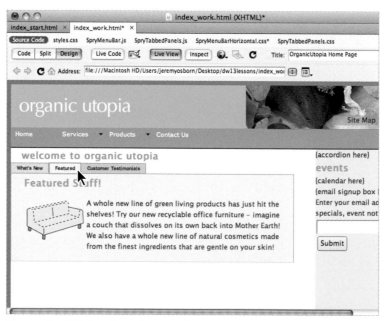

Your new Spry Tabbed panels set after moving the page contents to each of the three tabs (shown in Live View).

If you want to change which panel is open by default, you can use the Default Panel drop-down menu on the Property Inspector to determine which tab and panel are loaded first.

11 In the CSS Styles panel, locate and expand the style sheet named SpryTabbedPanels.css, which was attached when you added the tabbed panel group. Like the Spry Menu bar, the tabbed panel has a dedicated style sheet that you can modify to change its appearance.

12 Select the rule named *.TabbedPanelsTab* to display its properties. Click on the background-color value, and type **#88B036** (dark green)., then press Enter (Windows) or Return (Mac OS). This changes the color of the non-active tabs.

Modify the TabbedPanelsTab rule to change the appearance of non-active tabs.

13 Select the rule named *.TabbedPanelsTabSelected*. Click on the background-color value, and type **#CF9** (light green), then press Enter/Return. This changes the color of the currently selected tab.

14 Select the rule named *.TabbedPanelsContentGroup*. Click on the background-color value (#EEE) and type **#CF9** and press Enter/Return. This sets the background color of the entire panel to the same shade of green as the tab.

The panels height is currently being defined by the amount of content. If you wanted to override this you could set an explicit height for the panels.

15 Still within .*TabbedPanelsContentGroup*, click Add Property (below the properties list) this adds an empty field. Click on the drop-down menu to the right and choose the height property. In the new field that appears, type **250** (make sure px is specified) and then press Enter/Return. This increases the overall height of the content panels.

You can override the height of the panels by modifying the .TabbedPanelsContentGroup *style*

16 Choose File > Save. Then preview your page in the browser to see your tabs in action. There are a few other styles that you could modify here, but for now, you'll move on to the next Spry Widget: the Accordion Panel.

The Spry Accordion panel

At first glance, the Spry Accordion panel resembles a standard vertical menu bar. As the name suggests, however, each item contracts and expands to reveal a content panel where you can add text and images. The accordion panel allows you to have only one panel open at a time.

Accordion panels are great for navigation, tree-style navigation or lists, or organizing related content (such as a Frequently Asked Questions list) into a clean, panel-style format. As with the other Spry widgets, the Spry Accordion uses its own style sheet, which you can easily modify to make it match your current theme.

1 In the right-hand column, locate the placeholder text that reads {*accordion here*}. Select and delete the placeholder text, and leave your cursor in place.

2   From the Insert panel, click and add a new Spry Accordion at the cursor position.

The Spry Accordion added to the sidebar.

The Property Inspector below now displays the properties for the new widget.

3   On the Property Inspector, you see a list of the panels currently in your accordion (Label 1 and Label 2). Click the plus sign (+) above the list twice to add two new panels for a total of four. A label displays above each new panel.

4   Click on Label 2 and then press the up arrow twice to push Label 2 back under Label 1. This step is not mandatory, but it helps to keep your label order straight.

5   On your page, highlight the Label 1 text. Delete it and type **Food Products** in its place. Do **not** press Enter (Windows) or Return (Mac OS) after typing.

Type directly within the accordion labels to rename them.

5   Repeat step 4 for the Label 2, Label 3, and Label 4 tabs, renaming them **Clothing**, **Home Products**, and **Lifestyle**, respectively. Next, you'll add content to each panel that corresponds to its label.

6   In your Files panel, locate the text folder and expand it. Double-click and open the file named accordiontext.html. This contains the text you'll add to the accordion panel.

7   Select the text below the Food Products heading (don't include the heading itself), and choose Edit > Cut. Return back to your index_work.html page.

8   Hover over the Food Products label, and click the eye icon (👁) to expand it. Click inside the visible panel, and choose Edit > Paste to paste in the text from your content file.

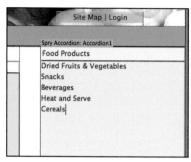

Paste the list of products in the Food Products category of the accordion.

9   Repeat steps 7 and 8 for the remaining paragraphs in the accordiontext.html file, pasting them into the Clothing, Home Products, and Lifestyle panels, respectively.

10 Under the CSS Styles panel, locate the attached stylesheet named SpryAccordion.css, and expand it to reveal its rules.

11 Select the *.AccordionPanelTab* rule. For the background-color property listed below, click on the color swatch and sample the green color from the header to set the background-color to #88B036 (green).

Using the eyedropper, sample the green from the header to apply it as a background-color for the Products category of the accordion.

To sample a color outside of the Swatches panel that appears, simply move the eyedropper anywhere on the screen.

12 Select the *.AccordionPanelOpen .AccordionPanelTab* rule. Click on the background-color value and type **#CF9**, then press Enter (Windows) or Return (Mac OS). This sets the open panel color to a light green,

13 Select the *.AccordionPanelContent* rule. Locate the height property shown in the Properties list, and change its value from 200px to **100px**. This changes the height of the content panels when shown.

There are a few more styles to change before you are done styling the accordion. One of the default styles for this widget is a Focused style which defines the appearance of the accordion when it is selected. By default it is blue, so you will change this now.

14 Select the *.AccordionFocused .AccordionPanelTab* style in the CSS Styles panel. Here you will match the background color you set in step 11. Click the color value for the background-color property and type **#8CD031**, then press Enter/Return to commit the change.

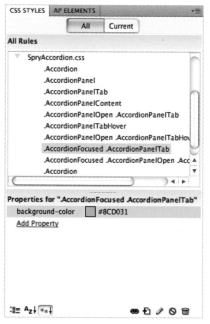

Setting the .AccordionFocused .AccordionPanelTab *style.*

15 Select the *.AccordionFocused .AccordionPanelOpen .AccordionPanelTab* style. This rule defines the appearance of any panel tab that is open. Click the color value for the background-color property and type **#CF9** to set it to the same light green used in step 12.

16 Choose File > Save to save your page. If the Copy Dependent Files dialog box appears, press Yes to allow Dreamweaver to copy any necessary files for your new widget to the site folder.

17   Choose File > Preview in Browser to see your new tabbed panel group in action. When you are done, close the browser and return to Dreamweaver.

The Spry Collapsible panel

This simple panel displays or reveals its contents when clicked, and is a great way to hide information that doesn't need to be visible at all times. You can think of the Spry Collapsible panel as a *piece* of the Spry Accordion that can only display a single panel and label.

You'll add a single Spry Collapsible panel to create a hidden e-mail signup form at the bottom of your page.

1   In the bottom half of the right column, locate the placeholder text that reads {*Email signup box here*}. Select and delete the placeholder text and leave your cursor positioned in its place.

2   On the Insert panel, locate and click the Spry Collapsible Panel button to add a button at your cursor position.

3   Select the text that reads *Tab* at the top of the panel, and type **Contact Us** in its place.

4   Below the panel, select the paragraph that reads *Enter your e-mail address to receive specials, event notifications and more!* and also select the form elements.

Move the content from the bottom of the right column into your new collapsible panel.

Choose Edit > Cut.

5   Select the word *Content* shown in the panel area of your collapsible panel, and paste the content you cut in its place. The text and form field now appear inside the panel.

6   In the CSS Styles panel, locate and expand the attached style sheet named SpryCollapsiblePanel.css. Select the rule named .*CollapsiblePanelTab* to display its properties.

7   Click the background-color value, and type **#88B036** to change the label's background color from grey to green.

You can also define the default appearance of the collapsible panel, in this case you would like it close by default.

8 Click the blue tab above the Collapsible panel to select it. In the Property Inspector, choose Closed from the Display menu to close the panel. Choose Closed from the Default state menu so that the panel will appear closed by default until clicked.

Use the Property Inspector to set the new panel's Display State and Default appearance to Closed.

9 Choose File > Save to save your page. When the Copy Dependent Files dialog box appears, click Yes to allow Dreamweaver to copy any necessary files to your site folder.

10 Choose File > Preview in Browser, and select a browser to test your page and see your new Collapsible panel in action. When you click the panel label, the sign-up text and form appears—click it again to close it.

11 Close the browser and return to Dreamweaver.

Working with Spry Data Widgets

In addition to what you've seen so far, the Spry panel includes a whole group of powerful data widgets that can read from an external XML file. This is perfect for creating pages and page elements (such as calendars, news, and blogs) that otherwise would require manual formatting.

You can connect XML information to a pre-configured data widget from the Spry panel (such as the Spry Table), or build your own display components using common page objects such as lists, tables, and div tags. You can even use CSS to format Spry data widgets so they blend perfectly with your existing design.

What is XML?

XML stands for eXtensible Markup Language, and is the standard now used to describe and exchange data between seemingly unrelated systems. XML, like HTML, uses a series of tags—however, that's where the similarities end. Unlike HTML, XML doesn't use a series of pre-defined tags; instead, XML developers create tags using names they understand and that are relevant to the data they're trying to work with.

A typical XML document may look like the following:

```
<meeting>

    <attendee>

            <name>John Smith</name>

            <dept>Payroll</dept>

            <extension>2225</extension>

    </attendee>

</meeting>
```

Each tag is referred to as a *node*; the nodes and structure of an XML file are referred to as a *schema*.

XML can exist on a web server outside your local site, or as a local XML file. How this XML file is created or where it comes from is up to you, and this will be different for every project. Because XML documents are plain text, they can be created in Dreamweaver, as well as a variety of other popular text editors.

Creating a Spry XML data set

Before you can add a data widget to your page, you must first create a Spry XML data set. These are pointers to XML data sources (such as an XML file in your site folder) that let Dreamweaver know where the file is and what information it contains. A single page can use multiple data sets, and you can manage all data sets from the Bindings panel.

1   Click the Spry Data Set button (🔲) at the top of the Insert panel's Spry category. The Spry Data Set dialog box appears.

2   At the top, choose XML from the Select Data Type drop-down menu. Type **events** as the Data Set Name.

3 Click the Browse button next to the Specify Data File field. When the Select XML Source dialog box appears, navigate to the *data* folder in your site's root directory. Select the events.xml file in the folder and press OK (Windows) or Choose (Mac OS).

The schema panel below displays the node structure of your XML document.

Pointing to the XML file to be used as a Data Set.

4 Click on the <event> node; the xData path below should read calendar/event.

This node is a *Row Element* which is a repeating node: this is appropriate because many events are held and they all have the same structure: Month, Date, Year.

5 Press Done to create the data set. You will now created data bindings to this data.

6   Choose Window > Bindings to display the Bindings panel, if it does not open automatically. This is where you can view and manage your data sets and see the nodes that they contain. You may need to expand the height of the Bindings panel to see the contents better.

The Bindings panel displays the data set of your XML file.

7   Choose File > Save to save your page. If you are prompted to Copy Dependent Files, press OK.

Adding a Spry Data Widget: The Spry Repeat List

Once you've created a Spry data set, you are ready to add a Spry Data Widget to your page. A Spry Data Widget is simply an HTML structure (such as a list or table) that is designed to build itself from information it finds in a Spry Data Set. Rather than having to manually add enough bullet points or rows, the widget builds as many as it needs to display the records found in a specific data set.

An easy way to display data from your new XML Data Set is by using a Spry Repeat List, which uses one of three HTML list styles (unordered, ordered, or definition list) to display data. As with any standard HTML structure, you can fine-tune its look with basic CSS properties. To get you started, the lesson file includes some pre-created classes that you can add to your list.

1   Locate the box in the right-side column of your page that begins with the header *events*. Select the placeholder text {*calendar here*} and delete it, leaving your cursor in its place.

2   Under the Spry category on the Insert panel, click the Spry Repeat List button to add a new list. The Insert Spry Repeat List dialog box appears.

3   From the Container Tag drop-down menu, you can choose one of three list types, or even use a form SELECT menu. Select the DL (Definition List).

> *A Definition List displays information in tiered Title/Definition sets. It is similar to a standard ordered or unordered list, except that each bullet contains a set of two pieces of information.*

4   From the Spry Data Set drop-down menu, select events, which is the XML data set you created earlier. The new list will build itself dynamically from information it finds in this dataset.

5   From the DT Column drop-down menu, select date. This corresponds to the date node found in your data set, and will display the date as the header for each list item created.

6   From the DD Column drop-down menu, select title. This will display the event title below the date in each list item created.

```
                    Insert Spry Repeat List

    Container tag:  [ DL (Definition List)  ▲▼ ]      (      OK     )

    Spry Data Set:  [ events                 ▲▼ ]      (    Cancel   )

    DT Column:      [ date                   ▲▼ ]      (     Help    )

    DD Column:      [ title                  ▲▼ ]
```

Add a new Spry Repeat List in the right column of your page. Choose the DL (Definition List) as your structure, and set it to display the date and title fields from your XML file.

7   Press OK. If a dialog box appears prompting you to Add a Spry Region, make sure to press Yes. Without it, the data will not load into the widget.

> *If you forget to add a Spry Region, or need to recreate it, you can use the Spry Region button, found underneath the Spry category of the Insert panel. Just make sure that any Spry Data Widgets are placed inside the new region!*

8   A new Spry Region is added to your page, as well as a new definition list. You will see placeholders for the information in your data set. When you preview your page, these will be replaced with actual data from your data set.

The Spry Region displays placeholders for your data from your events data set loads dynamically into the list when the page is previewed.

9   Choose File > Save to save your page. Click the Live View button on the Document toolbar; the placeholder list on your page is now filled with calendar information from your XML file!

Styling and fine-tuning data widgets

Once you've added a data widget, you can fine-tune it by adding additional data fields, rearranging the order of data fields, and of course, styling it with some basic CSS. The lesson file contains an attached style sheet with some pre-created styles that you can assign to your new Spry Repeat List to give it some style. You will also add data fields to your list that aren't currently being displayed, such as the time and description for each calendar event.

Before you begin, make sure that you turn Live View off in the Document toolbar.

1   Locate your new Spry Repeat List in the right-side column, and click to position your cursor directly after the {date} placeholder text.

2   Add a space, and type a colon (:). You'll follow this colon with the actual event time from your XML data set, which the list is not currently using.

3   If it is not currently visible, choose Window > Bindings to display your Bindings panel. You'll see your events data set listed, as well as the data fields below it. Locate and select the time data field in the list—this contains the time for each event.

4   Click and drag the time data field from the Bindings panel, and release it next to the *{date}:* text on the page. This adds a placeholder for the time to your repeat list. It should read *{date}:{time}*.

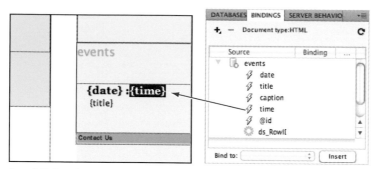

Drag fields from the Bindings panel to add placeholders to your repeat list. The new {time} placeholder will fill in the time information from your XML file.

5   Directly below the date and time, click to position your cursor after the *{title}* placeholder. Press Shift+Return to create a line break and put your cursor on the next line. Here is where you'll place the caption for each event.

6   On the Bindings panel, locate the caption field shown below your events data set. Click and drag it from the Bindings panel and place it in the new line you created on your page below the *{title}*. This adds a new placeholder for *{caption}*.

7   Now you'll use some pre-created CSS rules to dress up your list. Select the entire line in your list that reads *{date}:{time}*. On the left side of the Property Inspector, press the HTML button, if necessary, to switch to HTML view. Select *.eventDate* from the Class drop-down menu to apply it to the selected text.

Select text in your repeat list and apply a class from the Property Inspector to style it.

8   Select the text that reads *{title}*. Select *.eventTitle* from the Class drop-down menu to apply the rule to the selected text.

9   Highlight the text in your list that reads *{caption}*. Select *.eventCaption* from the Class drop-down menu to apply the rule to the selected text.

10 Choose File > Save to save your page. Click the Live View button on the Document toolbar to preview your list with the newly added data and CSS rules.

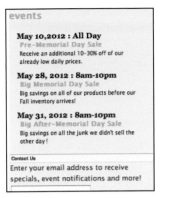

The finished and styled Spry Repeat List, shown in Live View.

11 Click Live View again to turn it off.

From this point, you can simply update the attached XML files without the need to modify the data widgets in any way. Because each Spry Data Widget populates dynamically, new data will flow into the widget each time the page is loaded.

Self study

As you can see, creating highly interactive web pages is made easy with Spry Widgets. Whether it's a fancy drop-down menu, or a dynamic list of events, the addition of a few widgets can make the difference between a good page and a great one. Further explore the different data widgets, and experiment with XML data from different sources. Identify areas on your site that could benefit from Spry Data Widgets, such as blog, news, or calendar pages, and follow the steps in these lessons to apply these same concepts to those pages.

Review

Questions

1   What are the four Spry Widgets that you can use for navigation and content presentation?

2   What is the significance of the Spry Assets folder that is copied to your site when using a Spry Widget?

3   What must first be created before you can use a Spry Data Widget?

Answers

1   The Spry Menu bar, Spry Accordion panel, Spry Tabbed panel, and Spry Collapsible panel.

2   It contains necessary support files such as CSS, JavaScript, and image files that your widgets need in order to function.

3   A Spry Data Set.

Lesson 14

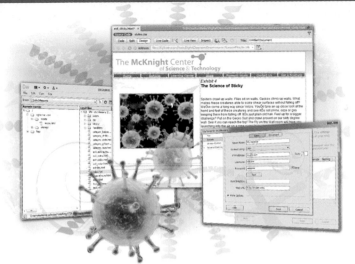

What you'll learn in this lesson:

- Uploading and managing files
- Optimizing pages for performance and search engines
- Using Site Reports
- Using the CSS Advisor & Browser Compatibility Check

Managing Your Web Site:
Reports, Optimization, and Maintenance

When it's time to release your web site to the world, you'll want to take some last steps to make sure your site works at, and looks, its best. Dreamweaver has a powerful set of reports, link checkers, and problem-solving tools to locate and fix any potential issues before final upload. When you're ready, the built-in FTP and synchronization features of the Files panel will get you up-and-running.

Starting up

Before starting, make sure that your tools and panels are consistent by resetting your workspace. See "Resetting the Dreamweaver workspace" on page 3.

You will work with several files from the dw14lessons folder in this lesson. Make sure that you have loaded the dwlessons folder onto your hard drive from the supplied DVD. See "Loading lesson files" on page 3.

Before you begin, you need to create a site definition that points to the dw14lessons folder from the included DVD that contains resources you need for these lessons. Go to Site > New Site, or, for details on creating a site definition, refer to Lesson 2, "Setting Up a New Site."

See Lesson 14 in action!

Use the accompanying video to gain a better understanding of how to use some of the features shown in this lesson. The video tutorial for this lesson can be found on the included DVD.

Working with the Files panel

You've already used the Files panel throughout this book to locate and open files within your site projects. In addition to serving as a useful file browser, the Files panel also serves as a full-featured file transfer application and synchronization tool. From the Files panel, you can upload your site to a web server, synchronize local and remote files, and manage files and notes between multiple designers.

Creating a remote connection

The Files panel uploads, retrieves, and synchronizes files between your local site and a web server. Typically, this is done using File Transfer Protocol (FTP), which connects to and allows interaction between your local machine and a web server. Before you can transfer files, you'll first need to establish a remote connection to the web server that stores your web site files.

You will not be able to proceed with this portion of the lesson if you do not have FTP information available for a web server. If you do not have this information or do not have a connection to the Internet, you may skip to the "Testing Site Integrity" exercise in this lesson.

To get started, make sure you have the following:

- **The FTP address of the web server and specific directory.** This would be provided by your web-hosting provider as part of your account details, or from your company or organization's IT department. A typical FTP address looks like *ftp.mysite.com.*

- **A user login and password for access to the server.** Most web servers require a user login and password for access. This information should be available from your web-hosting provider as part of your account details, or from your organization's IT department.

- **The specific directory to which your files should be uploaded.** In many cases, this is the main directory or folder that appears when you connect to your web server. However, in certain cases, you'll need to upload files to a specific directory other than the main directory.

- **The web address (URL) or IP address where you can view your uploaded files on the server.** Sample addresses would be *www.mysite.com/*, *www.mysite.com/2007/,* or *http://100.0.0.1.*

1   To begin creating a remote connection, choose Site > Manage Sites. The Manage Sites dialog box appears.

2   Select the Lesson 14 site definition (you set this up at the beginning of the lesson) and click Edit. If you haven't created a site definition for this lesson, make sure you do so now, as discussed in Lesson 2, "Setting Up a New Site."

3   The Site Setup window appears. Click on the Servers button to access the server setup screen. Click on the Plus button in the lower left.

Press the Add new Server button.

This opens up the Basic tab where you will need to add the required information to access your server.

4 Enter your specific FTP information in the text fields, as shown in the example figure. The Server Name should be a common sense label that will help you identify which site you are modifying. The FTP Address, Username and Password are the mandatory pieces of information.

Sample remote connection information. Your information should include an FTP address, login, and password, with a possible folder name.

5 Click the Test Connection button at the bottom of the panel to verify that Dreamweaver can connect to your server. If the information you've provided is valid and you have a live Internet connection, a dialog box appears, confirming that Dreamweaver has successfully connected to your web server.

A dialog box lets you know if your connection was successful. If you receive an FTP error, double-check your FTP information, and make any necessary corrections.

Certain servers may require a passive FTP connection to connect successfully. If you are certain your FTP information is correct, but experience a long delay or failure when connecting, check the Use Passive FTP checkbox in the Advanced tab, Remote Info category, and try again.

6   Press the Save button and you will see your site listed in the Server window.

Your site is now listed in the Server window.

7   Press the Save button in the Site Setup window. This may trigger an activity window that updates your site settings. Press Done in the Manage Sites dialog box, as you're now finished editing the site definition.

Viewing files on a remote web server

Once you've established a connection to your web server, you can expand the Files panel for a split view that displays both your remote and local files. You can easily drag and drop between both sides to upload or download files and update existing files.

1 If necessary, choose Window > Files to open the Files panel. Click the Expand button (⊡) at the top of the Files panel to ungroup and expand it to full view.

2 Locate and click the Connect button (🔌) above the left-hand column at the top of the panel. Dreamweaver attempts to connect to your remote server, and, if successful, displays all its files on the left side of the Files panel.

It's important to note that web servers can be configured in many different ways, and you may need to edit your site settings again once you have made a successful connection (in particular, the folder information). A discussion of the different ways that web servers might be configured is outside the scope of this book; if you have specific questions regarding your site, you should contact an IT professional or your web-hosting company.

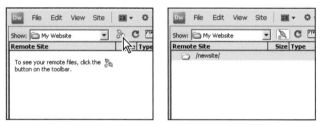

Click the Connect button to view files on your remote server in the left column of the Files panel.

Transferring files to and from a remote server with Get and Put

The built-in FTP and file transfer functionality of the Files panel makes it a snap to place files on your remote server or download files onto your local machine. This can be accomplished using the Get and Put buttons, or by dragging and dropping files between the Remote and Local file listings in the Files panel. Please note again, this exercise involves publishing your sample documents to a remote server, and therefore publishing them to the Internet; be very careful not to overwrite any pre-existing files that may be crucial to your web site.

1 Make sure you've connected to the remote server as described in the previous exercise, and that you can see your remote files in the left-hand column of the Files panel.

2   Select the index.html file from the local file listing on the right side of your Files panel, and press the Put button (⬆) at the top of the panel. Choose *No* when asked if you would like to include dependent files.

Select a file and click the Put button to upload it to the remote server.

When you transfer a document between a local and remote folder, a window may open, offering you the option of transferring the document's dependent files. Dependent files are images, external style sheets, and other files referenced in your document that a browser loads when it loads the document. This feature can be very useful: think of it as a way to make sure that any files which are linked to a particular document come along for the ride, however, for the purposes of this exercise, it will be unnecessary to transfer dependent files.

Alternatively, you can click and drag a file from the right (local) column to the left (remote) column.

Drag a file from the right column to the left to upload it to the remote server.

To get (download) a file from the remote server:

1   Make sure you've connected to the remote server as described in the previous exercise, and that you can see your remote files in the left-hand column of the Files panel.

2   Select the index.html file from the remote file listing on the left side of your Files panel, and press the Get button (⬇) at the top of the panel. Note that in your case this does not make a lot of sense since you just uploaded your index.html document.

You can update the local or remote file listing at any time by clicking the Refresh button (↻) at the top of the Files panel.

Using Check In/Check Out and Design Notes

If you're collaborating with others on a project, you'll want to set up an environment where everyone can edit files independently without overlapping or overwriting someone else's work. For these situations, the Check In/Out and Design Notes features can help you to manage workflow and communicate with others on a Dreamweaver site project.

Check In and Check Out

Dreamweaver's Check In/Check Out feature is a way of letting others know that you are working on a file and don't want it disturbed. When Check In/Check Out is enabled, a document that you're editing becomes locked on the remote server to prevent others from modifying the same file at the same time. If you attempt to open a file that's been checked out by another user, you see a warning that lets you know that the file is in use and who is currently working with it. Check In/Check Out doesn't require any additional software to run, and other Dreamweaver users can check out files if they also have Check In/Check Out enabled in their site definition.

The Check In/Check Out system does not work with a testing server. To transfer files to and from a testing server (if one is set up), use the standard Get and Put commands.

1   Choose Site > Manage Sites. Select the Dreamweaver site that you want to enable Check In/Check Out for and choose Edit.

2   In the Site Setup window, click on the Servers button, then select your site and click on the pencil icon at the bottom to edit the server settings.

3   Click on the Advanced button and then click on the Enable file check-out checkbox.

Type your name and email. This information will appear to other users who attempt to retrieve a file that you have checked out (as long as they are using Dreamweaver). Press Save and then press Save again to exit.

Enable check in/check out in the Site Definition panel to manage workflow between several users.

How does Check In/Check Out work?

Dreamweaver creates a lock (LCK) file for every document that is checked out; this basic text file contains the name and e-mail address of the user who has checked out the file. LCK files are written to both the remote server and local folder using the same name as the active file. When files are checked back in, the LCK files are deleted from both the remote server and local folder.

Although LCK files are not visible in the Files panel, they work behind the scenes to let Dreamweaver know what's checked out and what isn't. Checked-out files appear on both the local and remote file listings with a check mark next to them. Note that a colleague not using Dreamweaver can potentially overwrite a file that's checked out—however, LCK files are visible in applications other than Dreamweaver, and their appearance alone can help avoid any overwriting issues.

A user will be allowed to override your lock and switch checkout status to themselves. Make sure you establish rules with others about how to share and manage locked files.

Checking files in and out

When you check a file out, you are downloading it from the remote server to your local root folder, and placing a lock on the remote copy. Both your local copy and the remote copy appear with check marks next to them, which indicates that the file is currently checked out for editing. When you check a file back in, you are uploading the modified version to the remote server, and removing any locks currently on it.

1 Launch the Files panel and click the Expand button to expand it so that you can see both your local and remote files listed.

2 Select the file in your local folder that you want to check out, and use the Check Out button (🖐) at the top of the panel. Note that Dreamweaver overwrites your local copy of the file, as it needs to get the remote file from the server. The local and remote versions of the file appear with check marks next to them in the Files panel.

3 Open the checked file from your Local Files panel for editing. Make any necessary changes to the file, then save and close it.

4 From the Files panel, select the file again in the local Files panel and check it back in, using the Check In button (🔒) at the top of the panel. The file is uploaded to—and unlocked on—the remote server.

Check files out before modifying them so that others won't accidentally overwrite your work at the same time.

When you transfer a document between a local and remote folder, a window may open offering you the option of transferring the document's dependent files. Dependent files are images, external style sheets, and other files referenced in your document that a browser loads when it loads the document. For this exercise, it won't be necessary for you to transfer dependent files.

Your local copy becomes read-only, and appears with a padlock next to it. Next time you open the file for editing, Dreamweaver will automatically check out and get the latest copy from the server.

5   Collapse the Files panel to return it to the dock.

Using Design Notes

Design Notes store additional information about a file or media object in your Dreamweaver site. These notes can be for your own use, or they can be shared with others using the same root folder. Design Notes can be set to appear automatically when the file is opened, making it easy to display up-to-date information to others working on the same site. All Design Notes are stored as separate files in a _notes folder inside of your site's root directory.

What can be put in Design Notes?

Design Notes can contain any information that is important to the file or project; you can store design instructions, updates about the project, or contact information for project managers and supervisors. You can also store sensitive information that you ideally would not want in the file itself, such as the name of the last designer to work on the file or the location of important assets. You can even set the status of the file to indicate what stage of the revision the file is in.

1   To create a Design Note, under the Files panel, open the stores.html file from the current site.

2   Choose File > Design Notes. The Design Notes dialog box appears.

3   Type a message in the Notes field. If you wanted to insert the current date stamp, you could click the Calendar button (🗒) above the Notes field. If you want the note displayed when the file is next opened, check *Show when file is opened*.

The Status menu is used to set the document status; this can be useful in letting other collaborators know the revision stage of the current document.

4   Press OK to create the Design Note.

To view a Design Note, choose File > Design Notes when a file is open in the document window. As mentioned earlier, you can also choose to have Design Notes automatically appear when the file is first opened.

Design Notes can also be created or viewed directly from the Files panel; right-click (Windows) or Ctrl+click (Mac OS) a document in the files list and choose Design Notes from the contextual menu.

Sharing Design Notes

By default, Design Notes are stored only in the local site folder, and are not automatically copied to the remote server. However, you can share Design Notes with other collaborators by having Dreamweaver automatically upload and update them on the remote server.

1   Choose Site > Manage Sites. Select your site from the Sites panel and choose Edit. The Site Setup window appears.

2   Click on the Advanced Settings options and choose Design Notes from the left.

3   Under the Design Notes panel, check *Enable Upload Design Notes for sharing.* Design Notes are now copied and updated on the remote server so that other users can share them.

4   Choose Save to update the site definition, then press Done to close the Manage Sites dialog box.

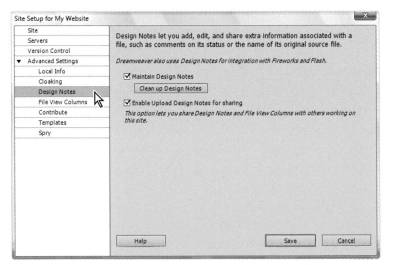

Set up Design Notes for sharing so that other Dreamweaver users can see and modify Design Notes on the remote server.

Displaying Design Notes in the Files panel

A convenient way to view and access Design Notes is by enabling the Design Notes column in the Files panel. An icon that can be used to open and edit Design Notes accompanies documents that have an associated Design Note. This feature also allows you to see all available Design Notes at a glance.

1   Choose Site > Manage Sites. Select your site from the Sites panel and choose Edit. In Advanced Setting options, choose File View Columns from the left.

Use the Site Definition panel's File View Columns category to show Design Notes in both the local and remote file listings.

2   Double-click the Notes item from the list and click the Show checkbox and then press Save.

3   Choose Save to update the site definition, then press Done to close the Manage Sites dialog box. You will likely see the Background File Activity window appear, wait for this to complete. A Notes column appears in the Files panel; a Notes icon (💬) is displayed next to each file that currently is associated with a Design Note.

Testing site integrity

Catching potential issues on a page before your visitors do is key to ensuring success from the start. Broken links, display issues, or unreadable pages can make the difference between a great first impression and a poor one. To look for and address problems before you publish your site, Dreamweaver provides many useful tools that can point out potential hazards and, in some cases, help you find the solution.

Using Check Links

The Check Links feature detects any broken links between pages in your local site and will identify orphaned files that are not linked to or used by any document within the site.

1   From the Files panel, double-click and open the index.html document.

2   Choose File > Check Page > Links.

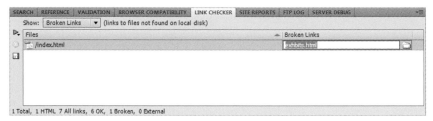

Choose File > Check Page > Links to check for broken links in the current document.

3   The Link Checker panel appears; you see one listing here. A link to the exhibits.html page is misspelled; you need to fix the error.

4   Click on the link name under the Broken Links column. The link name becomes editable.

Clicking on the link in the Broken Links column allows it to be edited.

5   Click on the folder icon to the far right. A Select File dialog box appears. Select the file **exhibits.html** and then press Choose. In the Link Checker tab, press Enter (Windows) or Return (Mac OS), and the broken link disappears.

6   Close the Link Checker panel by right-clicking (Windows) Ctrl+clicking (Mac OS) on the panel and choosing Close Tab Group. Save and close the current document.

Checking links sitewide

Check Links can be used on a single document, multiple documents (through the Files panel), or an entire local site at once.

1   Choose Site > Check Links Sitewide.

2   The Link Checker panel appears; by default, any broken links are displayed. All the broken links here are referencing the same incorrect link to category_books_cds.html. This could have happened if you or a collaborator on the site changed the name of the file within the operating system or another web editor.

Choose Site > Check Links Sitewide to check for broken links throughout the current local site. The Link Checker panel opens and displays any broken links found.

3   To view external links, choose External Links from the Show drop-down menu at the top of the panel.

External links are displayed, but aren't validated by Dreamweaver. The Link Checker can only validate links between local documents and files.

4   To view orphaned files, choose Orphaned Files from the Show drop-down menu at the top of the panel. Orphaned files are files that are not currently being linked to in your site. This may include stray multimedia files that have not been added to a page yet. You will not be doing anything with these files at this moment.

5   Choose Broken Links from the Show drop-down menu to return to the broken links report. Click on the first of the broken links shown to edit it. Click on the folder icon and browse through your site folder to locate the category_bookscds.html file. Select this file, press OK and then press Enter (Windows) or Return (Mac OS).

Adjust a link directly from the Link Checker panel to correct it sitewide.

6 A dialog box appears, asking if you'd like to make the same correction throughout the entire current local site. Press Yes. Behind the scenes Dreamweaver will go through all the pages and automatically update the correct link. This feature is an amazing timesaver as you don't even have to open the files to make the changes!

Viewing Link Checker results

If and when the Link Checker returns results, you can jump to any problem document to view and fix any issues. The Link Checker panel's Show menu (located at the top of the panel) toggles between three different Link Checker reports: Broken Links, Orphaned Files, and External Links.

Broken Links lists links that point to files not found within the local site. To jump to a page that contains a broken link, double-click the filename shown in the left column of the Link Checker panel. To correct a link directly from the Link Checker panel, click the link shown under the Broken Links column of the panel to edit it. Type in the proper page name or use the folder to browse to the proper file. If you edit a broken link this way, Dreamweaver can apply the same correction throughout other pages on your site.

Orphaned Files are any pages, images, or media files not linked to, referenced, or used by any files in your site. This report can be useful in identifying unused files that can be cleaned up from the local site, or pages that should be linked to (like a site map) but were overlooked.

External Links lists any links to outside web sites, pages, or files; and like the Broken Links panel, allows you to directly edit them or jump to the page that contains them. It's important to note, however, that Dreamweaver does not validate external links—you will still be responsible for double-checking these links on your own. You'll also notice that e-mail (mailto:) links are included in this list.

Generating site reports

Dreamweaver's site reports feature is an indispensable asset for detecting potential design and accessibility issues before publishing your site to the Web. Reports can be generated in several categories to give you a virtual picture of health, and the opportunity to locate and fix minor or major issues across an entire Dreamweaver site. These issues can include missing alternate text or titles, CSS issues, and recommendations for better accessibility practices, based on the W3C's Web Consortium Accessibility Guidelines (WCAG).

Reports can be generated for a single page, selected documents, or the entire current local site. Any results open and display in the Results panel, where you can see a list of issues and the pages on which they are located.

1   To run a site report, choose Site > Reports. The Reports dialog box opens, displaying two categories of reports: Workflow and HTML.

It is not necessary to have a document open in order to run sitewide reports.

Workflow reports display information about Design Notes, check in and check out operations, and recently modified files. HTML reports display potential design, accessibility, and display issues, based on best practices and W3C/WCAG accessibility guidelines.

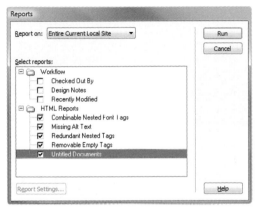

Choose Site > Reports, and select the reports you'd like to run in the Site Reports dialog box.

2   In the Reports panel, check all the reports under the HTML category. At the top of the panel, select Entire Current Local Site from the Report on drop-down menu.

3   Click Run in the top-right corner of the Reports panel. The Results panel appears, displaying any potential issues. Note that depending on the size of your site and number of issues found, it may take a few moments for all results to display.

4   Leave the Results panel open; you'll learn how to read and address issues in the next exercise.

The Results panel displays issues found across your entire current local site.

Understanding report results

At first glance, you may be overwhelmed at the amount of information returned by site reports. Keep in mind that many of the listings returned are recommendations or possible issues that should be looked into. Learning to read these site reports a little more closely will enable you to decide which items are crucial to your site's performance, requiring immediate action. Listings are displayed with three distinct icons.

ICON	NAME	USE
?	Question Mark	These listings suggest possible accessibility issues that should be investigated. Many of these issues have a reference to a specific W3C/WCAG guideline.
X	Red X	These listings indicate a failure to meet a certain guideline or requirement. Possible listings could include missing header information, deprecated HTML markup, or page titles that are not defined properly.
⚠	Warning Sign	Warnings indicate missing information that may be potentially detrimental to a site's performance, such as missing ALT text for images.

Addressing a listed item

After you've sifted through the report results, you'll want to use the Results panel to address items listed in the Site Reports tab.

1   Go to the Site Reports tab on the Results panel. Click the Description column header to sort the results. Scroll to the very bottom of the page until you see several listings accompanied by warning signs.

2   Find the listing for the store.html document, and click the More Info button (ⓘ) on the left edge of the Results panel for a detailed description, and recommended course of action.

File	Line	Description
⚠ ex1_aeronautics.html	28	Warning: Missing "alt" attribute
⚠ ex2_trains.html	28	Warning: Missing "alt" attribute
ex4_sticky.html	28	Warning: Missing "alt" attribute
⚠ ...ter.html	28	Warning: Missing "alt" attribute
⚠ index.html	14	Warning: Missing "alt" attribute
⚠ store.html	66	Warning: Missing "alt" attribute

Select a listing and click the More Info button to display a detailed description about the issue found.

The Description dialog box shows that an image on this page is missing the ALT attribute and alternate text.

3   Press OK to exit the Description dialog box and return to the Site Reports tab of the Results panel. Double-click the store.html listing to open the page for editing. The line where the issue begins should appear highlighted in Split view.

4   Select the large image in the middle of the page (giftcardpromo.jpg), and, in the Property Inspector, type **MKI Gift Cards are now available!** in the Alt field and press Enter (Windows) or Return (Mac OS).

Select the problem image and enter text in the Alt field to rectify the problem.

5   Save and close the page, and close the Results panel.

A full listing of accessibility guidelines, or WCAG, for web page designers and developers is available at the World Wide Web Consortium (W3C) web site at W3.org.

Saving reports

In a case such as this, when you have numerous warnings or suggestions, you might want to save them for future reference. Reports can be saved as XML for import into databases, existing template files, and archival files. You can sort report results using the Results panel before saving them.

1   If necessary, choose Window > Results > Site Reports to open the Site Reports tab.

2   Click on any column header to sort reports by type, page name, line number, and description.

3   Click the Save Report button (▣) on the left edge of the Results panel. When the Save Report dialog box appears, assign the report a name, and choose a location for the file.

4   Save and close the page, and close the Results panel.

The Browser Compatibility Check

When you format page content or create layouts with CSS, you'll want to be certain that your pages appear consistently across a variety of browsers. Some combinations of HTML and CSS can unearth some nasty display bugs in specific browsers. In fact, some browsers may not support certain CSS properties at all. To seek out and fix any potential CSS display problems, you'll use Dreamweaver's new Browser Compatibility Check (BCC) reports in conjunction with the CSS Advisor.

The CSS Advisor

An addition to the reporting tools in Dreamweaver CS5 is the CSS Advisor, which provides descriptions and solutions for CSS problems found during the BCC. Located in the lower-right corner of the Browser Compatibility Check panel, the CSS Advisor provides a direct link to the CSS Advisor section of Adobe's web site to find a fix for any CSS issues found and displayed in the Results panel.

1   To use the CSS Advisor, from the Files panel, locate and open the ex5_water.html document for editing.

2   Choose File > Check Page > Browser Compatibility.

Choose File > Check Page > Browser Compatibility to run the BCC for this document.

3   The Results panel opens and displays any errors or issues in the Browser Compatibility Check tab. Items returned indicate any potential CSS display issues; each result is accompanied by a confidence rating icon that tells you how likely it is that the problem will occur. This page should return one error.

4   Because the error listed is within the external style sheet you will need to open it and run the check again. Click on the styles.css button at the top of your document and choose File > Check Page > Browser Compatibility. The errors found refer to a CSS property *filter* which would affect the rendering of this page in a number of different browsers. If you navigate through the styles.css style sheet you can locate the property on line 26.

The Browser Compatibility Check tab on the Results panel displays a single error and description.

5   By default, the BCC checks for issues in the following browsers: Firefox 1.5; Internet
     Explorer (Windows) 6.0 and 7.0; Internet Explorer (Macintosh) 5.2; Netscape Navigator
     8.0; Opera 8.0 and 9.0; and Safari 2.0. You can modify the target browsers and versions
     by choosing Settings from the green Run button (▸) on the BCC panel.

Optimizing pages for launch

Although page optimization is discussed at this point in the book, it is by no means an
afterthought. A big part of preparing a site for success involves making it accessible to users with
special needs, such as those who are visually impaired, or preparing it for indexing by various
search engines. In addition to clean design and well-written content, pages can be optimized
through the use of keywords, descriptions, and often-overlooked tag attributes, such as alternate
text (alt) for images and a page's Title area. Combined, these pieces of information facilitate site
usability and visibility in several essential ways.

Search engine visibility and Search Engine Optimization

A big part of a web site's success stems from its visibility. Visibility comes through good
advertising, networking with other sites, and, above all, proper indexing and listings on the Web's
major search engines. Search engines can be a key to generating business and visits to your
site, but only if your web site can be easily found. Major search engines such as Google (which
powers AOL, MySpace, and Netscape searches), Yahoo! (which powers AltaVista and others),
and LiveSearch (formerly MSN Search) use a variety of factors to index and generate listings for
web sites. Many of these factors start at home, or more appropriately, on your home page.

Titling your documents with the *<title>* tag

Each document's head area contains a *<title>* tag, which Dreamweaver automatically inserts
with any new HTML/XHTML document. At its most basic, the *<title>* tag sets a display
title for a page that appears at the top of the browser window. You can modify the *<title>* tag
contents using the Title text field that sits at the top of your document window. By default, each
new document is issued the default title of Untitled Document. The *<title>* tag and its contents,
however, can be a powerful and effective way to assist search engines in indexing your page.

What makes a good title?

A good document title ideally should include keywords that describe your site's main service,
locale, and category of business or information. In addition to the obvious—your company's
name—think about the categories you would want your site to appear under on a web
directory or as the result of a web search. For instance, the McKnight Institute would ideally
want users looking for science museums or exhibits in the Philadelphia, Pennsylvania, area to
find them first. A possible title could be: The McKnight Institute: Science Museum, Educational
Exhibits and Attractions, Philadelphia, Pennsylvania.

This title contains several important keywords that describe the Institute's offerings, and features the Institute's name and location. In addition, re-shuffling these phrases and words produces several other search terms that could be beneficial to the Institute, such as:

* Science Exhibits

* Philadelphia Museum

* Pennsylvania Attractions

Avoid the rookie mistake of including only your company name in the document title. Remember, web searchers who haven't used your business before will only search by terms that apply to the service they are seeking (for example, wedding photographers, Washington, D.C.). Even the most recognized names on the web, such as eBay and Amazon, include generic search terms in their page titles.

To add a title to your web page:

1   From the Files panel, select and open the index.html document to open it for editing.

2   Locate the Title text field at the top of the document window. It currently displays the default title of Untitled Document. Select its contents and type **The McKnight Institute: Science Museum, Educational Exhibits and Attractions, Philadelphia, Pennsylvania** and press Enter (Windows) or Return (Mac OS).

Add a well-constructed title to the index.html page to make it more search-engine and bookmark friendly.

3   Choose File > Save to save the document, and then choose File > Preview in Browser > [Default browser] to open the document in your system's primary browser.

4   Note the title that now appears in the bar at the top of the browser window. Close the browser window and return to Dreamweaver.

The most basic purpose of the <title> tag is to display a title at the top of the browser window. If used properly, it can also be used as a powerful hook for search engines.

While there is technically no limit to title length, the W3C's Web Consortium Accessibility Guide recommends that page titles be a maximum of 64 characters to be considered 'well-defined.' Titles exceeding this length may generate warnings in the Site Reports Results panel. Longer titles may also appear truncated (cut off) when displayed in some browser windows.

Bookmark-ability: another benefit of the *<title>* tag

It's common for users to bookmark a site or specific page they've found so that they can easily return to it. Every browser has a bookmark feature, which allows users to mark and display favorite sites in an organized list; sometimes, favorite sites are listed in a Bookmarks bar in the browser window.

The document title determines the text that appears with a bookmark, so it's important to consider this when creating a good document title. Using a vague or non-descriptive title (or even worse, the default Untitled Document text) can make it impossible for a user to remember which bookmark is yours. A good title appears as a descriptive bookmark in a browser's Favorites list or Bookmarks bar.

Adding meta keywords and descriptions

While Search Engine Optimization (SEO) is a broad topic that's far beyond the scope of this book, good SEO methods begin at the design level. Search engines use a variety of factors to rank and list web pages. Keywords and descriptions can help specify the search terms that are associated with your site and how it's listed. The HTML *<meta>* tag enables you to associate any page with a specific list of search terms, as well as a brief description of the page or the web site itself. Like the *<title>* tag, *<meta>* tags are placed in the *<head>* section of a page, and can be added from the Common Insert bar on the right side of your workspace.

1 If it's not already open, open the index.html document for editing.

2 From the Common Insert bar, choose the Keywords button from the Head tags group.

3 When the Keywords window appears, add a comma-separated list of search keywords that you'd like associated with this page, or the site in general. While there is no general consensus on the limit of how many keywords you can use, common sense says that you should be able to categorize your site in roughly 20 keywords or fewer. For example, type **The McKnight Institute, science museum, technology exhibits, attractions, family attractions, philadelphia, pennsylvania museums**. Press Return (Windows) or Enter (Mac OS) to add the keywords.

From the Common category of the Insert bar, choose the Keywords object from the Head tags group and enter a list of keywords in the resulting dialog box.

4 Now you'll add a description that a search engine can use to summarize your page when creating a listing for it. Choose the Description button from the Head tags group on the Common Insert bar.

5   When the Description dialog box appears, type in a brief descriptive paragraph (fewer than 250 characters, including spaces). For example, type **The McKnight Center is a family-oriented education center and museum that explores the history of technology and scientific discovery through hands-on exhibits and events**. Press OK.

Add a short description that search engines can use to display a caption for your site listing.

6   Choose File > Save, then choose File > Close to close the file.

Describing images with alternate text

Each image placed in your page can feature alternate text, which describes that image and also acts as a placeholder in its absence. Alternate text is added with the alt attribute of the *<img>* tag, and, for each image, alternate text can be specified using the Alt field located on the Property Inspector. In the past, alternate text was used as a placeholder for an image that failed to load, or for larger images downloading through slow dial-up connections.

With increased download speeds and the widespread availability of high-speed Internet access, this usage of the Alt attribute has been given a lower priority because of two more popular uses: accessibility and search engine visibility. Accessibility is an important part of web page design, and refers to a page or collective web site's usability by people with disabilities. Alternate text provides a way for disability assistants such as voice browsers, screen readers, and other specialized browsers to interpret and describe images and graphics included on a page. Visually impaired users frequently make use of screen readers to 'speak' the contents of a web page out loud.

Search engines such as Google Images make use of alternate text to provide information about image listings. The more accurate and concise the description, the more likely it is that users will find what they are looking for on your site. Also, well-indexed images are another hook that allows users to find your site—for example, a user searching for an image of a scientific nature may discover many of the images on the MKI site through an image search.

1   To add alt text to your page, first locate and open the ex4_sticky.html page from the Files panel.

2   Select the single image located in the middle of the page (stick.jpg). If necessary, choose Window > Properties to open the Property Inspector.

3   On the Property Inspector, locate the Alt text field. Type the words **The Science of Sticky Exhibit at MKI**, and press Return (Windows) or Enter (Mac OS). Leave the image selected.

Add alternate text for a selected image using the Alt field located on the Property Inspector.

4   Switch to Code view by clicking the Code button in the upper-left corner of the document window. Note the highlighted section of code, which should include an *<img>* tag. The tag will appear with an alt attribute with your new text set as its value.

```
24        </tr>
25        </table></td>
26      </tr>
27      <tr>
28        <td colspan="2"><img src="assets/ImageAssets/stick.jpg" alt="The Science of Sticky Exhibit at
          MKI" width="283" height="212" hspace="25" align="left" /></td>
29        <td align="left" valign="top"><p><font size="3" face="Arial, Helvetica, sans-serif"><em>
Exhibit
30      4</em><br />
31      <strong>The Science of Sticky</strong></font></p>
32        <p><font size="2" face="Arial, Helvetica, sans-serif"><br />
```

The newly added alternate text, shown in Code view. Alternate text is added using the <img> tag's alt attribute.

5   Click the Design button at the top of the document window to return to Design view, and choose File > Save to save your page.

Rather than manually searching for missing titles or alternate text, use Dreamweaver's site reports, as shown earlier in this lesson, to generate listings of instances of missing alternate text throughout your site.

6   Choose File > Close to close the file.

Launching your site

Before launching your site for the public—and to ensure that your site works at, and looks, its best—take a moment to go over this pre-flight checklist.

Site Launch Checklist

☐ Enter FTP or upload information and test your FTP connection.

☐ Check links sitewide and repair missing or broken links and images.

☐ Run site reports and address crucial issues. Put special emphasis on:

  ☐ Missing document titles

  ☐ Missing alt text

  ☐ Invalid markup that may cause display issues

☐ Open the homepage (index.html, and so on) and navigate through your site, using menus, links in copy, and linked images to check page flow. Do this in several browsers, and, if possible, on both Windows and Macintosh platforms.

☐ View your home page and major section pages in a web browser in the three most common screen resolutions: 640x480, 800x600, and 1024x768.

Uploading your site

At this point, if you have been following along without having access to a remote FTP server, you will now require one to continue this lesson.

1   If you're ready to upload your site to the remote web server, make sure that the Files panel is open (Window > Files).

2   Click the Expand button (⊡) at the top of the Files panel to display it in two-column expanded view.

3   Click the Connect button (⚬) above the left (remote view) column to connect to your remote web server.

You need to have created a valid connection, as described earlier in the lesson.

Once a successful connection is made, the remote files (if any) display in the left-hand column.

4   In the right column, click and select the Folder icon at the very top of the file listing. This should be the root folder, and displays the current site definition title (Site Dreamweaver Lesson 14, for example).

Select the root folder of your local site and click the Put button to upload the entire site to the web server.

5   Click the Put button at the top of the Files panel to copy the entire current local site and all included files to the current directory on the remote server. A dialog box appears with the message, *Are you sure you wish to put the entire site?*

6   Press OK to begin copying the files to the remote server. A progress bar continues to display until all files have been successfully copied.

The entire web site has been successfully uploaded to the server, and displays in the remote view on the left.

7   Collapse the Files panel to return it to the dock.

Getting help and using the reference guides

Whether you are seeking a solution to a Dreamweaver-specific problem, or looking up the appropriate CSS rule to format a page item, you can use Dreamweaver's built-in Help system and integrated reference guides. In addition, the Help menu provides direct links to many online resources and Adobe support areas where you can seek help from Adobe professionals and the Dreamweaver user community.

1   To access the Help system, choose Help > Dreamweaver Help. The Adobe Help Viewer panel appears.

The Help menu.

2   Enter a search term at the top of the panel, or browse by topic on the left-hand side of the panel.

3   For more help options and a searchable knowledge base, choose Help > Dreamweaver Support Center. For the Dreamweaver support forums, choose Help > Adobe Online Forums.

The Reference panel

Dreamweaver's Reference panel is like a full library of technical books, including reference guides for HTML, CSS, JavaScript, and Dreamweaver-friendly, server-side languages such as ColdFusion and JSP.

1 To open the Reference panel, choose Help > Reference.

2 From the menu at the top left corner of the panel, select the *Usablenet Accessibility Reference* from the Book menu.

3 Click on the Rule menu and a list of various guidelines to help you make your web sites more accessible is listed. Choosing any topic reveals detailed information in the window below.

Suggested next steps

Congratulations on launching your first Dreamweaver site project! There's nothing more exciting than having your hard work on the web, and available for the world to see. The important thing to remember is that your web site should not be static; part of maintaining a successful web site requires continuously evolving it to meet the needs of your viewers, and keeping the content fresh and new.

Whether your site is for business, pleasure, or self-promotion, be sure to solicit feedback from friends, family, and colleagues after you've launched. Alert a small and trusted group about the launch by sending out an e-mail, mailing a postcard, or posting a notice on a blog (sometimes this is referred to as the 'beta' stage). Feedback and constructive criticism (a little praise is okay, too) are the best ways to objectively know what needs improvement. You'll probably receive more feedback and suggestions than you can handle, so focus on points that are common across multiple users, and address any major issues before making a more public launch (for instance, to your entire client base).

Focus on focus groups

Focus groups are an excellent way to get non-biased feedback on a major new site or product launch, and they have been a regular practice in product marketing and research for years. A focus group is composed of a group of individuals who are brought together to analyze, try out, and comment on a specific product—in this case, your web site—for the purpose of obtaining feedback and testing the product's effectiveness.

Groups can be guided through certain portions or processes on the site, or may be encouraged to navigate it on their own. Afterwards, they are polled with specific questions about their experience, and the results are put together to form a picture of the site's usability, effectiveness, and impact. This may include questions such as the following:

- Did you feel the web site was easy to navigate? On a scale from 1 to 10, how would you rate the difficulty level in locating specific pages or topics?

- Did the design, including graphics and color themes, effectively help communicate the web site's offerings?

- On a scale from 1 to 10, how would you rate the quality of the written content on the site?

Focus groups are often interactive, encouraging participants to talk with each other and share their opinions. In some cases, a moderator may be used to regulate group discussions, and hand out questionnaires. Participants can be composed of a focused demographic group (for instance, 25- to 35-year-old technology professionals), or they can represent a diverse professional and demographic range.

Focus groups are reasonable for any size company to organize—even if it's just you and five friends—and are a highly effective way to find out what's currently working and what's not. Give it a try; you may find the results encouraging, surprising, or even slightly discouraging. The trick is to use this feedback wisely toward the main purpose of making a better web site, and you'll be glad you did.

Web site design resources

There is a vast amount of information, and many tutorial-based web sites, covering topics from web page standards to advanced CSS design. Here is a small sampling of some useful sites that can help you take your skills and knowledge further. Use these in conjunction with Dreamweaver's built-in reference guides and Adobe's online support forums:

W3C (World Wide Web Consortium) – *www.w3.org*

W3Schools – *www.w3schools.com*

A List Apart – *http://alistapart.com/*

Adobe's Dreamweaver Developer Center – *www.adobe.com/devnet/dreamweaver/*

CSS Zengarden – *www.csszengarden.com/*

maxdesign – *http://css.maxdesign.com.au/*

CSSplay – *www.cssplay.co.uk/www*

Self study

1   Import a site from a previous lesson from this book or import your own site, and run a site report for broken links, orphaned files, and so on.

2   Investigate Dreamweaver's CSS Advisor by examining various files from this lesson and previous lessons. Using the CSS Advisor is a great way to learn more about CSS and browser compatibility issues.

Review

Questions

1   What does FTP stand for, and what is it used for?

2   What three purposes do document titles serve, and why are they important?

3   What are three possible pre-flight checklist items you need to address before launching a web site?

Answers

1   File Transfer Protocol. FTP is used to connect to and transfer files between your local machine and a web server.

2   Document titles display a title at the top of the browser window, display in a user's bookmarks bar, and are an important hook for search engines.

3   **a.** Enter and test your FTP connection information in the Site Definition panel.

   b. Run site reports to rectify any potential design or accessibility issues, such as missing alternate text for images or empty document titles.

   c. Run the Link Checker sitewide to check for broken links between pages or incorrect image references.

What you'll learn in this lesson:

- Creating frames and framesets
- Setting frame properties
- Using the Frame panel
- Adding and editing frame content
- Using tables for layout purposes

Using Legacy Tools: Frames and Tables

Cascading Style Sheets (CSS) have become the standard for both formatting and positioning elements on a web page. It took time for CSS to become viable in code, however, and in the meantime, tables and frames were used to handle the majority of layouts in common pages. This lesson focuses on using the legacy tools necessary for working on frame- and table-based pages.

Starting up

Before starting, make sure that your tools and panels are consistent by resetting your workspace. See "Resetting the Dreamweaver workspace" on page 3.

You will work with several files from the dw15lessons folder in this lesson. Make sure that you have loaded the dwlessons folder onto your hard drive from the supplied DVD. See "Loading lesson files" on page 3.

Before you begin, you need to create site settings that points to the dw15lessons folder from the included DVD that contains resources you need for these lessons. Go to Site > New Site, or, for details on creating a site, refer to Lesson 2, "Setting Up a New Site."

See Lesson 1 in action!

Use the accompanying video to gain a better understanding of how to use some of the features shown in this lesson. The video tutorial for this lesson can be found on the included DVD.

Legacy sites

A quick note about this lesson: we present here techniques for creating web pages using HTML tables and frames for layout. These two methods are becoming less popular every year. Throughout this book we have attempted to point you in the direction of building modern web sites using HTML and CSS for layout, a more robust and efficient method.

This lesson was designed so users who wish to focus on frames may complete the first half of the lesson, but not the second. Alternatively, if you are solely interested in working with tables for layout, you may jump to the second half without completing the first half on frames.

How frames work

Frames provide a way to divide a browser window into multiple regions, each capable of displaying a different HTML document. A frameset is an HTML file that defines the layout and properties of a set of frames, including the number of frames, their size and placement, and the content that appears in each frame. When you open a frameset file, the browser also opens all relevant HTML documents and displays them in their respective frames.

Advantages and disadvantages of frames

If you have the time (and patience), it is possible to create a page design with a frame-like layout without using frames. That, however, might involve excessive steps, such as building navigation controls on every page within your site. Frames, when used correctly, can be useful for site navigation and can save you a good deal of time in the page-creation process.

Using frames is not always a good idea, however. Like many time-saving features used in web design, there are advantages and disadvantages of using frames for layout.

Here are some advantages to using frames:

- Using frames saves time and avoids repetitive work in page creation.

- The viewer's browser doesn't need to reload graphics used for navigation on every page.

- Frames enable parts of the page to stay stationary (like navigation), while other parts (such as content) are able to scroll independently.

Viewers can scroll through long content in a frame using built-in scroll bars.

Here are some disadvantages of using frames:

- Aligning content precisely in different frames can be problematic.

- Viewers won't be able to bookmark individual framed pages (unless you provide specific server code).

- Testing the navigation from frame to frame can be time-consuming, and many users find it difficult to navigate sites with frames.

- Framed documents are problematic for search engines.

- Documents may appear outside the context of their frame set, such as those displayed in results from a search engine.

- Frames make it more difficult to count page or ad views.

Despite these concerns, frames are still used in many sites and are supported by Dreamweaver, so it is important to understand them. Take these advantages and disadvantages into account when deciding whether to use frames when you create pages on your own.

Common frame usage

Frames are most commonly used for navigation, with one frame displaying a document containing navigation controls, and other frames showing pages with content.

In this lesson, you'll be building an interactive Exhibits page for a museum web site. It will consist of a frameset with three frames: a narrow frame on the left with navigation controls, a short frame along the top containing the museum's logo and title, and a large frame containing the actual (and changeable) page content. Each frame will act as a container for the page it's displaying, but the page will not actually be part of the frame. When you're finished, your frameset will look like this:

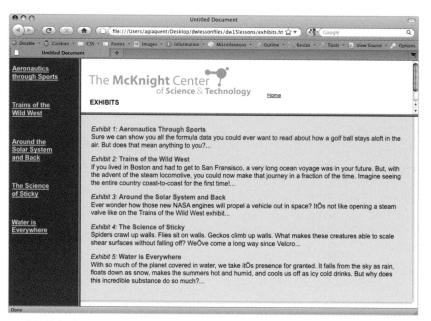

You'll build this frameset during this lesson.

Creating framesets

The best way to understand how frames and framesets work—and specifically how to work with them in Dreamweaver—is to create some.

There are two ways to create a frameset in Dreamweaver: you can choose from various predefined framesets, or you can design one from scratch. For this lesson, you'll combine both techniques, using a predefined frameset to begin, and then adding a *splitter* to customize the frameset's layout.

1   Choose File > New and click on Blank Page if necessary; then select HTML in the Page Type column and make sure *<none>* is selected in the Layout column. Press Create.

2   Make frame borders visible by choosing View > Visual Aids > Frame Borders.

View	Insert	Modify	Format	
Zoom In			⌘=	
Zoom Out			⌘−	
Magnification			▶	
Head Content			⇧⌘H	
✓ Noscript Content				
Table Mode			▶	
Visual Aids			▶	Hide All ⇧⌘I
Style Rendering			▶	
Code View Options			▶	CSS Layout Backgrounds
				✓ CSS Layout Box Model
Rulers			▶	✓ CSS Layout Outlines
Grid			▶	✓ AP Element Outlines
Guides			▶	✓ Table Widths
Tracing Image			▶	✓ Table Borders
Plugins			▶	Frame Borders
				✓ Image Maps
✓ Display External Files				✓ Invisible Elements
Color Icons				

Use the Frame Borders command to make your frame borders visible.

3   At the top of the Insert toolbar, choose Layout from the category drop-down menu.

4 Scroll down in the Insert toolbar to locate the Frames drop-down menu (⊟·), and choose Left Frame from the top of the menu. Your page is now divided into two frames by a light gray line.

Choose a prebuilt frame layout from the Insert toolbar (Left Frame).

By default, Dreamweaver is set up to prompt you to determine the Frame Tag Accessibility Attributes. This feature allows you to tag your frames so that they are more accessible to visually impaired viewers.

5 Choose mainFrame from the Frame drop-down menu, and type **Content** into the Title text field.

6 Choose leftFrame from the Frame drop-down menu, and type **Menu** into the Title text field. You can change both titles from within the same dialog box. Press OK.

Use the Frame Tag Accessibility Attributes dialog box to tag your frames so that they're more accessible.

Changing the names of the frame tags for accessibility is not the same as changing the names of the frames themselves. In the next exercise, you will learn how to select frames and rename them.

Selecting frames

As you view your document window in the Design view, you can click inside each of the two frames you've created and see a blinking insertion cursor there. If you want to change a frame's properties (including borders, margins, and scroll bar access), you'll want to select each frame individually.

1 Alt+Shift+click (Windows) or Option+Shift+click (Mac OS) inside the left (leftFrame) frame in the Design view to select the frame.

2 In the Properties panel, in the text field for Frame name, highlight the text leftFrame and type **Menu**. Press Enter (Windows) or Return (Mac OS) to apply this change.

3   Alt+click (Windows) or Option+Shift+click (Mac OS) inside the main (mainFrame) frame in the Design view to select the frame.

Notice that when a frame is selected, its borders are outlined with a dotted line. You'll change your individual frames' properties later in this lesson.

Selected frames are highlighted with a dotted line border.

4   In the Properties panel, in the text field for Frame name, highlight the text mainFrame and type **Content**. Press Enter (Windows) or Return (Mac OS) to apply this change.

Name your frames in the Property Inspector.

Frame names should be one word in length, and cannot contain special characters. (Underscores are permitted.) They are also case-sensitive.

Selecting framesets

Framesets have properties too, including frame dimensions, border color, and width. To access a frameset's properties, you'll have to first select the frameset itself. Click on the internal frame border (the light gray line separating your Menu and Content frames) to select the frameset.

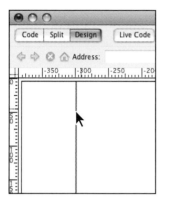

Click on the border between your frames to select the frameset as a whole.

The Frames panel

The Frames panel allows you to see the structure of your frameset more clearly than the document window allows. Its visual interface includes a thick border around the frameset, thin gray lines separating the frames, and a frame name clearly identifying each frame.

The Frames panel also allows you to more easily select frames and framesets than you can in the document window, by clicking on the desired frames in the panel itself.

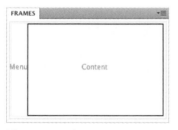

The Frames panel.

To select a frame or frameset in the Frames panel:

1 Choose Window > Frames, or press Shift+F2, to open the Frames panel.

2 To select the Content frame (which you named earlier), simply click on it in the Frames panel. Notice the selection outline that appears around the frame in the document window, as well as in the Frames panel.

3 To select the entire frameset, click on the border around the frameset in the Frames panel. A bold, black selection outline now surrounds the entire frameset in both the Frames panel and the document window.

Now that you have your frameset selected, you can move on to changing its properties.

Setting frameset properties

The dimensions, border width, and border color for the frames in your frameset are not set with the individual frames selected, but with the frameset itself selected. This is because your frames must always share the visible area of your page, and therefore, their sizes, borders, and so on, must be relative within the frameset.

Border properties

Using the Property Inspector, you can customize your frameset layout by adding borders of a particular width and color between your frames.

1 If necessary, click on the gray border separating your frames in order to reselect the entire frameset. The Property Inspector at the bottom of your screen now displays frameset properties, including the number of rows and columns in your current frameset.

The Property Inspector displays the properties of a selected frameset.

2 From the Borders drop-down menu, choose Yes to define a border between your frames. (The Default option allows the browser to determine how borders are displayed.)

3 In the Border width text field, type **6** to create a 6-pixel-wide border between your frames.

4 In the Border color text field, type the hexadecimal code **#666666** to make the border between your frames dark gray. You can also use the Color Picker to select the appropriate color swatch. Press Enter (Windows) or Return (Mac OS).

Now, you'll define the width of the frames in your frameset.

Frame dimensions

The Property Inspector allows you to further customize your frameset layout by specifying the dimensions of each frame relative to the other(s).

1 If they're not already visible, choose View > Rulers to gain access to your page rulers.

2 Right-click (Windows) or Ctrl+click (Mac OS) on either of the rulers (horizontal or vertical) that appear at the top and left side of your page. Choose Pixels from the context menu that appears.

Set your ruler units to pixels whenever you're designing for the web.

It's useful to work in pixels whenever possible in Dreamweaver, because you're designing your web pages to be viewed on a monitor, which is a pixel-based device.

3 In the Property Inspector, click the frame on the left side of the RowCol Selection area to select that frame's dimensions for editing.

Select the left side of the RowCol Selection area to edit that frame's dimensions.

4 To specify how much space a web browser should allocate to this frame, type **175** into the (Column) Value text field, press Enter (Windows) or Return (Mac OS) and choose Pixels from the (Column) Units drop-down menu.

Set the frame's width to a fixed value (175 pixels) in the Property Inspector.

This sets the left frame of your frameset, where your navigation controls will appear, to a fixed width of 175 pixels. Setting a frame's width to a specific pixel value is common when you want that frame to always be the same size, as in a navigation menu.

5 Click on the frame on the right side of the RowCol Selection area to edit that frame's dimensions.

6   To specify how much space a web browser should allocate to this frame, choose Relative from the (Column) Units drop-down menu.

Set the remaining frame's width by choosing Relative from the (Column) Units drop-down menu.

This sets the right frame of your frameset, where you want your changeable content to appear, to fill the remaining space in the browser window, relative to the 175 pixels used by the left frame.

Choosing the Percent option specifies that the frame selected should be a percentage of the total width of the frameset, for example, 50 percent of the total width of the browser window.

You now have a frameset with two frames, one of which is set to a fixed width of 175 pixels in any browser window, the other of which is set to fill the remaining space with HTML page content of your choosing. Next, you'll change individual frame properties within your frameset.

7   Choose File > Save Frameset. When the Save As dialog box appears, type **exhibits.html** into the Name text field. Navigate to the dw15lessons folder, and press Save.

Saving frames and framesets

As with everything else you create in Dreamweaver, it pays to save your frames and framesets early and often. It's also true that you won't be able to preview your frameset in a browser without first saving the frameset and all the content that appears in its frames. You can save these files individually or all at one time.

File	Edit	View	Insert	Mo:

New...   ⌘N
Open...   ⌘O
Browse in Bridge...   ⌥⌘O
Open Recent   ▶
Open in Frame...   ⇧⌘O
Close   ⌘W
Close All   ⇧⌘W
Save Frameset   ⌘S
Save Frameset As...   ⇧⌘S
Save All

When saving a frameset, you'll have at least three different files that will have to be saved as a result of creating frames. There's the frameset, which is the HTML container file that houses the frames, and then there are the individual HTML files that are contained in each frame.

To save a frameset:

1   Select the frameset in the Frames panel or in the document window.

2   Choose File > Save Frameset.

To save a frame's content:

1   Click in the frame to place an insertion cursor.

2   Choose File > Save Frame.

To save a frameset and all associated files:

1   Select the frameset.

2   Choose File > Save All.

Setting frame properties

Like frameset properties, you view and set frame properties in the Property Inspector. When you set properties such as borders, margins, and the visibility of scroll bars for a specific frame, these settings override properties that you set previously for the frameset as a whole.

1   Select the right (Content) frame of your frameset by Alt+clicking (Windows) or Option+Shift+clicking (Mac OS) on it in the document window.

2   In the Property Inspector, click on the Browse button (▣) to the right of the Src text field to navigate to the source file Teaser.html. Press OK (Windows) or Choose (Mac OS). This is one way of choosing the default content of the Content frame. You'll learn other ways later in this lesson. Press Don't Save when prompted to save changes.

3   Directly beneath the Src setting, choose Yes from the Scroll drop-down menu to ensure that scroll bars appear in this frame.

Add scroll bars by choosing Yes from the Scroll drop-down menu.

The Default option lets each browser use its default setting to decide whether scroll bars are included. Most browsers default to Auto (which you can also choose from this drop-down menu), which makes scroll bars appear only when there isn't enough room to view the content of the frame. Choosing No from this menu prevents scroll bars from appearing.

4   Click the No resize checkbox to prevent viewers from dragging your frame borders to resize them in a browser.

Prevent viewers from resizing your frames by choosing the No Resize option.

5   From the Borders drop-down menu, choose No to hide this frame's border when viewed in a browser. This overrides the frameset's border property.

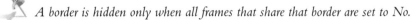

Hiding an individual frame's border overrides the frameset's border setting.

Choosing Yes from this menu shows the frame's borders, and choosing Default leaves this decision up to the browser. Most browsers default to showing borders, except when the frameset's border properties are set to No.

A border is hidden only when all frames that share that border are set to No.

6   The Margin Width and Margin Height fields in the Property Inspector set the space (in pixels) between the frame borders and the content. Set each of these to 25 pixels to give yourself some breathing room.

Setting the background color of a frame

The background color of a frame is not a property that you can set in the Property Inspector. To change frame background colors, you'll need to use the Page Properties dialog box.

1   Click inside the right frame to place an insertion cursor.

2   Choose Modify > Page Properties. The Page Properties dialog box appears.

3 In the Background color text field, type **#d7d7d7** to set the background color of your frame to a light gray.

Set the background color of a frame (d7d7d7) in the Page Properties dialog box.

4 Press OK to close the Page Properties dialog box and see the results.

Repeat these steps to change the Background color of the Menu frame to **#843432**.

Splitting a frame

There are two ways to divide an existing frame within your frameset into discrete frames. First, you can use a Split Frame command:

1 Click inside the Content frame to place an insertion cursor.

2 Choose Modify > Frameset > Split Frame Down. A new frame is created above the Content frame.

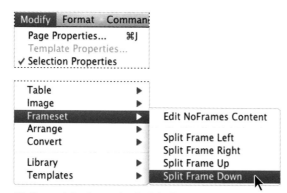

Divide an existing frame using the Split Frame Down command.

Dragging a frame border

A second way to divide an existing frame is to drag a frame border to split the existing frame in two:

1 Choose Edit > Undo to undo the previous frame addition. (You may have to do this twice.)

2 Alt+Shift+click (Windows) or Option+Shift+click (Mac OS) on the Content frame.

3 If necessary, choose View > Visual Aids > Frame Borders to make your frame borders visible.

4 Roll your mouse over the frame border at the top of the Content frame until you see the double-headed arrow (↕). Click and drag a frame border from that edge into the middle of the frame.

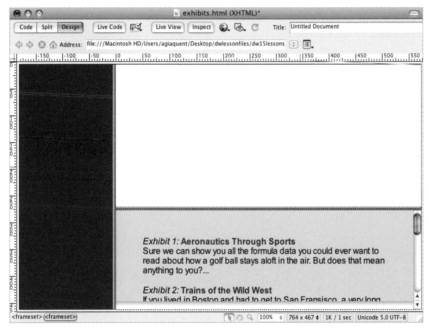

Drag a frame border to split an existing frame in two.

Once you have split a frame using either of these methods, you can reposition the border by clicking and dragging it to a new location in the frame, changing the space that is available for content.

5 Position your cursor over the border you just placed to split the frame.

6   Click and drag the border downward (or upward, depending on where you placed it) to the 100-pixel mark in the vertical ruler to the left of the document window.

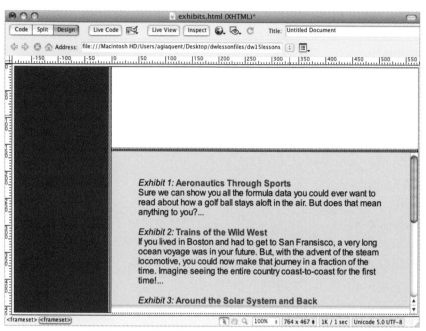

Drag a border to reposition it within the frameset.

You can use this new frame at the top of your frameset for the title and logo content. The page displayed in this frame will never change as the viewer navigates the site. (You'll set the default content of this frame, using the Open in Frame command later in this lesson.)

7   Select the new frame, using the Frames panel. In the Property Inspector, name it **Title**, and press Enter (Windows) or Return (Mac OS).

Now you're ready to add and edit frame content.

Specifying frame content

On your web page, you want the viewer to be able to click on a link in the navigation frame (called Menu), and have linked content appear in the main (Content) frame on the right.

The content of the Menu and Title frames, however, remains unchanged. To set the default content for each of these unchanging frames, you'll use the Open in Frame command.

1   Click in the Menu frame to place an insertion cursor.

2   Choose File > Open in Frame, or press Ctrl+O (Windows) or Shift+Command+O (Mac OS).

3   Navigate to the dw15lessons folder on your desktop and select the HTML page Menu.html. The base content for the Menu frame has been created for you.

4   Press OK (Windows) or Choose (Mac OS) to specify the initial content of the Menu frame. Press Don't Save when prompted to save changes.

5   Repeat steps 1 to 4 to specify the initial content of the Title frame. Insert the Title.html file here.

6   Finally, to make these HTML pages the default content displayed when the frameset is opened in a browser, click on any of the frame borders to select the frameset, then choose File > Save Frameset.

Targeting frames

In a framed document, you must target links for them to open a document in another frame. Targeting is simply a way of specifying in which frame Dreamweaver should open the linked content.

In Lesson 3, "Adding Text and Images," you learned how to link content from one HTML page to another. For this lesson, the links from items in your menu to their corresponding pages have been made for you. Your job is to target these links to the frames you created earlier in the lesson.

1   Use the Preview/Debug in browser button (⊚) to preview the Exhibits frameset in your browser. Notice that the frame pages you instructed Dreamweaver to display by default are showing in each of their respective frames. Note that if you don't see your pages for the Menu and Title, you may need to return to Dreamweaver, select the frames and use the Point to File tool for the Src field to point to the respective pages. Choose Save All and preview again.

2   Click on the first link, *Aeronautics through Sports*. Notice that the linked page doesn't appear in the Content frame as desired, but instead replaces the menu. This is because the link you clicked is not targeted to the Content frame.

3   Close your browser and return to the Design view in Dreamweaver.

4 In the menu frame, drag your cursor over the *Aeronautics through Sports* link to select it.

5 Click on the HTML button in the Property Inspector at the bottom of your screen. The Link field shows that this text is correctly set to link to the Aeronautics.html page when clicked. The Target field to the right is blank.

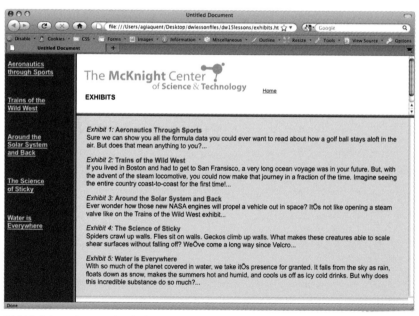

Note that the link is intact, but no specific frame has been targeted.

6 To target the Content frame when this link is clicked, click on the drop-down menu next to the Target text field and choose Content from the list. You have now ensured that this page appears in the Content frame of your frameset.

7 Use the Preview/Debug in browser button (●) to preview the Exhibits frameset in your browser. Click on the *Aeronautics through Sports* link to see the content display in the proper frame. If you do not see the change, close the browser window and return to Dreamweaver, and then preview in the browser again.

8 Repeat steps 1 to 7 for each link in the Menu frame, targeting the Content frame for each linked HTML page.

Multiple links can be targeted to display HTML content in different frames.

Now that you've learned to use frames at a higher level, let's look at some alternatives.

Linking to outside web pages

In the last exercise, you targeted links so that several pages from your local root folder were displayed interchangeably in the Content frame of your frameset. You're not limited, however, to linking only to local HTML pages when you target frames. You can link to outside, or remote, pages as well.

1   In the bottom-right corner of your Title frame, click and drag to highlight the word *Home*.

Always give the viewer a way back to your home page by creating a link back to it.

2   In the Property Inspector, click in the Link text field and type **Teaser.html**.

Set the link for the Home *text.*

This links the *Home* text to the home page, but the page content replaces the default content in the Title frame, because you haven't yet targeted the Content frame.

3   Preview the frameset in your browser and click on the *Home* link to confirm it.

4   Return to Dreamweaver. In the Property Inspector, choose Content from the Target drop-down menu to target that as the frame in which to display the page content.

5   Preview the frameset in your browser and click on the *Home* link once more to confirm that it is properly targeted.

Using _top to replace a frameset

You might have noticed that other choices are available in the Target drop-down menu in the Property Inspector. These choices offer other options for the frame in which a linked document should appear:

_blank opens the linked content in a new browser window (similar to a pop-up window), and leaves the current window behind it untouched.

_parent opens the linked content in the parent frameset of the frame in which the link appears. This option usually replaces the entire frameset.

_self opens the linked content in the current frame, replacing any existing content in that frame. (As you saw in the last exercise, Dreamweaver does this by default.)

_top opens the linked content in the current browser window, replacing the current frameset.

Content target using the _top command replaces your current frameset in a browser window.

As you've seen, you can also select a named frame (if you've defined any) to open the linked document in that frame.

For this exercise, you'll use the _top target to open the home page in the current browser window, replacing the frameset you've just built. This is often done to ensure that the page doesn't appear to be a part of your site, while the information is still delivered.

1 In the Title frame of your frameset, click and drag to reselect the *Home* link you targeted earlier.

2 The Property Inspector should show the target of this link as the Content frame. Change this by choosing _top from the Target drop-down menu.

The _top command overrides your frameset settings.

3 Preview the frameset in your browser and click on the *Home* link to confirm that the home page opens in the browser window, not the current frame, as desired.

Adding *<noframes>* content

Some web browsers aren't capable of displaying framed pages. Dreamweaver allows you to create content to display in these older or text-based browsers by storing the content in the frameset file wrapped inside a *<noframes>* tag. Only content enclosed in a *<noframes>* tag is displayed when a user opens a framed page in a browser that doesn't support frames.

1   Choose Modify > Frameset > Edit NoFrames Content. In the Design view, a blank screen with the title *NoFrames Content* replaces your frameset.

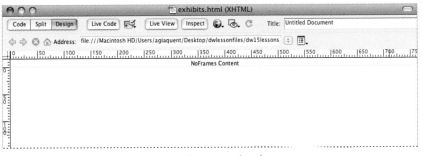

Adding noframes *content ensures that everyone has access to the information on your page.*

2   Enter or insert page content the same way you would normally. This content shows only when the page is opened in a browser that doesn't support viewing of your frames. The advantage of adding *<noframes>* content in this manner is that the content lives within your frameset file, and doesn't require the creation of an additional page file.

Now that you've learned how to work with framed (and non-framed) content, you can use this knowledge to inform your decisions as you explore another layout method, the use of tables. Choose File > Save All to save all your documents.

Using tables for layout

If you've used a spreadsheet or a program such as Microsoft Word, you probably already have an idea of how tables work. Put simply, tables represent a way of organizing content using headers, rows, and columns. When tables are used for web page layout, the borders between rows and columns can be made invisible, allowing you to position content in ways that were previously impossible using basic HTML.

Tables were originally included in HTML so that academics would have a means of organizing content on web pages. Cascading Style Sheets (CSS) were later introduced to handle all the formatting issues associated with HTML, so that HTML could remain focused on conveying information, not stylistic interests. However, by the time CSS had gained enough ground in web design circles, tables had already been used to handle layout in the majority of web pages. This is partly because reluctant developers took time to convert, and even today many programmers still only use table design. Thus it's important to know how tables function in a web page.

Tables versus CSS

How do you make an informed choice when it comes to page layout? Each method has its advantages and disadvantages.

One advantage of tables is their flexibility and ease of use. Dreamweaver's standard and layout design modes offer several ways to manipulate tables. Another advantage of tables is that they're universal—even older browsers can recognize them.

On the downside, tables can be bulky and very restrictive when it comes to layout possibilities. Tables are an older technology that is becoming less common in terms of design trends. Another issue is that although all browsers recognize tables, they don't all treat tables in the same way. Layouts can vary from one browser to the next, depending on how the table is formatted.

With Cascading Style Sheets (CSS), you have to-the-pixel positioning, flexibility, and you can place content wherever you want fairly easily. CSS also provides you with more ways to modify page appearance in terms of formatting color, margins, borders, and so on.

The disadvantage with CSS is that because it is a newer technology, many older browsers don't support it. Even newer browsers have chosen to support CSS at different levels over the years, which can cause pages to display inconsistently from browser to browser.

Inserting a table

You will start by designing the web site's home page using tables. You'll find that you don't have to use just one table on a page; you might have multiple tables to accommodate different facets of your page layout. You can even go so far as to nest one table inside another, with each having different characteristics.

In case you're wondering why you would even use tables, have you ever tried to work without them on a blank page? You can't just drag things and place them where you want them; the code doesn't work that way. Tables are one of the elements that will allow you to get your images and text right where you want them. They're also a way to provide consistency to your layout.

1   In the Files panel, double-click the index.html page to open it.

2   If your rulers aren't visible, select View > Rulers > Show.

View	Insert	Modify	Format
Zoom In			⌘=
Zoom Out			⌘−
Magnification			▶
Visual Aids			▶
Style Rendering			▶
Code View Options			▶
Rulers			▶
Grid			▶
Guides			▶
Tracing Image			▶
Plugins			▶
✓ Display External Files			

Rulers submenu:
✓ Show   ⌥⌘R
Reset Origin

✓ Pixels
Inches
Centimeters

Making rulers visible.

3   You can use guides in Dreamweaver to help establish consistent positioning in your layout. From the vertical ruler on the left side of the screen, click and drag out a guide. Because you're designing for monitors with a desktop resolution set to 800 (width) by 600 (height) or larger, place the guide at the 750-pixel mark of the top horizontal ruler.

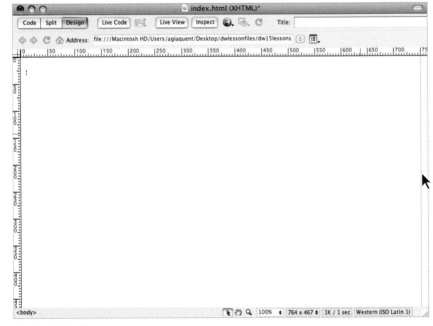

A ruler guide in Dreamweaver.

You didn't drag a guide out to the 800-pixel mark on the ruler because of the space that the Internet browser takes up. For instance, in Internet Explorer or Netscape, the scroll bar on the right side of the browser window absorbs some of the window's horizontal space. Some browsers also include a set of menu options on the left with different buttons for accessing bookmarks and other functions.

4 In the Title window in the Document panel, type **The McKnight Institute Home Page** as your page title. Press Enter (Windows) or Return (Mac OS).

You'll find different ways to insert tables, including using the menus along the top of the screen, or through the Insert panel.

5 Select Insert > Table, and the Table dialog box appears. Set the number of rows to **6** and columns to **3**. Set the Table width to **750**, making sure that the drop-down menu is set to pixels. Next, type **0** into the Border thickness text field. Leave the None header option selected, and the Caption and Summary fields blank. Press OK to insert the table.

The Table dialog box.

6 Choose File > Save to save your work.

Selecting tables

Selecting tables can be a little cumbersome until you get used to it. Before you add images and text, you will need to select the various table components and modify some of their basic physical attributes.

1   Place your cursor at the top of the table border; the cursor turns into a down arrow (↓) and the column is highlighted. Click to select a column in the table.

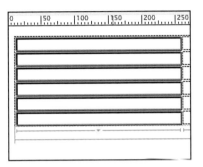

A selected column.

2   Place your cursor on the left side of the top row; this time, the cursor turns into an arrow facing to the right (→), with the row highlighted. Click to select the row.

A selected row.

3 To select a column on the table, place your cursor at the bottom of the first column. Click on the arrow there and choose Select Column.

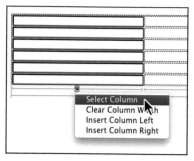

Selecting a column.

4 You can also use tags to select a table and its components. For example, click anywhere inside one of the table cells. Note the tags listed at the bottom-left corner of the page window. Select each tag—<*tr*>, <*td*>, <*table*>—and different parts of the table become selected.

Using tags to select portions of a table.

5   To select a cell, hold down the Ctrl (Windows) or Command (Mac OS) key and click on the cell. To select multiple cells, continue to hold Ctrl or Command and click the other cells you want to simultaneously select.

6   There are many options for selecting an entire table. First click on the *<table>* tag in the lower-left corner below the document window. This selects the entire table. Next, move your cursor to the upper-left corner of the table and click when the table icon (⯆▦) appears next to your cursor. You can also use the menus, click in any of the table cells, and select Modify > Table > Select Table.

Modify	Format	Command

Page Properties...	⌘J
Template Properties...	
✓ Selection Properties	

Table	▶	Select Table
Image	▶	Merge Cells ⌥⌘M
Frameset	▶	Split Cell... ⌥⌘S
Arrange	▶	
Convert	▶	Insert Row ⌘M
		Insert Column ⇧⌘A
Library	▶	Insert Rows or Columns...
Templates	▶	
		Delete Row ⇧⌘M
		Delete Column ⇧⌘–
		Increase Row Span
		Increase Column Span ⇧⌘]
		Decrease Row Span
		Decrease Column Span ⇧⌘[
		Clear Cell Heights
		Clear Cell Widths
		Convert Widths to Pixels
		Convert Widths to Percent
		Convert Heights to Pixels
		Convert Heights to Percent

Using menu commands to select an entire table.

Modifying tables

Now that you know how to select a table, you can modify its appearance by changing several of its attributes, including, size, color, number of columns and rows, border thickness, and more.

The right side of the table extends past the guide you placed earlier at the 750-pixel mark. Now, you'll modify the table so that it aligns properly with the guide.

1   Place your cursor on the right edge of the table until it turns into a double-pronged arrow (↖).

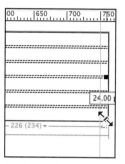

Use the double-pronged arrow to modify the width of the table.

2   Click and drag to the left to adjust the table's width. Drag your cursor so that the width matches the position of the guide. This modified table measures 740 pixels wide. You can view your table's width by selecting the table, and then checking the guide at the bottom of the table or checking the W (width) text field in the Property Inspector.

Modify the table's width from the Property Inspector.

You also can modify table width by typing in the value you want in the W (width) text field of the Property Inspector, with the table selected.

Setting table borders

The border value also affects a table's appearance, and it determines whether the table is visible or invisible when viewed in a browser. The border value for this table is set to 0; with that value, the table will be invisible in a browser.

1   Select the table, and in the Property Inspector, change the border value to **1**. Press Enter (Windows) or Return (Mac OS).

2   Preview the page in a browser by pressing the Preview/Debug in browser button (●) on the Document toolbar, and you see the table on the page. Exit the browser and return to Dreamweaver.

3   Because you'll be using the table as a layout tool only, make it invisible again by changing the border value back to 0. You'll change other attributes—such as cell color—later, when you start to add table content.

Merging cells

The next problem to address is where the content will go and how it will fit inside the cell. Luckily, you can merge cells, divide them, and nest one table inside another, so you can customize your table in a number of ways.

In this exercise, you'll merge the cells in a table row to accommodate a graphic you'll be placing in the row.

1   Select the top row of cells, using one of the selection methods you learned earlier.

2   In the Property Inspector, click the Merge Selected Cells button (□) in the bottom-left corner. The three cells merge into one big cell, with plenty of room for the graphic.

The Merge Selected Cells button.

3   Choose File > Save to save your work.

Nesting a table inside a row

The second row is where you'll place the menu. There are seven different menu items, so you'll need a cell for each one. Because three columns are established for some of the other content that you will add later, nesting a table inside this row gives you the flexibility you need for the menu items.

1 Select the second row, and then click the Merge Selected Cells button in the Property Inspector.

2 Click inside the cell in the second row and select Insert > Table. The Table dialog box appears. Set the number of rows to **1** and columns to **7**. Type **100** into the Table width text field, and select percent from the drop-down menu. Leave the other settings as they are and press OK.

Table
Table size
Rows: 1   Columns: 7
Table width: 100 [percent]
Border thickness: 0 pixels
Cell padding: ▦
Cell spacing: ▦
Header
None   Left   Top   Both
Accessibility
Caption:
Summary:
Help   Cancel   OK

Using the Insert Table command to insert a table inside a row from another table.

Pixel-based tables are of a fixed size, so if a user resizes their browser window, the table will not resize accordingly. A table based on percentages, however, will resize based on the size of the browser window, so you'll see the table and its contents stretch as the browser is stretched. Because you nested the percentage-based table into a pixel-based table, you won't see any change if the browser is resized.

Specifying column widths

You can set up specific column widths if you want to designate a specific amount of space for column content.

1 Select the table, and then select the leftmost column by placing your cursor on the bottom of that column, clicking on the arrow, and choosing Select Column.

2 In the Property Inspector, type **175** into the W (width) text field. Press Enter (Windows) or Return (Mac OS).

3 Repeat steps 1 and 2 for the column on the right. Don't add any values for the middle column. When you're finished, your table should look like this:

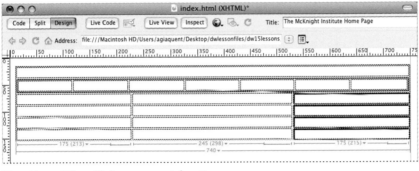

Your table, in which you'll place your menu information.

4 Create an area for the second menu at the bottom of the page by clicking in the center cell in the bottom row, then choosing Insert > Table. The settings you established for the last table are saved in the Table dialog box. Leave them as they are and press OK.

5 Choose File > Save to save your work.

Now that you have a basic table, you're ready to start adding some content. You'll modify cells later to accommodate some of the other information you'll be adding.

Adding content to tables

You can add any content to a table the same way you add content to a page; tables just give you more control in terms of placement.

1 Click in the top cell in the top row, and choose Window > Assets to access the Assets panel.

Open the Assets panel.

2 Select the mcknight.gif file from within the images folder in the Assets panel and insert it into the cell. This image file contains the logo you'll use for your museum web site. Type **logo** when you are asked to add an Alternate text tag. Press OK. You see the cell stretch to accommodate the size of the logo.

*Type **logo** in the Alternate text field of the Image Tag Accessibility Attributes dialog box.*

3 Click in the first cell in the second row and type **Home**.

4 Click in the next cell to the right and type **Exhibits**.

5 Click in each of the remaining five cells, and type the following headings into each cell:

Learning Center

Store

Museum Hours

Contact Us

Get a Brochure

To accommodate the content, the cells resize as you type. When you're finished, your table should look like this:

The table after adding text to the remaining cells.

Now you'll specify a width for each cell to make sure the sizing is consistent.

6 Click inside the first cell where you typed in the word *Home*. In the Property Inspector, type **100** in the W (width) window. Do the same for the remaining cells in the menu.

Set the width to 100 in each of the cells containing text.

7   Now you'll add more text content by nesting another table, then copying and pasting text that was supplied to you as part of the exercise.

8   Click in the middle cell in the third row and choose Insert > Table. Set the number of rows to **4** and columns to **1**. Type **375** into the Table width text field and choose pixels from the drop-down menu. Leave all other settings the same and press OK.

Adjust the settings for another nested table.

9   Click inside the cell you just nested the table into so that the cell becomes active. If this proves difficult, try clicking to the right of the table you just nested or select the *<td>* tag at the bottom of the document window.

10 In the Property Inspector, select the Vert (vertical alignment) drop-down menu and choose Top. This setting adjustment will keep the nested table at the top of the cell. This works for anything you place inside a cell, including text and images.

Adjust the cell's settings from the Property Inspector.

Next, you'll copy and paste the text content for the nested table.

11 To add the text content, choose Window > Files to open the Files panel, if it's not already open.

12 Open the Assets folder, then the Text Assets folder by clicking on the triangle to the left of each folder.

13 Double-click the home_page.txt file to open it in Dreamweaver. Click and drag to select the text about halfway down the page that reads *Welcome to MKI*.

```
6    Learn
7    It's not slime, ooze or goo th
     exhibit and crawl around on ou
8
9  ▼ Welcome to MKI
10   Welcome to The McKnight Instit
     visual and tactile experiences
11
12   Exhibits
13   At MKI, it's not just learning
     image with lots of text to dem
     learning about aerodynamics th
     around the solar system, playi
```

Select the text that reads Welcome to MKI.

14 Choose Edit > Copy. Click on the index.html tab in the top-left area of the page panel to return to the index.html page.

15 Click inside the top cell of the table you just inserted, then choose Edit > Paste.

Paste the Welcome to MKI text in the top cell of your new table.

16 Click on the home_page.txt tab in the top-left corner of the page window to return to the text file you copied from earlier. Highlight the paragraph just below the *Welcome to MKI* text and copy it.

17 Return to the index.html page and paste the paragraph of text into the cell below the *Welcome to MKI* text.

Paste the paragraph from home_page.txt into index.html.

Continue this process for the next header, *Exhibits*, along with the body text that goes with it, until your table looks like this:

Copy and paste the header and body text for the Exhibits section.

18 Choose File > Save to save your work.

Adding another table

You're probably starting to get some ideas about how you can incorporate tables into your own layouts. To reinforce some of the concepts you've learned so far, let's create another nested table.

1   Click in the first cell in the third row (the cell to the immediate left of the Welcome copy) and choose Insert > Table. In the Table dialog box that appears, set the number of rows to **4** and columns to **1**. Type **175** in the Table width text field and select pixels from the drop-down menu. Leave the other settings as they are and press OK.

The table you inserted is in the middle of the cell; once again you'll need to establish the cell's vertical alignment.

2   To establish this cell's vertical alignment, click inside the cell so that it becomes active. In the Property Inspector, click on the Vertical alignment drop-down menu and choose Top.

3   Click on the home_page.txt tab in the top-left corner of the page window to return to the text file you copied from earlier. Highlight the word *Discover*, and copy it by choosing Edit > Copy, or by using the keyboard shortcut Ctrl+C (Windows) or Command+C (Mac OS).

4   Click inside the top cell of your newly nested table and paste the text by choosing Edit > Paste, or by using the shortcut Ctrl+V (Windows) or Command+V (Mac OS).

5   Return to the home_page.txt file and select the paragraph below the *Discover* text you copied and pasted in step 3. Copy and paste the paragraph of text into the cell under the *Discover* text.

Copy and paste the Discover paragraph.

6 Finish the rest of the copy for the sidebar, using the *Learn* header and body copy to complete the information. When you're finished, your table should look like this:

Copy and paste the Learn *header and body copy.*

7 Choose File > Save to save your work. Preview your page in a browser by pressing the Preview/Debug in Browser button (●) at the top of the document window.

If the text you inserted into the nested tables seems a bit crowded, you can adjust some of the table attributes to give the content more breathing room.

Close browser and return to Dreamweaver.

8 Select the nested table that contains the Discover and Learn sidebar information. An easy way to do this is to click inside the nested table and select the second table tag in the bottom-left area of the page window.

In the Property Inspector are two windows that allow you to adjust cell spacing. The CellPad window allows you to enter a value that determines how much space is inside the cell between the edge of the cell and the content. The CellSpace value determines how much space is between the cells.

9 With the sidebar table selected, type **5** in the CellPad text field. The text in the table now has a little bit of a buffer between it and the edge of the cell.

Use the Property Inspector to give your sidebar text a bit more room.

10 Select the table in the center column that contains the *Welcome to MKI* text, and apply the same CellPad value of **5** for that table.

11 Choose File > Save to save your work. Preview the page again by using the Preview/ Debug in browser button in the Document toolbar. Note the difference in text spacing. Now you'll add another image to spice up the page a bit.

12 Click in the cell to the right of the *Welcome to MKI* text.

13 In the Assets panel, select the 3D_surface.jpg file from the Picture Assets folder within the Assets folder and insert it into the cell. Type **3D picture** as the Alternate text tag.

14 Once again, the picture shows up in the middle of the cell. Place your cursor below the inserted image and set the Vertical alignment to Top in the Property Inspector.

 Sometimes you'll want to modify graphics to fit table columns and rows. Don't just click and drag the images inside the cells, as this will create a stretched look. A better approach is to note the column or row width, open the graphic you want to place, and adjust its size in a program such as Photoshop or Fireworks.

Formatting tables

In addition to adjusting table and cell size, you can change other attributes, such as color, and format text content inside cells. In this exercise, you'll format table cells, and attach a style sheet to help with the process. If you're unfamiliar with styles, refer to Lesson 4, "Styling Your Pages with CSS."

1 Choose Window > CSS Styles. In the CSS Styles panel, click on the Attach Style Sheet button (●) toward the bottom-right corner of the panel.

2 Click on the Browse button, make sure you're in the dw15lessons folder, and double-click the styles.css file.

3 Make sure that the Link radio button is selected, and press OK.

Attach External Style Sheet	
File/URL: styles.css [↕] Browse...	OK
Add as: ● Link	Preview
○ Import	Cancel
Media: [↕]	
You may also enter a comma-separated list of media types.	
Dreamweaver has sample style sheets to get you started.	Help

Select the styles.css file and press OK to attach this external style sheet.

The rightmost part of the top cell is a gray color, which doesn't match the color of the graphic, and gives the cell a kind of split appearance. You can match cell colors to graphics to tie everything together.

4   Click inside the topmost cell, which contains the mcknight.gif header graphic. In the Property Inspector, click the Bg color swatch (this window refers to the cell background) to bring up the Swatches panel.

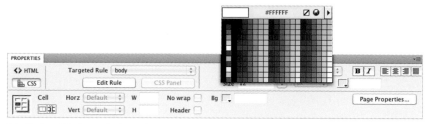

Modify the cell background color in the Property Inspector.

5   Move your cursor (which should now look like an eyedropper) and click on the white portion of the mcknight.gif file to sample the color. The cell turns white.

This is a great way to blend your graphics with page colors to make everything look seamless. You can set each cell to its own color, or set multiple cell colors simultaneously.

Now you'll format the menu, sidebar, and main content cells.

6   Click in the cell containing the word *Home*. In the Property Inspector, press the Bg color swatch and pick a color. This example uses color #00CC33. This cell will be different from the rest of the menu because this is the Home page.

7   Select the rest of the menu cells, from *Exhibits* to *Get a Brochure*. Choose a color from the Bg color swatch to apply it to all of the cells. This example uses color #CC9933.

8   Click inside the cell containing the word *Discover* and select a color from the Bg color swatch to assign the color to it. In this exercise, color #CCFF33 is used for the title text and #CCCC33 for the body text. Follow this procedure for each remaining text cell. For the table that contains the *Welcome to MKI* text, this example uses color #00CC33 for the headers and #00FF33 for the body copy. When you're finished, your table should look something like this:

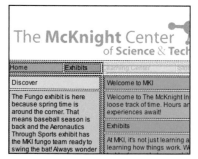

Style your tables by setting background colors for each cell.

The main cells are done, but they stick out from the rest of the page. You'll want to establish a color for the main table to tie everything together.

Working in the Expanded Tables mode

Selecting cells or content within cells can sometimes be cumbersome. This is especially true if there's no cell padding between the cells because you want to keep the table tight. The Expanded Tables mode makes selecting cells and cell content a bit easier by temporarily adding a visible border, cell padding, and cell spacing values.

To take advantage of this feature, go to the Insert bar and select the Layout category.

The Layout category of the Insert panel.

You see two buttons: Standard, which is the default mode, and Expanded.

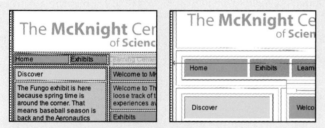

A table in the Standard mode, and in Expanded mode.

With a page that has a table within it open, click the Expanded Mode button. A dialog box appears that explains the purpose of the Expanded Mode.

Now you can see the border and cell values that have been added temporarily to make the selection process easier. Once you've made your selections and have done the work you need to do, click the Standard Mode button to return to your regular table settings.

9   Click inside the cell for the parent table (which is nesting all the other tables). In the Bg color swatch in the Property Inspector, pick an overall color for the table; this example uses color #FFCC00.

Modify the colors of the cells to make your site more appealing.

10 Choose File > Save to save your work, and then preview it in a browser by selecting the Preview/Debug in browser button (⊙) at the top of the document window. Close the web browser and return to Dreamweaver.

Now it's time to style the table cells.

11 Select the cells of the table that contain the menu items along the top of the page. Make sure you select the cells, not the table.

12 In the Style drop-down menu of the Property Inspector, choose the topmenu style to apply it to the cells.

Apply the topmenu style to your menu items.

13 Continue this process with the sidebar by clicking in the cell containing the word *Discover*. In the Style drop-down menu, select the style sidebarTitle.

14 Finish the process, applying the styles you think are appropriate to the remaining headers. Save your work when you're done.

One nice thing about this is that you can go back and make cell color adjustments very easily, or you can let the styles you create define everything for you!

The finished layout.

Self study

Try some of the following tasks to build on your experience with building and editing frames in Dreamweaver:

Create a new frameset and use the Bottom Frame preset to split the frameset into two frames. Add another frame, using the Split Frame Left command. Name the frames Left, Right, and Bottom, respectively.

Set the width of your Left frame to 30 percent, and the Bottom frame height to 150 pixels. Turn scrolling capability on in the Right frame. Explore the different looks that you can achieve by adding background and border colors to each of your three frames.

Build your own HTML page content for placement in these frames. Experiment with setting default content for these frames, and targeting different frames for this content when navigation links are clicked. For additional practice, create a *<noframes>* version of your frameset for browsers that don't support frames.

One way to learn how to take advantage of tables is to learn how other programs work in conjunction with Dreamweaver.

There's a process many web designers incorporate known as *slicing*, which involves cutting up an image in Photoshop or Fireworks, using slice tools. From there, the image is dissected into separate pieces that will load more quickly than one big image. You can then export the slices as separate images, along with a web page that does the layout for you, with each image automatically placed in a table.

To learn more about this time-saving process, start to investigate Fireworks, which tightly integrates with Dreamweaver to expedite the process.

Review

Questions

1   What are the advantages and disadvantages of using frames in a web page layout?

2   Why would you set a frame's width to a fixed value?

3   What would you do to ensure that a page shows in a specific frame by default when viewed in a browser?

4   What's the difference between a percentage-based table and a pixel-based table?

5   What setting in the Property Inspector determines whether a table is visible?

6   How can you import text so that the content will flow automatically into cells and columns?

Answers

1   Using frames saves time and avoids repetitive work in the creation of pages. In addition, the viewer's browser doesn't need to reload graphics used for navigation on every page. Frames also allow viewers to scroll through long pages of content in a frame, using built-in scroll bars. However, aligning content precisely in different frames can be problematic. Another disadvantage is that viewers won't be able to bookmark individual framed pages (unless you provide specific server code). Testing the navigation from frame to frame can also be time-consuming.

2   You would set a frame's width to a specific pixel value when you want that frame to always be the same size, as in a navigation menu. A fixed-width frame displays content at the same size in any browser window, whereas other frames will resize to fill the remaining space in your frameset.

3   Saving a frameset locks HTML page content into the frame you've defined when the frameset is opened in a browser. You also can't preview your frameset in a browser without first saving the frameset and all of the content that appears in its frames.

4   A percentage-based table will stretch to fit the size of the browser. A pixel-based table is fixed and will not resize.

5   The border value in the Property Inspector sets a border for a selected table. If the border value is 0 (zero), the table will not be visible when the page is viewed in a web browser.

6   By adding tabs and returns in the document to separate the text content and then importing the file as tabular data.

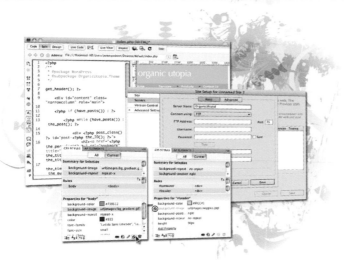

What you'll learn in this lesson:

- CMS support
- CSS Inspection tool
- CSS Enable.Disable
- Adobe BrowserLab
- PHP Code Hinting

Dreamweaver CS5 New Features

Dreamweaver's features evolve as the Web evolves. In this lesson, you'll take a tour of Dreamweaver's new features.

What's new in Dreamweaver CS5?

CS5 introduces many innovative design and coding features as well as improvements to Dreamweaver's flagship features. Perhaps the most significant change in Dreamweaver is its new support of Content Management Systems (CMS) and blogging platforms such as Wordpress, Joomla, Drupal and others. This change is most important for users who had frustrations previewing and testing their CMS sites in previous versions of Dreamweaver. The Live View feature introduced in Dreamweaver CS4 now has grown up and is a true native web browser that largely eliminates the need to make constant round trips to a browser for testing, even for dynamic scripting languages such as PHP and Coldfusion.

New support for Content Management Systems

Enjoy authoring and testing support for content management system frameworks like WordPress, Joomla!, and Drupal. Dreamweaver CS5 offers an easy way for designers to build sites in the Design view in a way that was not previously possible. A CMS/blog software like Wordpress provides users an easy way to publish content online and provides features such as automatic archiving and database integration. In the past, designers have been frustrated creating the page designs for a CMS in Dreamweaver because these systems generally rely on a relatively complex combination of dynamic pages (often php) that could not be previewed in Dreamweaver. For designers or users who are not code-savvy, the complexity of these files can be daunting. Dreamweaver can now help you discover the related files needed to put together the pages in your CMS framework.

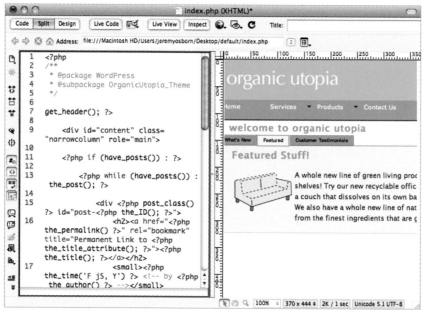

Previewing a Wordpress theme using Dreamweaver's new CMS support.

Dreamweaver will now preview the files of a CMS framework in the Design view (as long as you have a testing server defined) using the built-in Live View option. With this feature Dreamweaver CS5 also lets you interact directly with a database which means you can now test online forms, insert and modify database records and more.

CSS inspection

As CSS continues to grow in acceptance and use among designers and developers, web browsers have added features and plugins based on the users need to look at the code behind their pages. An excellent example of this would be the Firebug plugin for Mozilla's Firefox browser. This tool allows users to peek at the visual model and structure of a page. Dreamweaver now has a similar capability with the CSS Inspect tool. Clicking on this tool allows you to see the relationships between the elements on your page, most significantly margins and padding. With these tools on hand, the author of a web page can quickly diagnose the layout of a page simply by hovering over a page, and then if interested, can click on an item to reveal the code.

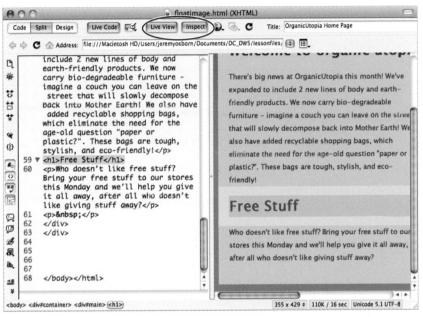

In the Inspect mode, mousing over the elements in Design view reveals the HTML and CSS code.

CSS Enable/Disable

On par with the CSS Inspect feature is the new CSS Enable/Disable feature. This feature allows you to isolate one or more CSS rules and then temporarily disable them. Disabling a property is as easy as clicking a property in the CSS Styles panel and then pressing the CSS Enable/Disable button. Clicking the button again turns the property back on. You can think of this feature as a tool to help you understand how any particular property (or properties) are affecting elements on your page. Whether it be testing column layout or experimenting with CSS font properties, the CSS Enable/Disable feature is a handy tool in the designer's toolbox.

The CSS Enable/Disable button allows you to selectively turn CSS properties on and off.

Preview pages using Adobe Browserlab

Adobe BrowserLab is a useful tool for testing page layout across multiple platforms and for different browsers. Traditionally, users on the Mac platform would need a Windows machine in order to test their pages on Windows web browsers and by extension, users on Windows would need a Mac OS machine to do the same. This workflow is not particularly efficient, and diagnosing browser differences is not made easy. BrowserLab is part of Adobe's CS Live service, an integrated set of web-based utilities. After setting up an account on CS Live, you can use BrowserLab to preview both local files as well as live pages online. Once logged into BrowserLab you can test and compare your pages using different browser versions and platforms.

Adobe's BrowserLab service is an integrated part of Dreamweaver.

Site setup and support for multiple servers

Gaining access to the new CMS capabilities of Dreamweaver has been made a bit easier with the new Site Setup window. Users who are not working with a site that uses a scripting language will have an easier and quicker time creating a new site to get up and running. For more advanced users, there is now the ability to define multiple servers as part of the site setup. A common use for this would be to have two servers set up: the currently live site (1) and the testing server (2). This capability makes it easier for the experimenting and testing of a site to take place without a lot of downtime.

The new Site Setup window provides benefits for beginners and advanced users alike

PHP Code hinting

More advanced users who use the scripting language PHP more often will be happy to learn that Dreamweaver CS5 now has much improved support for PHP syntax, this includes code completion and syntax checking as well as full support for all core functions, constants, and classes. PHP code hints have also been improved substantially.

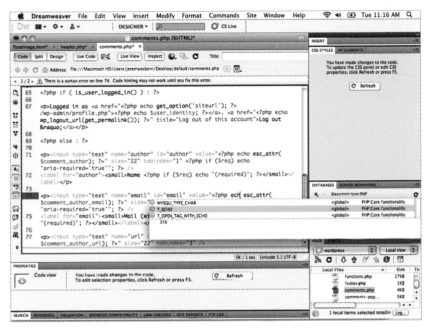

PHP Code hinting is better than ever in Dreamweaver CS5

Other new features

Business Catalyst Integration

Adobe's Business Catalyst is an online service that provides a variety of features such as online store/shopping cart capabilities, email marketing, web form functionality, analytics extension and more. With the Business Catalyst extension in Dreamweaver you can login to Business Catalyst and synchronize multiple sites at once. Dreamweaver can be used to access and edit the style module used on your Business Catalyst connected sites.

Subversion

Dreamweaver now has improved support for Subversion, a version control system similar to CVS and Visual Sourcesafe (VSS). Subversion is typically used by companies to maintain a team environment on larger projects that require changes to be logged, and versions to be controlled. Without Subversion, if you wanted to maintain versions, you would have to do the work yourself—maintaining folders and copies of previous versions. With Subversion, all files are kept on the Subversion server. Changes are tracked so that you can restore your project to any previous state.

CSS Starter Pages

CSS Starter pages have been around Dreamweaver for a few versions now, they allow you to get a jumpstart on building CSS layouts by choosing from a variety of pre-built page layouts which you then modify. In Dreamweaver CS5 the code for these starter pages is new and improved for modern web browsers with plenty of code commenting behind the scenes to help you start modifying your pages quickly.

Index

audio
    compressing, 231
    inserting, 229–231
    making web content interesting, 220
    overview, 219–220
Auto Indent option, 260
automatic margins, containers, 126

B

background color
    adding to sidebar, 166
    alternate row styling in CSS, 195
    Cascading Style Sheets (CSS), 293–295
Background color option, Page Properties dialog box, 45
background image, 137
Background image field, Page Properties dialog box, 46
Background text field, Page Properties dialog box, 45
Balance Braces button, Coding toolbar, 262
banner, web, 220
BCC (Browser Compatibility Check)
    CSS Advisor, 354–355
    overview, 353–354
    site management and FTP, 8
    tables and boxes, 125
Behaviors panel, 298–300, 305
Bg color swatch option, Property Inspector, 408
Bindings panel, 329
_blank command, Target drop-down menu, 388
Blank Page category, New Document dialog box, 40
Block category, CSS Rule definition dialog box, 106
<body> tag
    creating and modifying styles, 99
    hierarchy of tags, 27
    HTML document, 20
    modifying, 115
    tag selector, 214
bold (<strong>) tag
    compound selectors, 107
    tag hierarchy, 27
bookmarks, 357
border attribute, <img> tag, 76–77
Border property, 193
border value, Property Inspector, 413
border-collapse property, 189–190
borders
    adding to elements, 145
    Box model, CSS, 123
    frame
        dragging, 383–384
        properties, 383–384
    overview, 142–143
    removing from HTML tables, 186
    tables, 193–194, 397
Box model, CSS
    <div> element, 123
    floated images, 154
    ID selector, 124–125
    margins, 123
    modifying attached style sheets, 115
    overview, 122
    padding, 123

 (break) tag, 26, 28
bracketed keywords, 18
break (<br>) tag, 26, 28
brightness, adjusting, 80–81
broken links, preventing, 83
Broken Links report, 350
Browse button, Hyperlink dialog box, 68
browser compatibility
    adding code for IE 6, 168–169
    applying finishing touches, 169–170
    page layouts, 168–170
Browser Compatibility Check (BCC)
    CSS Advisor, 354–355
    overview, 353–354
    site management and FTP, 8
    tables and boxes, 125
Browser Compatibility Check tab, Results panel, 354
browser hacks, 152

browser, web
    previewing pages, 65–66
    XHTML 1.0 Transitional, 17
Browserlab tool, 419
built-in FTP, 11
bulleted lists, 71
Business Catalyst Integration, 421
buttons
    Add new Server, 337
    Advace Formatting CSS, 268
    All, CSS Styles panel, 169
    Anything, Validate Form dialog box, 302
    Apply Comment, 263
    Balance Braces, 262
    Browse, Hyperlink dialog box, 68
    Code View, 51
    Collapse Full Tag, 262, 264
    Collapse Selection, 262, 265
    CSS, 93
    Current, 91
    Design View, 50, 95, 275–276
    Detect Size, 225
    Disable/Enable CSS Property, 147
    Draw AP Div, 123, 132
    Email address, 302
    Expand, 344
    Expand All, 262
    Format Source Code, 263
    Freeze JavaScript, 13
    Get/Put, 11
    HTML, 59
    Indent Code, 263
    Insert, 258
    Insert Div Tag, 123
    Insert Rows radio, 181
    Italic, 74
    Line breaks radio, 286
    Line Numbers, 263
    Live View, 66, 312, 316, 318, 333
    Merge Selected Cells, 397
    Move or Convert CSS, 263
    New CSS Rule, 103, 191
    New Library Item, 240
    Open Documents, 262
    Ordered List, 72
    Outdent Code, 263
    Play, Property Inspector, 222
    Plus, Behaviors panel, 299
    Preview/Debug in Browser, Document toolbar
        adding tables, 406
        adding text fields, 282
        closing Hyperlink dialog box, 70
        Draw AP Div tool, 132
        formatting tables, 410
        inserting sound, 230
        previewing page, 228
        setting table borders, 397
        targeting frames, 385–386
    Recent Snippets, 263
    Refresh
        Assets panel, 246
        Files panel, 342
        Property Inspector, 64
    Remove Comment, 263
    Reset, 290–291
    Select Parent Tag, 262, 264
    Show All Events, 300
    Show Code Navigator, 262
    Show Set Events, 303
    Site Root, 309
    Source Code, 98
    Split
        changing workspace, 62
        creating gallery page, 76
        placing images in HTML, 21
        tag structure and attributes, 18
        whitespace rules, 25
    Split View, 52
    Spry Region, 330
    Submit, 290–291
    Syntax Error Alerts in Info Bar, 263

Wiley Publishing, Inc.
End-User License Agreement

READ THIS. You should carefully read these terms and conditions before opening the software packet(s) included with this book "Book". This is a license agreement "Agreement" between you and Wiley Publishing, Inc. "WPI". By opening the accompanying software packet(s), you acknowledge that you have read and accept the following terms and conditions. If you do not agree and do not want to be bound by such terms and conditions, promptly return the Book and the unopened software packet(s) to the place you obtained them for a full refund.

1. **License Grant.** WPI grants to you (either an individual or entity) a nonexclusive license to use one copy of the enclosed software program(s) (collectively, the "Software") solely for your own personal or business purposes on a single computer (whether a standard computer or a workstation component of a multi-user network). The Software is in use on a computer when it is loaded into temporary memory (RAM) or installed into permanent memory (hard disk, CD-ROM, or other storage device). WPI reserves all rights not expressly granted herein.

2. **Ownership.** WPI is the owner of all right, title, and interest, including copyright, in and to the compilation of the Software recorded on the physical packet included with this Book "Software Media". Copyright to the individual programs recorded on the Software Media is owned by the author or other authorized copyright owner of each program. Ownership of the Software and all proprietary rights relating thereto remain with WPI and its licensers.

3. **Restrictions on Use and Transfer.**

    (a) You may only (i) make one copy of the Software for backup or archival purposes, or (ii) transfer the Software to a single hard disk, provided that you keep the original for backup or archival purposes. You may not (i) rent or lease the Software, (ii) copy or reproduce the Software through a LAN or other network system or through any computer subscriber system or bulletin-board system, or (iii) modify, adapt, or create derivative works based on the Software.

    (b) You may not reverse engineer, decompile, or disassemble the Software. You may transfer the Software and user documentation on a permanent basis, provided that the transferee agrees to accept the terms and conditions of this Agreement and you retain no copies. If the Software is an update or has been updated, any transfer must include the most recent update and all prior versions.

4. **Restrictions on Use of Individual Programs.** You must follow the individual requirements and restrictions detailed for each individual program in the "About the CD" appendix of this Book or on the Software Media. These limitations are also contained in the individual license agreements recorded on the Software Media. These limitations may include a requirement that after using the program for a specified period of time, the user must pay a registration fee or discontinue use. By opening the Software packet(s), you agree to abide by the licenses and restrictions for these individual programs that are detailed in the "About the CD" appendix and/or on the Software Media. None of the material on this Software Media or listed in this Book may ever be redistributed, in original or modified form, for commercial purposes.

5. **Limited Warranty.**

    (a) WPI warrants that the Software and Software Media are free from defects in materials and workmanship under normal use for a period of sixty (60) days from the date of purchase of this Book. If WPI receives notification within the warranty period of defects in materials or workmanship, WPI will replace the defective Software Media.

(b) WPI AND THE AUTHOR(S) OF THE BOOK DISCLAIM ALL OTHER WARRANTIES, EXPRESS OR IMPLIED, INCLUDING WITHOUT LIMITATION IMPLIED WARRANTIES OF MERCHANTABILITY AND FITNESS FOR A PARTICULAR PURPOSE, WITH RESPECT TO THE SOFTWARE, THE PROGRAMS, THE SOURCE CODE CONTAINED THEREIN, AND/OR THE TECHNIQUES DESCRIBED IN THIS BOOK. WPI DOES NOT WARRANT THAT THE FUNCTIONS CONTAINED IN THE SOFTWARE WILL MEET YOUR REQUIREMENTS OR THAT THE OPERATION OF THE SOFTWARE WILL BE ERROR FREE.

(c) This limited warranty gives you specific legal rights, and you may have other rights that vary from jurisdiction to jurisdiction.

6. Remedies.

(a) WPI's entire liability and your exclusive remedy for defects in materials and workmanship shall be limited to replacement of the Software Media, which may be returned to WPI with a copy of your receipt at the following address: Software Media Fulfillment Department, Attn.: *Adobe Dreamweaver CS5 Digital Classroom*, Wiley Publishing, Inc., 10475 Crosspoint Blvd., Indianapolis, IN 46256, or call 1-800-762-2974. Please allow four to six weeks for delivery. This Limited Warranty is void if failure of the Software Media has resulted from accident, abuse, or misapplication. Any replacement Software Media will be warranted for the remainder of the original warranty period or thirty (30) days, whichever is longer.

(b) In no event shall WPI or the author be liable for any damages whatsoever (including without limitation damages for loss of business profits, business interruption, loss of business information, or any other pecuniary loss) arising from the use of or inability to use the Book or the Software, even if WPI has been advised of the possibility of such damages.

(c) Because some jurisdictions do not allow the exclusion or limitation of liability for consequential or incidental damages, the above limitation or exclusion may not apply to you.

7. U.S. Government Restricted Rights. Use, duplication, or disclosure of the Software for or on behalf of the United States of America, its agencies and/or instrumentalities "U.S. Government" is subject to restrictions as stated in paragraph (c)(1)(ii) of the Rights in Technical Data and Computer Software clause of DFARS 252.227-7013, or subparagraphs (c) (1) and (2) of the Commercial Computer Software - Restricted Rights clause at FAR 52.227-19, and in similar clauses in the NASA FAR supplement, as applicable.

8. General. This Agreement constitutes the entire understanding of the parties and revokes and supersedes all prior agreements, oral or written, between them and may not be modified or amended except in a writing signed by both parties hereto that specifically refers to this Agreement. This Agreement shall take precedence over any other documents that may be in conflict herewith. If any one or more provisions contained in this Agreement are held by any court or tribunal to be invalid, illegal, or otherwise unenforceable, each and every other provision shall remain in full force and effect.